EGYPT: A TRAVELLER'S ANTHOLOGY

Other books by the author
Embassy to Constantinople – The Travels of
Lady Mary Wortley Montagu (editor)
Exploring Rural England and Wales
The Railway Route Book
Children's Guide to London

EGYPT
A Traveller's Anthology

Compiled by
Christopher Pick

JOHN MURRAY

Copyright in the introduction, editorial matter
and compilation
© Christopher Pick 1991

First published in 1991 by
John Murray (Publishers) Ltd
50 Albemarle Street, London W1X 4BD

The moral right of the author has been asserted

British Library cataloguing in Publication Data
Egypt: a traveller's anthology.
1. Egypt. Description & travel, history
I. Pick, Christopher, *1948*–
916.204

ISBN 0-7195-4715-6

Typeset and printed in Great Britain by
Butler and Tanner Ltd, Frome and London

For Peter,
with love

Contents

Illustrations

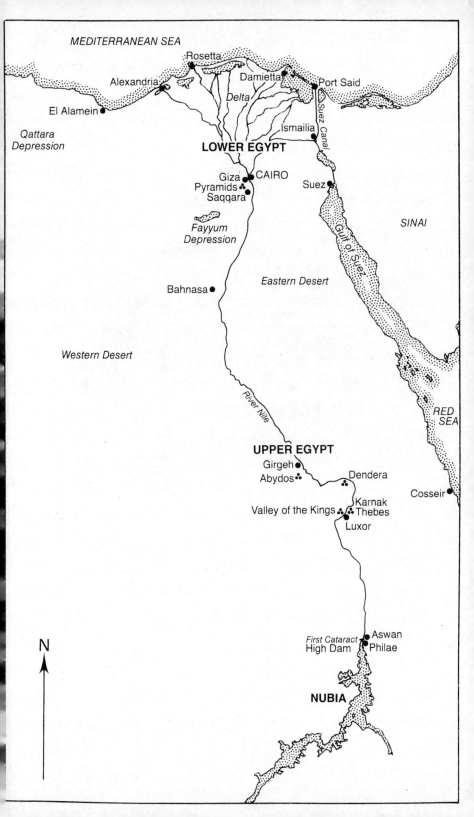

Introduction

THE massive physical remains of the ancient dynasties of Egypt have always aroused interest in the western world. The sheer size of the pyramids, tombs and temples and their setting on the very edge of the desert; the incomprehensible signs and symbols that covered them, evidence of a long-vanished but highly sophisticated civilization; the fascinating mysteries of the ancient mummies; the antiquities brought back by merchants and pilgrims – all created intense curiosity. Yet, until the eighteenth century, Egypt itself was scarcely visited by travellers from western Europe. The number of visitors increased during that century, and some compiled detailed accounts of their journeys, with illustrations, measurements of the monuments examined, and descriptions of scenery and people encountered. Even so, Egypt remained an exotic, mysterious destination, well beyond the scope of the traditional Grand Tour.

The decisive event that increased public knowledge of Egypt was Napoleon's invasion in 1798. A party, 167 strong, of *savants* – scientists, cartographers, surveyors, botanists, architects, geologists and a large group of artists – accompanied Napoleon's army. Their job was to record as much information as they could concerning both ancient and contemporary Egypt. They were remarkable companions to a military expedition, and produced, in *La Description d'Egypte*, published in twenty-four volumes between 1809 and 1813, an exhaustive text illustrated with a vivid collection of paintings and drawings. Many of the plates were the work of the expedition's chief artist, Vivant Denon, who had already had a great success with an autobiographical account of his travels in Egypt, *Voyage dans l'haute et basse Egypte* (*Travels in Upper and Lower Egypt*), much quoted in this book.

Napoleon's expedition, though it soon ended in ignominious retreat, helped to establish French influence in Egypt that remained strong throughout the nineteenth century and even today has not entirely disappeared. In France, along with Denon's book and the *Description*, it created a fashion for Egyptian styles and artefacts. Much the same happened in Britain, which had invaded Egypt in 1799 in order to chase the French out. The Rosetta Stone, a spoil of victory acquired from General Menou of the defeated French forces, was put on display in the British Museum in 1802, along with other acquisitions, to considerable public interest. This marked the apogee of the 'Egyptian Revival' style in the decorative arts and fashion. The exploits of another traveller, the larger-than-life Giovanni Belzoni, who penetrated the second Pyramid (see p. 108), discovered several tombs in the Valley of the Kings, and uncovered the temple of Ramesses II at Abu Simbel (see p. 203), stimulated another wave of interest. Belzoni's *Narrative of Operations and Recent Discoveries . . . in Egypt and Nubia* was published in 1820, and the following year a spectacular exhibition was staged in the Egyptian Hall in London's Piccadilly, with the statue of the Young Memnon, which Belzoni had removed from Luxor, as the centrepiece.

In Egypt the pattern for the large part of the nineteenth century was now established. Though the last British forces left in 1807 and the Pashas were all but formally independent of the Sultan in Constantinople, British and French influence continued to be felt. The French presence was strongest in education and the arts, notably archaeology, the British in matters such as policing, finance, defence and public works. However, in the 1850s and 1860s, when it came to the construction of the Suez Canal, it was the French who supported the project from the first, against considerable British opposition.

Egypt now quickly became a popular destination on an extended grand tour of the Near East through Greece, Turkey and the Holy Land. Diplomats, painters, architects and writers, and a good number of curious travellers, began to reach Alexandria and Cairo, and then ventured up the Nile at least as far as Thebes. The French writer Chateaubriand arrived in Egypt as early as 1806–7 (though his was a fairly cursory visit, and Nile floods prevented him from visiting the Pyramids). In 1831 Benjamin Disraeli toured Cairo and the Nile with gusto, recording his impressions, and by then he was one of many. To be sure, there were difficulties – demands for *backshish*, unreliable and unpunctual guides and Nile boat crews, poor hygiene – but nevertheless Egypt seemed a relatively secure place to explore, and in which to experience the sensations of the Orient.

There were many Americans among this early wave of travellers in Egypt. John Ledyard, the first American to reach Cairo, died there in 1788 before he was able to embark on his explorations on behalf of the Association for Promoting the Discovery of the Interior Parts of Africa. In the ten years following the opening of the US Consulates in Alexandria and Cairo in 1832, at least sixty-five Americans are known to have visited Egypt; the recollections of some of them – Mrs Kirkland, Mrs Haight, the Reverend Stephen Olin – are quoted later in this book.

Some of the particular attractions of Egypt have already been suggested: the fascination of the monuments of the Pharaohs and, increasingly, of the details of everyday life in ancient times as revealed by archaeologists; and the opportunity to sample, in relative ease and safety, the contemporary Eastern way of life. Another important attraction was Egypt's scriptural associations. Visitors looked forward to seeing the sites of some of the most famous Old Testament events. Painters of biblical scenes in particular (such as Frederick Goodall, the sole object of whose first visit in 1858 was to 'paint Scriptural subjects') found in the contemporary scenery and people of Egypt a fruitful source of inspiration and material. Another artist, William Müller, wrote: 'Egypt is full of scriptural subjects, and a Holy Family is found in every Arab village.'

The works of other artists, such as the prolific David Roberts, who visited in 1838–9, helped to popularize the country. His aim was to present contemporary Egypt as realistically as possible. The designer Owen Jones used drawings made on his Egyptian journeys in the design of the Egyptian Court erected in London's Crystal Palace in 1854.

While most tourists, at least until well into the nineteenth century, could expect to carry home some ancient artefacts and papyri for their private collections, archaeologists and hunters of antiquities represented another, rather different category of Westerner in Egypt. A number of celebrated Egyptologists such as John Gardner Wilkinson (author of the pioneering *Manners and Customs of the Ancient Egyptians*) and the Prussian Richard Lepsius made detailed site surveys and recorded inscriptions and monuments, and the French scholar Jean François Champollion successfully deciphered the ancient Egyptian hieroglyphs. However, not until the appointment in 1858 of the French Egyptologist Auguste Mariette, to establish the Antiquities Service and found the Egyptian Museum, did any real control begin to be exercised over archaeological investigations and the export of antiquities. Until then, little attention had been paid to the systematic excavation and recording of sites, and it was still to be a long time before archaeology evolved into the precise science (aided by imaginative inspiration) it is today.

Most visitors stayed for a winter season, which allowed adequate time to sail as rapidly as possible up the Nile to Thebes, and on into Nubia to Abu Simbel, before returning at a more leisurely pace, examining the monuments *en route*. Exceptional visitors stayed for years, often adopting Egypt as their second country. Edward Lane, who spent many years in Egypt for his health, produced a great number of paintings of everyday life, as well as writing *Manners and Customs of the Modern Egyptians* and translating the *Thousand and One Nights*. During his third lengthy stay in the 1840s (when he was joined by his sister Sophia Poole, see p. 53), he started to prepare his massive *Arabic Lexicon*. Health was also the reason why Lucie Duff Gordon settled in Egypt. Her *Letters from Egypt*, perhaps the single most sympathetic book on Egypt, demonstrate a lively and warm sensibility towards Egyptian life.

The pattern of visitors began to change in the last quarter of the nineteenth century. The introduction of steam power turned the months previously required for the Nile voyage into weeks. Thomas Cook's package holidays (spacious as they may seem by present-day standards) brought a different type of visitor to Egypt in increasing numbers. The pull of the ancient monuments was as strong as ever, though, aided by the success of Amelia Edwards' highly readable account of her voyage, *A Thousand Miles Up the Nile*, first published in 1877. Through her book and her indefatigable work for the Egypt Exploration Fund (later Society), which she founded five years later, she did more than perhaps any other individual both to secure the future of Egyptological research and to popularize its findings.

Following the establishment of British rule in 1882, a governing élite was superimposed on Egypt. While its members lived very much according to British traditions and customs, once again the more sensitive acquired a profound understanding and love of Egypt. These shine from the writings of such people as Ronald Storrs, Mabel Caillard and Mary Rowlatt, whose family lived and worked in Egypt for five generations.

Travel to Egypt may have lost its sense of the exotic and adventurous by the turn of the century, but interest continued unabated, receiving an enormous boost from the massive worldwide publicity that accompanied the discovery of Tutankhamun's tomb in 1922. A huge variety of people came to visit or live in Egypt, of whom this book can only represent a few. Later, in the soldiers stationed in military headquarters behind the lines in Cairo or in the forefront of the desert campaign, the Second World War brought another category of more or less willing visitor. Cairo, which had always enjoyed a superficial cosmopolitanism, seemed, to a certain category of Westerner at least, almost an extension of social and literary London. Many writers found material in the juxtaposition of the experience of battle and the strange vividness of Egyptian life.

Western influence dwindled rapidly after the end of the War. Following the British withdrawal in 1952 (and in 1956 even from the military zone alongside the Suez Canal), for the first time for more than a century and a half Egypt found itself free of direct foreign involvement. For some two decades, as the new state established itself, tourism remained relatively small-scale, but today, as it has for two centuries, the grandeur of the monuments of ancient Egypt and the fascination of Egyptian life continue to attract ever-increasing numbers of visitors.

The aim of this collection is simple: to offer the reader, whether travelling on the ground or at home in the proverbial armchair, a selection of the most interesting and entertaining writings by visitors to Egypt. Like all compilers of antholo-gies, I have had to make a number of relatively arbitrary decisions, largely for reasons of space. I start in 1798 with Vivant Denon as he accompanies the French forces up the Nile, thereby omitting the accounts written by eighteenth-century travellers; and I finish more or less in 1956, though I have slipped in a few more recent extracts where these seem to add to the story. I also decided, with much regret, to ignore fictional writing set in Egypt, though I realize full well that in doing so I run the risk of omitting some of the most sympathetic and penetrating insights into both land and people. Even so, I have been left with far more material than I can possibly find room for.

Introduction

For advice and ideas, I am especially grateful to Patrick Conner, Jacqueline Fisher, Charles Newton, and Roger Hudson of John Murray, and also to Suzanne Bosman for translating extracts from French for me. My wife and children have happily put up with my preoccupation with Egypt, and my thanks go to them. This book could not have been written without the resources of many libraries and the willing help of their librarians. I would particularly like to thank the staffs of two, the London Library and Upper Norwood Public Library, without whom my work would have been immeasurably more difficult.

Christopher Pick
London
June 1990

I

Precepts for Travellers

Three journeys to the East make one feel that guide-books are not sufficiently explicit as to such details as are here given, and this must be my apology for venturing to give the following bits of advice.

1. As to dress. Dress as you would in England in early summer, but take a good wrap: flannel shirts and flannel belt; mornings and evenings are often chilly. Wear boots rather than shoes, because there are such things as asps in Egypt; and brown rather than black, because of the heat. Cream for cleaning these boots, should be taken out from England, as it is not always procurable abroad, and if not used, the boots are soon spoiled by the dry hot sand. Canvas leggings for men, and a light serge skirt (walking length) for ladies, are advisable, because donkeys are dirty and tombs are dusty. Wear a sun helmet, or (better) a soft, grey felt wide-awake, double thickness. Take a strong white English-made umbrella, lined with green or blue, and a pair of glasses – smoked, not blue – for use when riding over desert-sand.

2. As to food, everything can be got in Cairo, except good English tea. On no pretext be induced to drink Nile water, when at anchor; avoid it at all times, unless boiled. The Nile is the drain of all Egypt. Dwellers on the banks of it know that it contains a parasite which is a troublesome customer, if it takes up its abode in the human body. Light claret and St. Galmier and other mineral waters can be obtained for you by Gaze or Cook. Never let flies settle on your face; they may bring ophthalmia. Use lotion at the first symptom.

3. Medicines. Pyretic saline, quinine, Dover's powder (these last in the form of pills), chlorodyne, a roll of plaster, lint, a bit of oil-silk, a box of mustard leaves, compound colocynth pills, an eye-douche and eye-lotion obtained in Cairo, are all that is necessary. For use amongst natives, a box of eye ointment (red oxide of mercury). Good doctors are at Luxor and on the Nile steamers; and in case of typhoid, most devoted nursing, with the best possible medical skill, can be obtained at the German Deaconesses' Hospital in Cairo. If ill, do not stay in the hotel, but remove at once, under doctor's orders, to the hospital.

4. Take a reel of magnesium wire; there is great difficulty in obtaining a satisfactory lamp for the continuous burning of magnesium wire. Procure a tin reflector, like a stable lantern, to hold five candles, with socket and long stick. This enables the traveller to see the more interesting drawings and sculptures, which are generally best preserved on the upper parts of tombs and temples.

Good writing and drawing materials, note-books, &c., are not obtainable in Cairo.

The little 'Kodak' camera is very useful for instantaneous photographs of figures, &c.

5. Donkeys. In Cairo, engage and pay for your donkeys through the hotel porter. Examine for raw place under broad belt and under tail, before engaging. If you find a donkey falls, change him; he will do it again. On going up Nile, see the ladies' saddles, and have them marked before leaving, or you may be put off with native-made instead of English-made saddles, which are often unusable, and the straps of which are generally rotten. See that your side-saddles are not whisked off from your steamer, as you return, on to another steamer passing up.

6. Dragomen. However well recommended, never expect your dragoman to know anything about Egyptian history or the monuments up Nile. Go, knowing what you want to see, and insist on seeing it. Refuse to allow your dragoman to take 'a squeeze' for you from any of

the monuments. He is generally very ready to do so, and much damage has been done in this way.

In Cairo it will save you time and expense to engage a dragoman for the day. He knows the mosques best worth seeing, and can get all the necessary orders, and will easily save you his day's pay at the bazaars.

7. In dealing with the people, treat them as gentlemen. The Eastern, who is always polite, appreciates this. He understands a joke also. One often escapes the importunity of those who ask for 'bakhsheesh' by nodding, and saying with a smile, 'Boókra,' which means 'To-morrow.' Above all things, remember the religion of Muhammad is a real thing in Egypt. Show deference to religious belief and custom, and a becoming reverence when you enter any of their mosques. To avoid missing interesting scenes, ascertain the days of religious festivals.

8. If you want to see the monuments, remember that this cannot possibly be done in a crowd. Travellers by small steamer or dahabîeh will have the best of it in this matter.

It is well to ask if there is any peasant in the neighbourhood, who has been in the employ of one or other of the explorers of late years. These men have exact memories, and can often point out to you objects of interest that you would otherwise miss. Make a public example of any one in your company you catch defacing a monument, either by scribbling his name or by taking fragments of it away. Posterity will bless you.

9. As to scarabs, never purchase, except at the Gîzeh Museum, unless you are an expert. Nineteen out of twenty, offered for sale up Nile, were manufactured in the scarab-makers' shops, and buried or worn next to the skin by the vendor, to give the appearance of age, and colour.

As to papyri, do not refuse a portion of one – it may contain a valuable text. If you obtain possession of one that has not been unrolled, do not attempt to unroll it, or allow the man from whom you buy it to do so; but take it to your national museum, let the authorities examine it, and if important, leave it with them. It is necessary to allow scholars of the Egyptian language the fullest possible access to any texts that are discovered.

10. It will save you much perplexity, and add to the pleasure of the Nile voyage, if you have made yourself familiar, beforehand, with the main historical facts and characteristics of the various epochs and dynasties; if you know the cartouches of the more important kings; and if the leading features and symbols of the ancient Egyptian religion and divinities, the localities of the various gods, and the general arrangement of temple worship, are grasped . . .

The best books for those who would study the Egyptian monuments and history are the Egyptian collections in the various national museums. Travellers, before starting for the Nile, should, if possible, have visited the British Museum and the Louvre, and before sailing up river, should make a point of spending some considerable time in the Gîzeh Museum.

Canon Hardwicke D. Rawnsley, *Notes for the Nile.* 1892.
See p. 130.

2

First Impressions

At nine o'clock, turning the end of a chain of mountains which formed a promontory, the French suddenly
beheld the seat of the antique Thebes, in all its devel-
opement [*sic*]; Thebes, of which Homer has painted the
extent in a single word, the *hundred-gated* Thebes, a
poetic and empty expression, confidently repeated
through a series of ages. Described in a few pages dic-
tated to Herodotus by the egyptian priests, and copied
ever since by all other historians; celebrated for a succession of kings whose wisdom has placed them in the
rank of gods, for laws which were revered without being
understood, for sciences confided to pompous and enig-
matic inscriptions (those learned and earliest monuments of the arts, which time itself has forborne to
injure): this abandoned sanctuary, insulated by barbarism, and returned to the desert whence it was conquered;
this city, in a word, perpetually wrapped in that veil of
mystery by which even colossusses are magnified: this
exiled city, which the mind no longer discovers but
through the mists of time, was still a phantom so gigantic
to our imagination, that the army, at the sight of its
scattered ruins, halted of itself, and, by one spontaneous
impulse, grounded its arms, as if the possession of the
remains of this capital had been the object of its glorious
labours, had completed the conquest of the egyptian
territory.

Vivant Denon, *Travels in Upper and Lower Egypt*, 1803.

Having taken passage on board a vessel of the country for Cairo, we sailed up the canal, the shores of which presented nothing but sand and barrenness to the view. But how delightfully the scene was changed, when, on coming upon deck early the next morning, we perceived the vessel going slowly down the Nile! It was just before sunrise, and the softest hues were spreading all over the horizon. The shores were covered with groves of palm, among which were numerous villages, while here and there the white thin minaret rose into the air, and a universal stillness reigned throughout the scene. It was impossible to find oneself, for the first time, on this celebrated river, without the liveliest emotion. The boat stopped for some hours at the town of Foua. Having bathed in the river, I walked through the town: though so early, the shops were open, and fruit selling in the streets: more than one good Moslem, who had just risen from his bed, had taken his seat without his door, and with the Koran in his hand, was reading the Prophet's splendid promises, or teaching his child his prayers. Even in this town there were twelve mosques; and the Muezzin, from the top of the minaret, had begun to call to prayers. This cry, in so still a country as Egypt, and heard at the dawn or at night from a distance, has an effect the most beautiful and solemn that can be conceived.

John Carne, *Letters from the East*, 1830.

The sun has some heat and the flight is smooth later when I wake up and stroll aft to stand by the window and smoke. There are magnificent views of volcanic ranges and the fascination of tracing the Nile. Six miles below the Second Cataract we put down at Wadi Halfa to refuel. The river banks rush up to meet us and we feather along the water, pulling up neatly opposite the landing-stage. There is tea ashore in a garden with a profusion of roses and two tall purple bougainvilia. We are soon air-borne again and we have persuaded the pilot to take us a little off course for the antiquities.

So here is the City of Thebes printed in ruin upon the green carpets which spread along the shores of the river. Here effortlessly sliding beneath us are the colossi of Memnon unexpectedly standing amid cultivated fields. We fly low across the Valley of Kings and we skim down to meet the Nile water as the immemorial temples of Karnak flash by the windows. I have read and dreamed of these places, and now with a sergeant-pilot from Nottingham and the general who had my seat I press my nose against *Caledonia's* glass trying to recognise, identify and remember them all, their massive beauty in the sun, their pattern majestically outlined against the Nile's green aprons. All too soon we are water-borne, going ashore to face the pestering salesmen and the beggars outside Luxor's Winter Palace Hotel.

After refuelling we climb up and glimpse the Red Sea flashing intensely blue upon the starboard quarter: but mostly we follow the verdant pattern of the Nile's irri-gated fringes, the white squares of farms and the regular circles where oxen are turning the water-wheels. For the last lap I sit with the captain and pick out the Pyramids from a great distance. In the strong afternoon light Cairo spreads out warted along the river. The Pyramids seem closer, more domesticated, less arrogant than one had supposed. The two pilots begin to point out Cairo's good and bad features and we glide down towards the green lozenge of Gezira Island. My birthday treat – though they do not know it – is to remain in the cockpit during the landing. The water is grey; the air has an authentic January chill. We queue for customs examination upon a house-boat. Somebody behind me is saying: 'Well, you do see the country by flying.'

But that the Pyramids should be made to look small . . .

John Pudney, *Who Only England Know*, 1943.

First Impressions

During the voyage it had been possible to avoid intro-
spective enquiry, but as we lay off Port Said, motionless
and awaiting disembarkation, the confusion of motives
behind my actions rose to the surface, and after a while
I was troubled by these reflections. Then, after a day of
shimmering heat, a cooler evening breeze ruffled the
mirror of the apparently tideless waters. A soldier standing next to me, leaning against the railings of the main
deck and gazing at the dusty and barren hills opposite,
gave vent to a common feeling – what on earth am I
doing here? – by loudly announcing to nobody but
himself, 'The white cliffs of Dover browned off!' and
abruptly went below. At that moment, however, I was
not feeling quite that way. The mountains, the colour
of dusky moths' wings, changing to spectacular rose and
violet, became an invitation. The sun set swiftly, and in
the sky, now a deep and silent indigo, the stars came
out. Conscious of being alone, and like a shipwrecked
sailor responsible for my own fate, I experienced the
elation of solitude, and looked forward to the adventure
of the unknown.

Robert Medley, *Drawn from the Life*, 1983.

3

Alexandria

THE landing at Alexandria represented, until the era of air travel, the initial, much anticipated, prospect of the East. For many, the arrival was a disappointment. The city could never live up to the past glories her very name recalled. Thus Vivant Denon, one of the large party of scholars and scientists who accompanied Napoleon's expedition in 1798, on the eve of his landing at Alexandria.

When the long shadows of evening had marked the outlines of the city, I distinguished the two ports, the lofty walls, flanked by numerous towers, no longer inclosing any thing but heaps of sand, and a few gardens, the pale green of whose palm-trees scarcely tempered the ardent whiteness of the soil; the turkish castle, the mosks, their minarets; the celebrated pillar of Pompey; and my imagination went back to the past; I saw art triumph over nature; the genius of Alexandria employ the active hands of commerce, to lay, on a barren coast, the foundations of a magnificent city, and select that city as the depository of the trophies of the conquest of a world; I saw the Ptolomies invite the arts and sciences, and collect that library which it took barbarism so many years to consume: it was there, said I, thinking of Cleopatra, of Cæsar, and of Anthony, that the empire of glory was sacrificed to the empire of voluptuousness! After this, I saw ferocious ignorance establish itself on the ruins of the master-pieces of the arts, labouring to destroy them, and unable, notwithstanding, even yet to have disfigured those beautiful fragments which display the noble principles of their first design.

Vivant Denon, *Travels in Upper and Lower Egypt*, 1803.

FOR, as travellers soon realized, Alexandria was not the *real* Egypt they had been expecting. The city, founded by Alexander the Great in 332 BC as the era of ancient Egypt was ending, stands on the very rim of Africa, closer, through culture, tradition and geography, to Greece and the Levant than to the Egypt of the Pharaohs. The ruins were, of course, an essential part of the itinerary, but in the modern city, even when wide boulevards and squares and the new docks began to be built in the 1820s and 30s, there was little to attract the visitor. Small wonder, then, that many writers voice their feelings of anti-climax. Here are two: the French writer and politician Chateaubriand, on his way home after a Middle East tour in 1806–7, and Sarah Haight, a lively and sympathetic (if rather conventional) American lady who was doing a grand tour with her husband in 1836.

If I had been enchanted with Egypt, I thought Alexandria, on the contrary, the most dreary and desolate place in the world. From the terrace of the consul's house I could perceive nothing but a naked sea, breaking against a low and still more naked coast, harbours almost empty, and the Libyan desert stretching to the south as far as the eye could reach. This desert seemed, as it were, an extension of the yellow and level surface of the deep: you might imagine that you had before you but one single sea, one half of which was agitated and turbulent, and the other half silent and motionless. Modern

Alexandria every where mingling its ruins with the ruins
of the ancient city; an Arab gallopping among them
upon an ass; a number of half-starved dogs devouring
the carcases of camels on the beach; the flags of the
European consuls waving over their habitations, and
displaying hostile colours in the midst of tombs – such
was the spectacle here presented to my view.

Sometimes I took a ride with M. Drovetti to the old
town, to Necropolis, or to the desert. The plant which
yields soda scarcely covered the dry sand; the jackals
fled at our approach; a species of cricket chirped with a
shrill and disagreeable voice, painfully reminding you
of the villager's cot in this solitude, where no rural smoke
ever calls you to the tent of the Arab. This place has
become still more dreary since the English inundated the
spacious hollow which served Alexandria for a garden.
Nothing meets the eye but sand, water, and Pompey's
eternal pillar.

Chateaubriand, *Travels in Greece, Palestine, Egypt and
Barbary*, 1811.

This cannot be an *Egyptian* city. It never was. A
Greek conqueror was its founder, who built his splendid
capital upon the site of a former Greek trading town. In
its best estate it could only have been considered as a
beautiful Propylon, standing in advance of the great
ancient temple *Egypt*, and in comparison with the
immense antiquity of the latter but a modern work; more
elegantly classic in its proportions and ornament, though
falling far short of the majestic and mysterious grandeur
of the principal edifice.

I am impatient to get to the *Great River*; to feel myself
floating upon those waters which, after rising in vapours
from the salt sea now before me, float in mid air, and
are carried by the winds to the mountains of the tropics;
there condensed among their high and chilly peaks, to

descend in torrents upon the plains of Ethiopia. Thence rushing by the cavern temples of Nubia, leaping over the granite ridges of Syene, they divide the Theban capital in twain, and, laving the shores of Memphis, reach the sea again, to take another annual circuit to the end of time.

We take our departure hence to-morrow. A new and fruitful field is now before me; and however often it may have been reaped by others who have preceded me, there is, doubtless, an abundance of rich gleanings which I may be able to gather into my garner. Whatever portion I may hereafter send to you, may you, after winnowing away the chaff, find a few golden grains of the corn of the Egyptian valley.

Sarah Haight, *Letters from the Old World*, 1840.

NOT everyone reacted in so negative a way. Some were beguiled by the confusing sensations of the East. Arriving on his first visit to Egypt in 1858, the painter Frederick Goodall found himself torn between the practical demands of seeing to luggage and finding a dragoman (the interpreter-cum-guide essential for all independent travellers in Egypt) and his desire to absorb the local colour.

Sir Lewis Pelly, my travelling companion from Paris, told me many years afterwards, that he never saw any one so nearly cracked as I seemed to be immediately after the landing at Alexandria. I *did* feel almost cracked, but I had urgent business on hand and no time for rhapsody. I had to attend the Custom House and claim my heavy luggage, which had been forwarded from London many weeks before, and engage my dragoman, whom I found extremely useful and attentive . . .

Consul Green invited me to dine with him, and in the

meantime I wandered about with my pocket sketch-book, jotting down everything I thought worthy of making a note of, and finishing up at the camp of the pilgrims from Mecca – a most extraordinary sight – waiting for the steamer to take them on to Tunis, Algiers, and Morocco. My dragoman told the people whom I was sketching, that I was only an officer of the steamboat putting down their names as passengers. Many of the pilgrims were suffering from ophthalmia, and came crowding round me for medicine. In a kind-hearted mood I went back to the hotel for sulphate of zinc, and when I returned, the people came unpleasantly close, holding out shells for a few drops of the medicine. I told Consul Green what I had done, and he said if he had known where I was going he would have warned me, as the camp was full of fever and disease ...

During a donkey-ride through the town I saw enough subjects to last a lifetime. The children's school impressed me as a beautiful subject, the wee Turks squatting on the ground outside the house, and the turbaned schoolmaster seated in the doorway teaching them the Koran, the little fellows repeating it after him. The wells, with the animated groups round about them, were beyond description. The women were not all veiled, and when filling their pitchers, or carrying them on their shoulders, reminded me of what I had read of the grace of the women of the ancient world. The men, too, with their water-skins, and the camels with theirs, formed such groups as I had never beheld even in a day-dream. It made me quite long to be at work. I could not refrain from exclaiming aloud at the different scenes that met my eye – 'How beautiful!' 'How wonderful!' 'How gloriously picturesque!' 'What colour!' 'What costumes!' 'What character!' until my dragoman must have thought he had got charge of a lunatic. The fact was I was perfectly bewildered at the novelty of everything and felt absolutely convinced that the people had never been painted, that practically I was on virgin soil, with a free hand.

Frederick Goodall, *The Reminiscences of Frederick Goodall, R.A.*, 1902.

Alexandria

ALEXANDRIA's commercial and intellectual revival, stimulated largely by its increasing importance as a port ('founded upon cotton with the concurrence of onions and eggs', as the novelist E.M. Forster put it) lasted not much more than a century. Forster was posted there during the First World War to do Red Cross work, and subsequently returned to write a classic guidebook to the city. In this short essay, 'Between the Sun and the Moon', he reflects on the interplay of the city's past and present lives.

Of the three streets that dispute the honour of being Alexandria's premier thoroughfare the Rue Rosette undoubtedly bears the palm for gentility. The Bond Street (I refer to Rue Chérif Pacha) is too shoppy to be genteel, and the Boulevard de Ramleh competes from this particular aspect not at all. In its length, its cleanliness, and the refined monotony of its architecture, Rue Rosette outdoes either of its rivals. They are tainted with utility: people use them to get something or somewhere. But Rue Rosette is an end in itself. It starts in the middle of the town and no man can tell where it stops: a goal it may have, but not one discoverable by mortal leg. Its horizon, narrow but uninterrupted, ever unrolls into a ribbon of blue sky above the wayfarer's head, and the ribbon of white beneath his feet corresponds, and right and left of him are the houses that he thought he had passed a quarter of an hour before. Oh, it is so dull! Its dullness is really indescribable. What seem at first to be incidents – such as the trays of worthies who project from the clubs – prove at a second glance to be subdued to what they sit in. They are half asleep. For you cannot have gentility without paying for it.

The poor street does not want to be dull. It wants to be smart, and of a Parisian smartness. Eternally well-dressed people driving infinitely in either direction – that is its ideal. It is not mine, and we meet as seldom as possible in consequence. But friends of a higher social outlook tell me that, by a great effort, they can feel perfectly at home in the Rue Rosette – can transform the municipal buildings into Ministries, and the Consulates into Embassies, and arabias into broughams, can increase the polish on the gentlemen's boots and the frou-frou from the ladies' skirts, until the Rue Rosette becomes what it yearns to be – a masterpiece by Baron Haussmann, debouching in an Arc de Triomphe instead of a Police Station.

I have never been able to make that effort. When fancies do come here, they are of an older and friendlier civilization. I recall Achilles Tatius, a bishop of the post-classical period, who wrote a somewhat improper novel. He made his hero enter Alexandria by this very street one thousand years ago. It was not called the Rue Rosette then, but the Canopic Road, and it was not genteel or smart but presented throughout its length scenes of extraordinary splendour. Beginning at the Gate of the Sun (by the Public Gardens) it traversed the city uninterruptedly until it reached the waters of the Harbour (near Minet el Bassal), and here stood the Gate of the Moon, to close what the Sun had begun. The street was lined with marble colonnades from end to end, as was the Rue Nebi Daniel, and the point of their intersection (where one now stands in hopeless expectation of a tram) was one of the most glorious crossways of the ancient world. Clitophon (it was thus that the Bishop named his hero) paused there in his walk, and looked down the four vistas, over whose ranks rose temples and palaces and tombs, and he tells us that the crossways bore the name of Alexander, and that the Mausoleum close to them was Alexander's tomb. He does not tell us more, being in search of a female companion named Leucippe, whom he deems of more permanent interest, but there is no reason to doubt his statements, for Achilles Tatius himself lived here and dare not cause his characters to lie. The passage gleams like a jewel among the amorous rubbish that surrounds it. The vanished glory leaps up again, not in architectural detail but as a city of the soul. There (beneath the

Mosque of Nebi Daniel) is the body of Alexander the Great. There he lies, lapped in gold and laid in a coffin of glass. When Clitophon made his visit he had already lain there for eight hundred years, and according to legend he lies there still, walled into a forgotten cellar. And of this glory all that tangibly remains is a road: the alignment of the Rue Rosette. Christian and Arab destroyed the rest, but they could not destroy the direction of a road. Towards the harbour they did divert it, certainly; the great thoroughfare contracts into the Rue Sidi Metwalli and becomes heaven knows what in the neighbourhood of the Rue des Sœurs. But in its eastern stretch it runs with its old decision, and the limestone and stucco still throw over it the shadows that marble once threw.

Of the two gates there survives not even a description. They may have been masterpieces of art, they may have been simple entrances, but they must certainly have included shrines to the god and goddess who respectively guarded them. No one took much notice of the shrines. Paganism, even in the days of Clitophon and Leucippe, was dead. It is dead, yet the twin luminaries still reign over the street and give it what it has of beauty. In the evening the western vista can blaze with orange and scarlet, and the eastern, having darkened, can shimmer with a mysterious radiance, out of which, incredibly large, rises the globe of the moon.

E. M. Forster, *Pharos and Pharillon*, 1923.

Two decades and a world war later, Lawrence Durrell, one of the many writers washed up by war in Egypt, captured the atmosphere of heady cosmopolitanism in his letters and, above all, in his celebrated novels of Alexandrine life, the *Alexandria Quartet*. Here he writes to the American novelist Henry Miller in 1944.

Alexandria

BRITISH INFORMATION OFFICE,
1, RUE TOUSSOUM, ALEXANDRIA,

May 23

Dear Henry

... I am in charge of a goodish sized office of war-propaganda here, trying to usher in the new washboard world which our demented peoples are trying 'to forge in blood and iron'. It's tiring work. However it's an office full of beautiful girls, and Alexandria is, after Hollywood, fuller of beautiful women than any place else. Incomparably more beautiful than Athens or Paris; the mixture Coptic, Jewish, Syrian, Egyptian, Moroccan, Spanish gives you slant dark eyes, olive freckled skin, hawk-lips and noses, and a temperament like a bomb. Sexual provender of quality, but the atmosphere is damp, hysterical, sandy, with the wind off the desert fanning everything to mania. Love, hashish and boys is the obvious solution to anyone stuck here for more than a few years. I am sharing a big flat with some nice people, and atop it I have a tower of my own from which the romantics can see Pompey's Pillar, Hadra Prison, and the wet reedy wastes of Lake Mareotis stretching away into the distance and blotting the sky.

This is the world of the desert Fathers and the wandering jews; the country eaten away like the carious jawbone of a mummy. Alexandria is the only possible point in Egypt to live in because it has a harbour and opens on a flat turpentine sealine – a way of escape. At the moment I am in mid-stream fighting my way through the rapids of a love affair with Gipsy Cohen, a tormented jewish-greek ...

It's funny the way you get woman after woman: and exactly what it adds up to I don't know: each more superficial than the last Gaby, Simone, Arlette, Dawn, Penelope ... but only Gipsy Cohen burns black and fierce under her Tunisian eyebrows; the flavour is straight Shakespeare's Cleopatra; an ass from Algiers, lashes from Malta, nails and toes from Smyrna, hips from Beirut, eyes from Athens, and nose from Andros, and a mouth that shrieks or purrs like the witching women of Homs or Samarkand. And breasts from Fiume. And what the hell?

But their sex here is interesting; it's madly violent but not WEAK or romantic or obscure, like anglo-saxon women, who are always searching for a tintype of their daddies. It is not preconceived but taken heavily and in a kind of war – not limp northern friendship – but fierce and glaring, vulture and eagle work with beak and claws.

Well, the last few days we've driven out through Bourg El Arab, and slipped down through the battle-fields to a long beach where the real Mediterranean comes up in great green coasters and sky is smothered down to violet, all lambent and turning your body in water to a wonderful rose. The sea citron-green cold and pure with sandy floor; for the first time in four years I felt I was in Greece. Bathing naked. At our back the dunes running away to the deserted crusader fort, nibbled battlements misty and like a mirage. Thousands of empty rounds of ammunition, dirty bandages, twisted wreck of enemy tanks, lumber. Strange atmosphere this deserted battlefield with the sea inking in the edges of the sky and the old fortress glowing like a jewel. On the road an occasional Bedouin with his camel. And palms like old camel-flesh trees clicking stiffly in the wind. Strange transition to Cavafy's Alexandria, and a letter from George Seferis saying that he is feeling happier and happier now that he has dropped propaganda.

There is not much else to tell you that can be conveniently written; forgive the mad haste of this. I must see what the world-fronts are saying on the radio. Gipsy is coming for a drink at one. Life is long, art short, as Goethe did not say.

Wonder when it will all end? Do write again soon won't you?

Lawrence Durrell, *The Durrell-Miller Letters, 1935–80*, 1988.

THE war was the final, overblown moment of Alexandria's second flowering. After the 1952 Revolution, British and French, Greeks and Italians, Christians and Jews gradually left, trade dwindled, and Alexandria found itself beached once more, an inappropriately Mediterranean city in a determinedly Arab land. The journalist David Holden recalls a visit in 1963.

A sandstorm threw a golden pall over Alexandria when I was there again the other day. A vicious, unseasonal storm, three months earlier than the usual *khamsin*, it stiffened the hair with a dung-like crust and smothered even the sight and sound of the sea. Palm trees waved overhead like wraiths and men vanished behind yellow veils as they crossed the street.

Next morning the wind had backed to the north-west and under a clearing sky the Mediterranean was lashing the corniche with the cold fury of a northern sea. Spray cascaded off the tiers of bathing huts beneath the sea wall; the cafés on the rocky promontories were awash and the tall flats that straggle for miles between Ramleh and Montazah Bay were shuttered tight against the wind.

This was Alexandria out of season, when the city turns its back upon the sea, as a sheep puts its rump to a blizzard. Behind the wave-drenched promenades the narrow streets of Alexandria's dockland were pullulating with the introverted life of peasant Egypt, but upon the boulevards and gardens of the European city a great desolation had descended. The ornate villas of the *quartier Grec* were almost visibly brown at the edges, withdrawn and wilting, their gardens ragged with wind-blown paper and creepers too long untrimmed. Behind the rattling doors of the cafés in the Place Zaghloul a few old men crouched over silent games of *tric-trac*. In the bar of the Cecil Hotel, where the potted palms once danced in the hearty fug of British officers on leave from the Western desert, the barman nodded on his stool in solitary boredom.

Since I first knew it a few years ago, Alexandria out of season has always been a little chilly and forlorn, like a pensioner waiting for the warmth of summer to bring back the blood to her cheeks. But this time the chill seemed to strike deeper, to smell less of winter than of death. The peasants in the back streets were the teeming maggots in the corpse.

There is a paradox here, of course. Like every other town in Egypt, Alexandria is growing in numbers. One-and-a-half-million people find a home somewhere within its boundaries now and more are coming every year, thrust off the land of the Nile valley by the pressure of their own fecundity. In summer, when the heat in Cairo is oppressive, half-a-million more arrive for a breath of Mediterranean air. The promenades then are thick with holiday-makers, the public gardens loud with the wail of transistor radios, the beach huts and cafés bursting with young Egypt – dark, shapely and emancipated, with not a veil or a tarboosh to be seen. All this is not dead. It is frighteningly alive – a resurgent Egypt, flooding down the Nile to the Mediterranean shore, as Europe so recently poured its energies the other way. With the turn of the tide the city of Cavafy, Forster, and Durrell has not yet physically disappeared like the city of Alexander when the Arabs arrived, but it has just as effectively ceased to be. In the 10 years since Farouk stepped into exile aboard his yacht, from the terrace of the palace at Ras el Tin, European Alexandria has been washed into history.

This is not something for which Gamal Abdul Nasser must take all the blame. Like Algiers and Tunis – or Leptis Magna and Cyrene – Alexandria was one of those grappling hooks that Europe cast upon Africa in a time of imperial expansion. With the decline of her power, the hooks were cut away again. As soon as World War

II was over the writing was on the wall for Alexandria's
European community, and the far-sighted were already
getting out. In their heyday, Europeans and Jews
together may have numbered 200,000. By 1945 there
were less than 150,000. If there are more than 30,000
now I should be surprised. Since 1952 at least 70,000
must have gone. The British and French have almost
totally disappeared, cleared out in the aftermath of Suez.
So have the Jews, who alone numbered scores of thousands. The Italians, the Maltese, and some inde-
terminate Levantines hang on in handfuls here and
there, and the Greeks, who formed the biggest of all
the European colonies and gave the city much of its
distinctive Mediterranean flavour, may muster as many
as 20,000 still. But 10 years ago there were 50,000 Greeks
in Alexandria, and even after Suez, when the Greek
pilots stayed to help the Egyptians in the canal and *enosis*
in Cyprus was still a lively possibility uniting Athens to
Cairo in opposition to the British, many of them believed
that the European exodus would never include them.
'That was our mistake,' said one of them this time. 'The
others got out when they still could. The British and
French even got paid for leaving, thanks to Anthony
Eden. But we must pay for staying.' And pay they do,
as the government in Cairo snatches up the economic
reins that used to lie so profitably in Alexandrian hands,
and firmly asserts that Egypt is for the Egyptians now.
Not for nothing, after all, is Nasser the first true Egyptian to rule his country since Alexander arrived. For
most of the 2,300 years in between Egypt has been either
milked or spurned by foreigners; now an Egyptian is
milking and spurning them.

The Alexandrian cotton market, once one of the great
commodity markets of the world and the channel for
three-quarters of Egypt's foreign earnings, has been
nationalised. The bourse is empty and the brokers are
out of business. Barclay's *DCO* and the *Credit Lyonnais*
are now the Bank of Alexandria and the Misr Bank. The
Mohammed Ali Club, once the *Athenaeum* of Alexandrian society, has become a 'Government Cultural

Centre.' The grotesque royal palace at Montazah is an empty casino. The British Cricket Club ground has been acquired by Alexandria University as a hockey pitch, the Avenue Belgique is now the Avenue Lumumba, and members of the Yacht Club may not take their boats beyond the harbour mouth lest they set sail for Cyprus with their valuables in an effort to get away from it all.

The Alexandrian telephone book reads like a Levantine requiem. Bianchi and Bassilis, Athanassacopoulos and Papadopoulos, Zarb and Zerbini, Karam, Smouha, Moscatelli and Salvago, Marcopolis and Marcantonaki – most of them gone already, and the rest hoping that they will be next to invite their friends to a farewell party. For those that remain, embedded in the ruins of their own past, Pastroudis' café is still a source of bitter solace, with its memories of the old days; and elderly Greek couples still turn up of an evening at the Union Bar to dine on practically the only decent European food still cooked in Egypt – for the kitchen suffers along with the salons and the bank balances when history is on the move.

But for all of them life has really ended already. They are simply seeing out their last years in the ivory towers of heightened memory and straightened circumstances. There is the Comte Patrice de Zogheb, for example, a true Alexandrian if ever there was one, with a French wife, Danish nationality, Italian title, and Syrian descent, an old Etonian and an amateur of the arts, squatting in his penthouse in the middle of the city and contemplating with the bland resignation of his 72 years the sequestration of all his property and the decline and fall of everything he was born to. 'Come on Sunday to my *Messiah*,' he said. 'I've done it every year for a quarter of a century, you know. Of course, it's only on gramophone records now – but the British Consul-General will open the proceedings.'

There is Stelios Comoutsos, a Greek waiter with a passion for history, who has spent his life's savings digging up the pavements of his native city in a fruitless search for the tomb of Alexander. There is Jimmy, whom nobody but his mother knows by any other name and whom his father may never have known at all. 'I'm half-Irish meself' says he, lurking in a doorway of the Place Zaghloul. Jimmy likes to call himself a guide, claiming nameless delights at his command; and once, before I knew any better, I accepted his offer of an introduction to the Bombay Speller, thinking that I might meet some exotic fakir washed up on these shores long ago, like Jimmy's father perhaps, among the wrack of the British Empire. But instead I was taken to see the monumental column erected in honour of the Emperor Diocletian and known to Alexandrians as Pompey's Pillar – the most pointless but imposing of the few remaining relics of the earlier Empire that began Alexandria's legend.

That Empire, too, was submerged by alien tides; and before Europe reclaimed Alexandria through Bonaparte and Mohammed Ali, the pearl of the Mediterranean had declined into a fishing village. Its latter-day revival has been of shorter duration than its early glory. Events move faster now than then, and a single century of European prosperity is all the modern city has enjoyed. It is easy to be too sentimental about its fate. Modern Alexandria produced nobody to compare with Euclid and Eratosthenes, Plotinus and Athanasius. It reflected the harsher qualities of 19th-century imperialism as well as some of the sybaritic sophistication of the Levant. It was a base for rapacious adventurers and war profiteers, for merchants and bankers, consuls and concubines – the middlemen of diplomacy, trade, and culture. It was not, essentially, a creative city; yet it did create its own legend as a glorious, decadent paramour among cities – a whore of the golden east. In our more puritan, bread-and-butter century, however, paramours are no longer highly thought of, especially when they come with the wrong passport. Working wives are more the thing.

Yet Alexandria deserves its mourners; and one evening on my last visit I talked to one of them, a true lover of his native place. He was a Greek, of course, and for two hours, while the sand-storm rattled the shutters outside, he went through the rubble of his city's past with a nostalgic sieve, catching in the mesh of his memory a score of remarkable figures and institutions, and sighing with pleasure over the visions that my curiosity had compelled him to recall. Suddenly he stopped, as if the memories had become unbearable, and flung up his hands, palms outwards, in a gesture of despair. 'Gone!' he cried, in a voice of deep severity, 'All gone! Tonight we are historians. We speak now only of history.'

I left him and went out into the storm, with the sand stinging my eyes and throat, and around me the ghosts of an Alexandria that is always out of season now.

David Holden, 'Letter from Alexandria', *Encounter*, August 1963.

4
The Journey to Cairo

ALL too eager to leave behind the disappointments of Alexandria, the traveller was now faced with the tedious journey to Cairo. So near, and yet so far! With an unfavourable wind and an unwilling crew, the trip could last a frustrating five or six days. At least the opening of the Mahmoudieh Canal in 1820, built in a matter of months by gangs of forced labour, brought a direct link between Alexandria and the Nile. Until then, a desert journey, much feared (though usually without reason) by the novice visitor, was necessary to reach the Nile at Rosetta. Even so, there was all the bother and confusion of changing on to a larger Nile boat at Atfeh.

In Alexandria travellers generally stayed sheltered from local life, which provided no more than a tantalizing and colourful backdrop to the ruins. Now, on this voyage, they were brought face to face for the first time with all the constant irritations, for Europeans, of travel in Egypt: the unreliability, the demands for backsheesh, the sheer slowness of everything. These are complaints heard time and time again, especially by travellers with a fixed timetable, such as Mrs Haight.

Before leaving Alexandria we had made arrangements for one of the regular line boats, belonging to a company of merchants there, in which, being doubly manned and ably commanded, the trip was made in the least possible time. Our friends sent on an express to *Adfe*[Atfeh] (where the canal intersects the river), to retain for our exclusive accommodation the company's boat, about to sail the next day.

We then embarked on board the canal-boat with all our effects, and, on arriving at the river, found that our arrangement for the boat had been frustrated by some friends of other parties concerned in the line, who had been made aware of our express, and had sent another in advance of it, or, perhaps, bribed our own. We found that our boat had gone some hours, and the agent of the company had supplied our order with a little *kanjee*, which, as he said, had the recommendation of being new, and not requiring to be sunk to rid it of vermin before it was fit for use. There being a fine north wind at the time, we naturally supposed that we could run the short distance to Cairo in a day and a half; so we made a virtue of necessity, and embarked cheerfully, with an assurance from the agent that only six hands were necessary, as we should not have to *tow* the boat a mile.

We ran on a few hours in gallant style, stemming the current at the rate of five or six miles per hour. When sundown came, the wind fell; and then it is the duty of the crew to get out with their tow-line and drag the boat along the shore, taking advantage of all the eddies. No such thing, however, with us. Our captain gave the order for supper; and as after that an Arab must sleep, and there is no waking him without the whip (which part of the performance we had not yet learned), we lay quietly moored alongside the bank all night; next morning there was no wind; the men dragged during the morning one mile per hour. During the afternoon a little breeze for a short time; sundown found us fast to a stake again; thus one day was gone, and only twenty miles were made ... The fact is, we were regularly cheated by these villains. The gentlemen began, as usual with them, to encourage the captain and crew, by promising them '*backshee*,' and all the time giving them meat, coffee, and tobacco. This was very injudicious. They should have given them nothing, or else, to finish their breakfast, a dessert of supple bamboo should have followed, by way of quick-

ening their digestion. The sly dogs thought, and with
good reason, too, that the more days they took to reach
Cairo, the more days of good cheer for them. So, for
once, our weapons of liberality were turned against us;
and in requital for our kindness to them, they determined to bestow upon us as much of their good company
as we could possibly endure, together with that of all
their domestic establishment of rats, spiders, cock-
roaches, and other nameless creeping creatures, as plen-
tiful as the dust from which the good book says they
sprang in days of old.

Sarah Haight, *Letters from the Old World*, 1840.

IN 1849, not long after the introduction of steam ships on
the Nile, there occurred an intriguing historical might-have-
been. Among the crowds who fought for a place on the
steamer were two young people in their late twenties. They
were Gustave Flaubert (soon to achieve notoriety as a novelist), who had come to Egypt to find inspiration for his writing;
and Florence Nightingale (soon to achieve fame as a nurse),
who had come to Egypt after rejecting a suitor her family
had considered most eligible. They did not meet, but maybe
Flaubert's remarks about an 'English family' refer to the
Nightingale party. Here are their observations, Flaubert's
made from his bed on deck, Florence's from the cramped
communal ladies' cabin.

Leave on a boat towed by a small steamer carrying only
its engine. Flat, dead banks of the Mahmudiyeh; on the
shore a few naked Arabs running, from time to time, a
traveller trots by on horseback, swathed in white in
his Turkish saddle. Passengers: ... an English family,
hideous; the mother looks like a sick old parrot (because

of the green eyeshade attached to her bonnet) ... At 'Atfeh you enter the Nile and take a larger boat.

First night on the Nile. State of contentment and of lyricism: I gesticulate, recite lines from Bouilhet, cannot bring myself to go to bed; I think of Cleopatra. The water is yellow and very smooth; a few stars. Well wrapped in my pelisse, I fall asleep on my camp-bed, on deck. Such rapture! I awoke before Maxime; in waking, he stretched out his left hand instinctively, to see if I was there.

On one side, the desert; on the other, a green meadow. With its sycamores it resembles from a distance a Norman plain with its apple-trees. The desert is a reddish-gray. Two of the Pyramids come into view, then a smaller one. To our left, Cairo appears, huddled on a hill; the dome of the mosque of Mohammed Ali; behind it, the bare Mokattam hills.

Arrival in Bulak, confusion of landing, a little less cudgeling than at Alexandria, however.

From Bulak to Cairo, rode along a kind of embankment planted with acacias or *gassis*. We come into the Ezbekiyeh [Square], all landscaped. Trees, greenery. Take rooms at the Hôtel d'Orient.

Flaubert's travel notes from *Flaubert in Egypt*, translated and edited by Francis Steegmuller, 1972.

MY DEAREST PEOPLE,
Here we are, our second step in the East. We left Alexandria on the 25th, at seven o'clock A.M. Were towed up the Mahmoudieh Canal by a little steam-tug to Atfeh, which we reached at five P.M. The canal perfectly uninteresting; the day gloomy. I was not very well, so I stayed below from Alexandria to Cairo. At Atfeh, as we were seventy people on board a boat built for twenty-five, Mrs. B. and I plunged out, without a plank, upon the bank, and ran across the neck of land which still

separated us from the river, to secure places in the *Marchioness of Breadalbane*, which was waiting to take us to Cairo. Then first I saw the solemn Nile, flowing gloomily; a ray just shining out of the cloudy horizon from the setting sun upon him. He was still very high; the current rapid. The solemnity is not produced by sluggishness, but by the dark colour of the water, the enormous unvarying character of the flat plain, a fringe of date trees here and there, nothing else. By six o'clock P.M. we were off, the moon shining, and the stars all out. Atfeh, heavens! what a place! If you can imagine a parcel of mud cones, about five feet high, thatched with straw, instead of tapering to a point, a few round holes in them for windows, one cone a little larger than the rest, most of them grovelling up the bank, and built in holes – that is Atfeh, and the large anthill is the Governor's house.

On board our steamer, where there is no sleeping place, but a ladies' cabin, where you sit round all night, nine to the square yard, we have hardly any English, no Indians, for luckily it is not the transit week. Our condition is not improved physically, for the boat is equally full of children, screaming all night, and the children are much fuller of vermin; but mentally it is, for the screams are Egyptian, Greek, Italian, and Turkish screams; and the fleas, &c are Circassian, Chinese, and Coptic fleas.

Mr. B. comes down into the cabin, and immediately from off the floor a Turkish woman rose in her wrath, adjusted her black silk veil, and with her three slaves, who all put on theirs which were white, sailed out of the cabin like a Juno in her majestic indignation, and actually went for the night on board the baggage steamer which followed us. She was the prettiest woman I ever saw, more like a sylph than a Juno, except on that occasion, and sat in her close jacket and trousers, with a sash round her waist, when with us ...

At two o'clock the moon set, and the stars shone out. At six the bright and morning star Venus rose; presently the pyramids appeared, three, against the sky, but I could not muster a single sensation. Before ten we were

anchored at Boulak; and before eleven, with our baggage
on camels, ourselves with the Efreet running before us,
the kourbash [whip] cracking in his hand (it is impossible to conceive anything so graceful as an Arab's run),
we had driven up the great alley of acacias from Boulak
to Cairo to the Ezbekeeyeh and the Hôtel de l'Europe.

I would not have missed that night for the world; it
was the most amusing time I ever passed, and the most
picturesque.

Florence Nightingale, *Letters from Egypt*, edited by Anthony
Sattin, 1987.

THE opening of the railway in 1855 (built by Robert Ste-
phenson, the celebrated British railway engineer) brought
Cairo within a few hours of Alexandria and removed the
worst frustrations of this part of the Egyptian journey. The
train was taken by the French poet Théophile Gautier, who
was in Egypt to attend the opening of the Suez Canal in
1869.

A railway station in Egypt is not intrinsically Egyptian
in character, resembling rather all the railway stations
one can imagine. But the crowd which throngs it
immediately reminds the traveller that he has left
Europe. At the sight of those bronzed complexions,
those high-cheekboned faces smiling sphinx-like, those
long flowing robes, those tunics tied at the waist with
camel hair cord, like those of the biblical shepherds,
those intricate turbans, those red caps of floss silk, those
mask-like faces with long trailing beards, you quickly
realise that you are not at the Gare de l'Ouest about to
buy a ticket for Auteuil, Versailles or Saint Germain.

That morning there was the most appalling crush of
cawas, dragomans, servants, railway employees, tourists

and native travellers, whose ranks were broken at every moment by fellahin carrying trunks and huge parcels on their backs which they kept in place by a cord tied across their brow, or by the passage of carriages. Everyone followed the progress of his luggage across this prodigious throng with understandable anxiety. The notices on the walls written in Arab were no help and any dialogue was reduced to sign language. But soon an officer of the Khedive who seemed to speak every language intervened and graciously acted as interpreter for the French, English and German visitors. As if by magic, all difficulties disappeared and order reigned amongst this inevitable confusion . . .

The train carriages, made in England, are painted white with the classes designated in English and Arabic. The first-class carriages are fitted with large green leather armchairs. There is a false ceiling with a large space between it and the real ceiling to cut down the heat from the sun and to stop the interior of the wagons being transformed into a rustic furnace where one would be roasted alive. In the middle a round opening forming a sort of air shaft serves to ventilate the carriage. Openings on the sides are also engineered to make the most of the slightest breeze. The door windows have venetian shutters instead of roller blinds. The second-class compartments communicate like those on Swiss railways, with one fundamental difference: at the end of the compartment there is a closed room which is set aside for the women like a sort of harem. We had already noticed this concession to Muslim protectiveness on the steam boats which serve the Levantine seaports. The third-class carriages, simple farm wagons covered with a roof, were literally crammed with fellahin, barabras, negroes and common folk of all types and ages. It is they apparently who provide the bulk of the railway's returns. They much appreciate this method of travelling even if few concessions to comfort have been made in the space set aside for them.

Everybody had just about managed to squeeze in more or less satisfactorily. No more frantic late-comers dashed around on the platform. The whistle of the engine emitted the shrill scream that the ear never gets used to and that always startles you even when you expect it. Throwing out a jet of steam, the locomotive lumbered into life and dragged forward its load, making a terrific metallic uproar as it went over the points.

We were off, and very soon we were going to realize a dream which we had long cherished. From our earliest days, we had longed to see Venice, Grenada, Toledo, Constantinople, Moscow and Cairo. The only town left on the list was the town of the Caliphs, and now barely four hours separated us.

Théophile Gautier, *L'Orient*, 1877, translated by Suzanne Bosman.

5
Cairo: the Nineteenth-century View

Now, as Gustave Flaubert and Florence Nightingale sensed, the Egyptian adventure was really beginning. Cairo was the largest, most cosmopolitan city of Africa. As Baedeker's *Egypt* for 1908 rightly, if somewhat stiffly, alerted its readers: 'The [Cairo] street scenes ... afford an inexhaustible fund of amusement and delight, admirably illustrating the whole world of Oriental fiction, and producing an indelible impression on the uninitiated denizen of the West.'

Here are two impressions, one written within a few months of its author's visit, the other recollected after fifty years. The first is from Benjamin Disraeli, who reached Egypt in May 1831 at the end of a tour of Spain and the Middle East some years before he entered the House of Commons; the second is from the Pre-Raphaelite painter, William Holman Hunt, remembering his first Egyptian tour in 1854.

Nothing can be conceived more animated and picturesque than Cairo during the early morning or at night. It seems the most bustling and populous city in the world. The narrow streets, abounding with bazaars, present the appearance of a mob, through which troops of richly dressed cavaliers force with difficulty their prancing way, arrested often in their course by the procession of a harem returning from the bath, the women enveloped in inscrutable black garments, and veils and masks of white linen, and borne along by the prettiest donkeys in the world. The attendant eunuchs beat back the multitude; even the swaggering horsemen, with their golden and scarlet jackets, rich shawls and scarfs, and shining arms, trampling on those around, succeed in drawing aside; but all efforts are vain, for at the turning of the street appears the first still solemn visage of a long string of tall camels bearing provisions to the citadel, a Nubian astride on the neck of the leader, and beating a wild drum, to apprise the people of his approach. The streets, too, in which these scenes occur are in themselves full of variety and architectural beauty. The houses are lofty and latticed, abounding in balconies; fountains are frequent and vast and richly adorned as Gothic shrines; sometimes the fortified palace of one of the old Mamlouks, now inhabited by a pacha, still oftener the exquisite shape of an Arabian mosque. The temples of Stamboul cannot vie with the fanes of Cairo. Their delicate domes and airy cupolas, their lofty minarets covered with tracery, and the flowing fancy of their arabesques, recalled to me the glories of the Alhambra, and the fantastic grace of the Alcazars and shrines of Seville and Cordova.

At night the illuminated coffee-houses, the streaming population, each carrying a lantern, in an atmosphere warmer and softer than our conservatories, and all the innocent amusements of an out-door life – the Nubian song, the Arabian tale, the Syrian magic – afford a different, but not less delightful scene.

Benjamin Disraeli, 'The Court of Egypt', *New Monthly Magazine*, June 1832.

Jugglers were at a little distance collecting a dense crowd, with a fringe of nimble children impatient at not having the best places as spectators, but quickly consoling themselves by the pursuit of rival mountebanks trading on the antics of a sufficiently ugly baboon; animals as they marched along and men on business were often chewing newly culled stalks of sugar-cane. Bedouin from the desert prowled stealthily like beasts of prey with sheathed claws; serpent charmers, with their noxious reptiles in hand or in open breast, invited patrons as they passed and re-passed, incredulous of want of *franghi* [European] fondness for their pets. Now a clamour of screeches with a burden of men's intoning voices heralded a funeral, with the corpse borne, face uncovered, dressed as the man was living yesterday in the market place. The cry of the widows and daughters was addressed to the silent principal of the scene, calling him by all his pet names to come back to them and theirs. The infants were riding on the mothers' shoulders, bewildered at the situation and forgotten, as the women tossed the dust on their own heads. Across an end of the square a religious procession of another tenor came upon the stage. It was less hurried and tempestuous; all the actors walked sedately, while the tom-tom sounded and the joy-cry rang out its peal of notes. This was a marriage company, with the child bride under a canopy of gold embroidery, walking with slowly shuffling feet. Mother and female relatives, dressed in old, harmonious-coloured, and traditionally decorated silks, attended the party. As the various groups passed along, through all the confusion, water-carriers rang their brass tazzi, and mingled their shouts in the name of the Prophet with those of other itinerant vendors of tempting drinkables and edibles. Above all swept the searching hawks, circling and crossing, and sometimes swooping down into the busy crowd to seize undefended prey. I stood at that window looking down upon mortal interests as much apart as the gods might survey mankind from the clouds. How swiftly transient, however, are the most slowly passing scenes! All the actors of that day have now passed away – the Pasha in his gorgeous carriage, with running footmen kurbashing the subservient pedestrians; the priests solemnising the procession of the *doséh*, on the return of the Sheik of the Saadeyeh, on his white horse, from Mecca; the devout who threw themselves down to be trampled upon, despite the chance of broken backs; the rude fellah, holding in his hand the long sugar-cane, all have passed off the scene now, taking nothing with them but the lesson sacred in their own hearts derived from the facts of the great drama in which they took part; now, fifty years after, their places are taken by new actors, and even the stage itself has been changed, yet how vivid and full of life are the memories I retain in my mind as though they had been interrupted only for a moment. I bless the meanest of the original actors for the delights they gave me, and may my benediction have some weight against the condemnation of the pious believer in perdition for all followers of Mahomet.

William Holman Hunt, *Pre-Raphaelitism and the Pre-Raphaelite Brotherhood*, 1905.

TRANSPORT in the Arab quarters was generally by donkey: a novel experience at first, though the novelty could soon wear off. Follow Stephen Olin, Methodist minister, President of the Weslyan University of the USA through the pullulating Cairo streets.

It is wonderful how a donkey makes his way along the densely-crowded streets. I have often thought it would be quite impossible to pass one of these living masses that block up the thoroughfares of Cairo; but, yielding myself to the guidance of the donkey and his driver, I always succeeded in finding a passage. The sagacious animal gallops quite up to the multitude, presses against them, and urges his way along carefully but surely. The boy cries out to those whose attention is too much absorbed. He thrusts with his rod at the camels, whose enormous loads threaten to sweep away donkey and rider, and seem to fill the whole street, urging them close to one side or the other. You jostle donkeys and their riders, or their leathern bags of water. You butt against women with enormous jars or trays upon their heads, and find yourself offering unintelligible apologies in English or French. Your knees and toes are perpetually coming in contact with persons standing before the stalls, often urging them in upon the premises of the tradesman with little ceremony. In the end, you succeed in your object you cannot tell how, having jostled everybody and been jostled by everybody, but without inflicting or receiving any serious injury. You have only got a foot wet by drippings from the huge leathern bottles of water on the back of a camel, or a grease-spot by wiping the pantaloons against a jar of oil, and the eyes and mouth filled with dust.

These are incidents that belong to a ride in the streets at any time. On a market or fête day the difficulties and liabilities are of the same kind, differing only in degree; but the additional exposure is compensated by the unwonted activity and odd sights which then give life and interest to the bazars. The stalls are much more thronged than usual, and, in addition to this, almost every person in the street has some article for sale, which he urges upon you with many earnest protestations of its good qualities and low price. One has a pair of pistols or a cimeter in his hand; another, his arms filled with yellow slippers or red caps; another has a girdle or a turban, which he raises aloft or waves in the air; a fourth carries a carpet and several pieces of showy calicoes upon his head. Almost every portable article of traffic is thus exhibited in the crowded street. The living mass is in constant motion. Every one is striving to attract attention to his own particular wares, by exhibiting them as conspicuously as possible, and by many vociferations. The scene is unique, and, for once or twice, highly interesting to the stranger.

Stephen Olin, *Travels in Egypt, Arabia Petraea and the Holy Land*, 1843.

To begin with, just being in Cairo was exotic enough: strange smells, sounds, faces, simultaneously repellent and yet profoundly attractive. Seemingly simple things were done in quite different ways: shopping for instance. Let the archaeologist and Arabist Stanley Lane-Poole explain:

Whoso would know what the townsfolk of Egypt are like should make acquaintance with the Cairo shopkeeper. The tradespeople are the conservative element in Egypt: it is they who keep up the old traditions and walk in the old paths. The upper classes are becoming daily less and less Oriental in outward appearance and habits, though it will take some time to Europeanise their minds. They dance with foreign ladies, wear Frankish [European] clothes, smoke cigarettes, enjoy French plays, and, but for their Eastern habits of tyranny, peculation, insincerity, and corruption, they might for all the world be Europeans. They have, indeed, retained one national feature, the red fez or *tarbûsh*; and the collection of fezes (for the Mohammedan never takes off his hat) in the stalls of the opera, and the veils of gauze stretched in front of the boxes on the grand tier, to hide the beauties of the harîm, are the only things in the Cairene opera that remind us that we are not in Paris. Even the national coffee cups are manufactured in Europe ...

Leaving the European quarter behind, and taking little note of the Greek and Italian shops in the renovated Musky, we turn off to the right into the Ghurîya – one of those larger but still narrow streets which are distinguished with the name of *shâri'* or thoroughfare. Such a street is lined on either side with little box-like shops, which form an unbroken boundary on either hand, except where a mosque door, or a public fountain, or the entrance to another street interrupts for a brief space the row of stores. None of the private doors or windows we are accustomed to in Europe breaks the line of shops. For a considerable distance all the traders deal in the same commodity – be it sugar-plums or slippers. The system has its advantages, for if one dealer be too dear, the next may be cheap; and the competition of many contiguous salesmen brings about a salutary reduction in prices. On the other hand, it must be allowed that it is fatiguing to have to order your coat in half-a-dozen different places – to buy the cloth in one direction, the buttons in another, the braid in a third, the lining in a fourth, the thread in a fifth, and then to have to go to quite another place to find a tailor to cut it out and sew it together. And as each dealer has to be bargained with, and generally smoked with, if not coffeed with, if you get your coat ordered in a single morning you may count yourself expeditious.

In one of these little cupboards that do duty for shops, we may or may not find the typical tradesman we are seeking. It may chance he has gone to say his prayers, or to see a friend, or perhaps he did not feel inclined for business to-day; in which case the folding shutters of his shop will be closed, and as he does not live anywhere near, and as, if he did, there is no bell, no private door, and no assistant, we may wait there for ever, so far as he is concerned, and get no answer to our inquiries. His neighbour next door, however, will obligingly inform us that the excellent man whom we are seeking has gone to the mosque, and we accordingly betake ourselves to our informer and make his acquaintance instead.

Our new friend is sitting in a recess some five feet square, and rather more than six feet high, raised a foot or two from the ground; and within this narrow compass he has collected all the wares he thinks he is likely to sell, and has also reserved room for himself and his customers to sit down and smoke cigarettes while they bargain. Of course, his stock must be very limited, but then all his neighbours are ready to help him; and if you cannot find what you want within the compass of his four walls, he will leave you with a cigarette and a cup of coffee, or perhaps Persian tea in a tumbler, while he goes to find the *desideratum* among the wares of his colleagues round about.

Cairo: the Nineteenth-century View

Meanwhile, you drink your scalding coffee – which is, however, incomparably delicious – and watch the throng that passes by: the ungainly camels, laden with brushwood or green fodder, which seem to threaten to sweep everything and everybody out of the street; – the respectable townspeople, mounted on grey or brown asses, ambling along contentedly, save when an unusually severe blow from the inhuman donkey-boy running behind makes their beasts swerve incontinently to the right or left, as though they had a hinge in their middles; – the grandees in their two-horse carriages, preceded by breathless runners, who clear the way for their masters with shrill shouts – 'Shemâlak, yâ weled!' ('To thy left, O boy!') 'Yemînik, yâ Sitt!' ('To thy right, O lady!') 'Iftah 'eynak, yâ Am!' ('Open thine eye, O uncle!') and the like; – the women with trays of eatables on their heads, the watercarrier with goat-skin under arm, and the vast multitude of blue-robed men and women who have something or other to do, which takes them indeed along the street, but does not take them very hurriedly. In spite of the apparent rush and crush, the crowd moves slowly like everything else in the East.

Our friend returns with the desired article; we approve it, guardedly, and with cautious tentative aspect demand, 'How much?' The answer is always at least twice the fair price. We reply, first by exclaiming, 'I seek refuge with God' (from exorbitance), and then by offering about half the fair price. The dealer shakes his head, looks disappointed with us, shows he expected better sense in people of our appearance, puts aside his goods, and sits down to another cigarette. After a second ineffectual bid, we summon our donkey and prepare to mount. At this moment the shopman relents, and reduces his price; but we are obdurate, and begin riding away. He pursues us, agrees almost to our terms; we return, pay, receive our purchase, commend him to the protection of God and wend our way on.

Stanley Lane-Poole, *Cairo*, 1892.

NOTHING in Cairo was more liable to stimulate an ambiguous mixture of fascination and disgust than the slave market, here described by William Müller, visiting Egypt to gather material for his paintings of local life.

The slave-market was one of my most favourite haunts, although no figure-painter. One enters this building, which is situated in a quarter the most dark, dirty, and obscure of any at Cairo, by a sort of lane; then one arrives at some large gates. The market is held in an open court, surrounded with arches of the Roman character. In the centre of this court the slaves are exposed for sale, and in general to the number of from thirty to forty, nearly all young, many quite infants. The scene is of a revolting nature; yet I did not see, as I expected, the dejection and sorrow I was led to imagine. The more beautiful of the females I found were confined in a chamber over the court. They are in general Abyssinians and Circassians. When any one desires to purchase, I not unfrequently saw the master remove the entire covering of the female – a thick woollen cloth – and expose her to the gaze of the bystander. Many of these girls are exceedingly beautiful – small features, well formed, with an eye that bespeaks the warmth of passion they possess. The negresses, on the contrary, have little to please; they disgust, for their hair is loaded with two or three pounds of a sort of tallow fat, literally in thick masses, and as this is influenced by the heat of the sun, it gradually melts over the body, and the smell from it is disagreeable in the extreme; yet in this place did I feel more delight than in any other part of Cairo: the groups and the extraordinary costume can but please the artist. You meet in this place all nations. When I was sketching – which I did on many occasions – the masters of the slaves could in no manner understand my occupation, but were continually giving the servant the price of the different slaves, to desire me to write the same down, thinking I was about to become a large buyer.

I only wish some artist would make this the spot of his studies, and paint the figures and groups.

William Müller, 'An Artist's Tour in Egypt', *Art Union*,
September 1839.

ANOTHER essential on the list of things to be done and seen was a performance by dervishes. Thomas Seddon, who was travelling with his fellow-painter William Holman Hunt, recounts one. ('Mr Burton' was Sir Richard Burton, soon to make his name as one of the few Europeans to undertake the pilgrimage to Mecca.)

Dec. 12, *Monday.* – The close of the Mooled e' Nebbee, or birthday of the prophet Mohammed, which has been celebrated by the Saadeeyeh dervishes the whole of the last week in the Usbekeyeh. This morning the sheikh rode over the prostrate bodies of the fanatics. After wandering about the fair with Fletcher, we met a Mr Burton, who, knowing the Arabic language thoroughly, has taken the dress. Finding the door of the sheikh's house open, we went in, and found a great many Europeans there, with a crowd of Arabs, Kawasses, dervishes, and men and boys of all nations. Seats were ranged on each side for the Europeans. We came in at about eleven, and had to wait more than two hours before the sheikh arrived. During the interval, a number of jugglers and serpent-tamers performed their evolutions. Two men, very wildly dressed, went through some very bad sword-and-buckler exercise. Then men came in with pointed iron spikes, about fifteen inches long, with a large knob of iron at one end, garnished with short chains. These they stuck in the corners of their eyes, and twirled them round; then they dug the pointed end against their heads and bodies; then a man lay down, and they placed the pointed end on his stomach, whilst a man stood upon it; then they held four or five on the ground, point uppermost, and the jugglers walked on them; they then brought in skewers, and thrust them through their cheeks and arms, and through the flesh on their bodies, having stripped to the waist. The performance began now to be very disgusting: they foamed at the mouth, and seemed to become intoxicated, falling back into the arms of those behind them, apparently fainting. One man howled, growled like a lion, and raved like a maniac. This continued for some time, when the serpent-men came in with the asps round their necks; and then some of the fanatics rushed on the snakes, and tore them with their teeth; and when four or five men held them each, they struggled fearfully, and tried to bite them. As the banners now appeared, the lower order of them lay down side by side on their faces, while the others, better dressed, took them by the legs and shoulders, and pressed them closely together. By the time that a compact mass was formed, half-a-dozen turbanéd dervishes, with long sticks, rushed in over them; and then the sheikh, on horseback, a man leading his frightened horse, who trod heavily and quickly, like a horse passing through a bog. He swerved, and trod on one man's head, and on the legs of others. The sheikh sat lying back, as if stupified and in pain, dressed in a huge green turban, and supported by a dervish on each side. Some of the men were lifted up as if hurt, and all seemed to be, or to sham an intoxicated ecstasy.

J.P.Seddon, *Memoir and Letters of the Late Thomas Seddon,*
1858.

SNAKE-CHARMERS numbered among the other exotic attractions of the city. The novelist Maxime du Camp, Flaubert's
travelling companion, invited one troupe to perform in his
hotel.

Along with jugglers and acrobats must be mentioned
the *psylli*, who are greatly feared in Cairo; snakes obey
them, they can drive them away or attract them at will.
Are they direct descendants of the *ophiogenes* of ancient
Egypt? Have they learned by hereditary transmission
the secret of the magicians who vied with Moses before
Pharaoh's throne? Or are they merely very clever presti-
digitators who play with snakes the way ours juggle
disappearing balls? I know not.

I was curious to see them at close quarters, to watch
their motions with unbiased eye, and, if possible, to
ascertain their methods; I had them come to my hotel.

They appeared as a trio: an old man, a young man, and
a boy of fifteen. They carried a knapsack that contained a
squirming mass – several scorpions, two vipers, and a
large black snake of a kind found in the Mokattam. The
boy took the snake, wrapped it around his body, lifted
it to his lips and let it glide several times between his
shirt and his bare skin. He spat into its mouth, and
pressed strongly with his thumb on the head of the
innocent reptile, which immediately became as straight
and stiff as a stick. This effect, surprising at first, is of
course very easy to obtain. All one has to do is exert a
violent pressure on the snake's brain (which is very
weak), and thus induce a cataleptic state: the snake is
immediately rendered immobile, so stiffened that it
cannot be bent, only broken.

At my request the charmer entered my room, walked
around it, and announced the presence of a viper. He
undressed in front of me as proof that there would be
no trickery, and striking the walls with a short stick he
began to utter a sad, monotonous, slow whistle. Then
he intoned a strange, imperious sort of incantation, only

to break off and resume his whistling, but more softly than before. He said: 'In the name of clement and merciful God, I adjure you! I adjure you! If you are within, if you are without, show yourself! Show yourself! I adjure you in the name of one so great that I dare not say it! If it is your will to obey, appear! If it is your will to disobey, die! die! die!' Then he thrust his arms forward and undulated his body without shifting his place. He stood at the door of my room, and as I watched I saw a small grayish snake come out, moving quite fast across the shiny matting. The charmer caught it up and proudly showed it to me, asking at once for '*baksheesh kebir*' – 'a big tip.' The thing was well done, I admit, but it did not convince me: the young man who uttered the spells could very easily have taken advantage of a moment of distraction on my part and dropped into the room a snake that he had been concealing in his armpit all along.

The charmer then proposed to immunize me for the rest of my life against all kinds of bites, and to endow me with the power to handle with perfect safety all animals no matter how venomous. I accepted with pleasure, hoping for some kind of magical ceremony, and put myself in the boy's hands. I sat down cross-legged before him, he took my hand, pressed my thumb, wrapped a snake around my wrist, and addressed me in words that were rapid and staccato: he lifted the snake to my ear; it bit me hard; with a finger he took the blood from the bite and spread it on the ground; then he breathed twice into my mouth, made me breathe twice on the large black snake, which he had wrapped around my neck, twice rubbed my bloody ear with his hand that he had moistened with his saliva, once again asked me for 'a big tip' – and the thing was done. Very simple, as you see: not a very perilous initiation.

Maxime du Camp, *Le Nil, Egypte et Nubie*, from *Flaubert in Egypt*, translated and edited by Francis Steegmuller.

THE aim of most Westerners, to get close to Egyptian life, was hard to achieve. Barriers of language and, even more insuperable, of religion and social customs intervened. Sophia Poole, by no means an unsympathetic observer, found that a visit to the baths provoked mixed feelings. She lived in Cairo for several years in the early 1840s with her brother, Edward Lane, author of the celebrated *Modern Egyptians*.

In the first apartment, each of us enveloped herself in a very long and broad piece of drapery, – which, but for its size, I might call a scarf, – and proceeded through a small chamber, which was moderately heated, to the principal inner apartment, where the heat was intense. The plan of this apartment is that of a cross, having four recesses; each of which, as well as the central portion, is covered with a dome. The pavements are of white and black marble, and small pieces of fine red tile, very fancifully and prettily disposed. In the middle is a jet of hot water, rising from the centre of a high seat of marble, upon which many persons might sit together. The pavement of each of the recesses is a few inches higher than that of the central portion of the apartment; and in one of them is a trough, into which hot water was constantly pouring from a pipe in the dome above. The whole apartment was full of steam.

On entering this chamber a scene presented itself which beggars description. My companions had prepared me for seeing many persons undressed; but imagine my astonishment on finding at least thirty women of all ages, and many young girls and children, perfectly unclothed. You will scarcely think it possible that no one but ourselves had a vestige of clothing. Persons of all colours, from the black and glossy shade of the negro to the fairest possible hue of complexion, were formed in groups, conversing as though full dressed, with perfect *nonchalance*, while others were strolling about, or sitting round the fountain. I cannot describe the bath as altogether a beautiful scene; in truth, in some respects it is disgusting; and I regret that I can never reach a private room in any bath without passing through the large public apartment.

I will turn to the more agreeable subject – the operation of the bath, which is quite luxurious. The sensation experienced on first entering the hottest chamber is almost overpowering – the heat is extremely oppressive; and at first I believed that I could not long support such a temperature; but after the first minute, I was relieved by a gentle, and afterwards by a profuse perspiration, and no longer felt in any degree oppressed. It is always necessary for each lady to send her own bathing-linen, a pair of high clogs, a large copper vessel for hot water, two copper bowls, and towels.

The first operation is a gentle kneading the flesh, or champooing. Next the attendant cracks the joints of those who desire to submit to this process. I confess I did not suffer such an infliction. Some of the native women after this are rubbed with a rasp, or rather with two rasps of different kinds, a coarse one for the feet, and a fine one for the body; but neither of these rasps do I approve. A small coarse woollen bag, into which the operator's hand is inserted, is in my opinion preferable. Next the head and face are covered with a thick lather, which is produced by rubbing soap on a handful of fibres of the palm-tree, which are called leef, and which form a very agreeable and delicate-looking rubber. It is truly ridiculous to see another under this operation. When her head and face have been well lathered, and the soap has been thoroughly washed off by abundance of hot water, a novice would suppose that at least *they* were sufficiently purified; but this is not the case: two or three of such latherings, and as many washings, are necessary before the attendant thinks her duty to the head and face accomplished. Then follows the more agreeable part of the affair, – the general lathering and rubbing, which is performed by the attendant so gently, and in so pleasant a manner, that it is quite a luxury; and I am persuaded that the Eastern manner of bathing is highly salubrious, from its powerful effect upon the skin.

When the operation was completed, I was enveloped in a dry piece of drapery, similar to the bathing-dress, and conducted to the reposing-room, where I was rubbed and dressed, and left to take rest and refreshment, and to reflect upon the strange scene which I had witnessed. I wish I could say that there are no drawbacks to the enjoyment of the luxury I have described; but the eyes and ears of an Englishwoman must be closed in the public bath in Egypt before she can fairly enjoy the satisfaction it affords; for besides the very foreign scenes which cannot fail to shock her feelings of propriety, the cries of the children are deafening and incessant. The perfection of Eastern bathing is therefore rather to be enjoyed in a private bath, with the attendance of a practised velláneh [bath attendant].

Sophia Poole, *The Englishwoman in Egypt*, 1844.

THE role of women, and in particular the nature of harem life, was the subject that above all provoked intense curiosity, stimulated by the groups of mysteriously veiled and shrouded ladies sometimes seen on the Cairo streets. By the nineteenth century, accounts of harem immorality and licentiousness had generally been discounted. Reality, as most visitors soon realized, was the most unstimulating monotony. Ellen Chennells spent five years in the 1870s as governess to the Khedive's daughter, Princess Zeyneb.

I could not help being struck even at this early stage with the different life led by a young married couple in the East and one in our country. My pupil's husband had been in love with her from a child, and was devoted to her after marriage as he had been before. Still they had no pursuits in common; they could not walk out together, ride, drive, or go to the theatre together, or have any mutual acquaintance. Any wish she might express was immediately gratified by him; he got a pretty little pony-carriage and pair of ponies and taught her to drive, but she grew weary in a few days of driving round the garden, with or without him, and gave up using it. One pet after another was given her; the poor child wanted liberty, as a bird pines in its cage, and cared for nothing else. When they went to the theatre or opera it was in separate carriages, and they sat in separate boxes. When any gentlemen came to see the Prince it was at the *selamlik*, and he could not introduce them to her. If any of her brothers came they were brought in at once, and the intercourse was a great pleasure both to them and to her. Some of them had been brought up in France and England, and they highly appreciated having as sister a charming young woman, full of the light graceful *badinage* which is always so attractive in the society of young people. But after all, the visits of the brothers were only occasional; there were a great many weary hours to get through. The Princess generally drove out towards evening, and Kopsès went with her. She had a very elegant carriage and fine horses, two *saïs* (pronounced *syces*) preceding with long sticks, and white dress terminating at the knee, and sleeves which the wind inflated as they ran, so that they looked like wings. There were also generally a couple of outriders in handsome uniforms, and two or three eunuchs on horseback, who, however, fell behind, not riding, as a few years before was the custom, in front of the carriage-windows, with the blinds drawn down. Now, the blinds were up and the carriage was nearly all windows, and the two pretty girls, in their bright dresses and transparent *yashmaks*, were distinctly visible. The other Princesses got similar carriages and drove out in the same style, and the Choubrah or Abbasieh road presented quite a lively scene, for the hack-carriages used by travellers do not produce an elegant effect. But last winter all this had passed away, and a harem carriage driven in such a style was an unfrequent sight! . . .

I had often heard people talk of the mystery in the harem, and the difficulty there was in knowing what went on within the walls, to those who lived in the outer world. This was true enough, but I soon observed there was no mystery amongst each other. What one knew (as a rule) everybody knew. The mistress was never alone; there was no place, however private, where her attendants could not penetrate. When visitors came, the chief slaves waited in the room, forming a semicircle at a slight distance, but within earshot. The only way to speak in private appeared to me to be under cover of the band playing, when the noise was deafening, and the voice could only be heard by the next neighbour. Where a foreign language was spoken, privacy was always ensured, and my dear little Princess was not a little pleased to be able to talk to her husband, to Kopsès, and to me, in French, which no one else understood; and to Kopsès and me also in English, which the Prince did not understand. I heard an anecdote concerning this custom of the constant presence of the attendants. A European went one day to visit one of the married daughters of his Highness, and as the Princess understood only Turkish and Arabic, the conversation was held in one of these languages. But the visitor had something private to say, and whenever the slaves were at a little distance she broached the subject, changing it as they approached. Her visit, however, came to an end before she had an opportunity of saying what she wished, and before leaving she said in the most polite phrases which she could use, 'I never could have believed that an Egyptian Princess would submit to such slavery as never to hear or to speak anything without the same being carried through the whole household.' The Princess was so struck with this that she gave orders that in future, whenever any European visitor should come to her, the slaves were to remain in the anteroom. These innovations were being gradually introduced during my stay in Egypt.

Ellen Chennells, *Recollections of an Egyptian Princess*, 1893.

ELLEN CHENNELLS had some limited success in educating her Princess, despite the many obstacles court life put in her way. More casual contacts proved less fruitful. Here is Mabel Caillard, daughter of the British Postmaster-General of Egypt, who spent most of her life in Egypt.

Among ladies the barriers of custom were almost as insuperable. The harem visits that I paid with my mother were received with an air of courteous acceptance rather than of welcome. The conversation, apart from the difficulties of language, was perforce confined to such subjects as might not offend the susceptibilities of either side, but more especially those of the women whose lives were bound up in a network of superstitions – so that you might cast the evil eye upon a child by merely praising its beauty, or blast a tree by too closely admiring its fruits, or in a hundred other ways inadvertently bring trouble upon a household where your only wish was to leave a good impression and to intrude not a minute longer than was necessary.

Dullness rather than mystery seemed, to the casual observer, to be the sum of existence in the harems, from visiting which one escaped, as from the appraising gaze of the black guardians of their jealous portals, with a definite sense of relief. The same heavy and comfortless formality pervaded all. I have seen Oriental interiors furnished luxuriously with silken divans piled with soft cushions, in stage plays and on the films; the harem ladies whom I visited in real life were perched on hard and somewhat high couches covered with dimity or brown holland, from under which there might protrude a pink or yellow satin corner of a bolster solidly stuffed with cotton. The gilt chairs, and even the ornamental tables, would be concealed beneath similar drab and dingy coverings, removed only on rare occasions to display the glory of their brocade or velvet upholsteries and their surfaces of marble.

Mabel Caillard, *A Lifetime in Egypt*, 1935.

FOR Egyptians and European residents and visitors alike, the annual ball given by the Khedive marked the culmination of the winter season in Cairo.

For many years the Khedive's ball was ... as brilliant a function as Oriental splendour and cosmopolitan fashion in combination could compass. His Highness received his guests at Abdin palace, in the first and largest of a long suite of rooms dazzlingly illuminated by immense, glittering chandeliers, and by the mirrors that lined the walls, flashing a thousand reflections. Gilt and damask in gorgeous contrast supplied the sumptuous furnishing; and a winter garden, reminiscent of Ismaïl Pasha's fancy for rare and exotic plants, afforded a dim refuge of coolness from the heated rooms.

The short drive to the palace took a couple of hours to accomplish, the queue of carriages beginning in the Opera Square and proceeding at a snail's pace up the narrow Abdin Street. On your arrival you were pounced upon by one of the dapper *maîtres des cérémonies* in waiting near the entrance, who, if you were a woman, offered his arm and rushed you up the grand staircase, during which breathless progress he contrived, with the utmost grace and affability, to elicit your name – which was murmured to the Khedive as you made your curtsey.

Then, if you were of sufficient importance, you were conducted to a seat at the side of the room to await the Khedive's procession to the ball-room; otherwise you were whisked off by your courtly guide and deposited in one of the ante-rooms, through which the procession would ultimately pass and absorb you into its tail.

In spite of the spaciousness of the ball-room the crush was terrific and dancing, in those days of frills and furbelows and spurs, was rather a *tour de force* than a pleasure. At one end of the room ran a gilded grating of intricate design, through which the ladies of the harem could watch the proceedings without being seen. I was initiated into the secret on hearing a mysterious rustle close behind me, as I paused with my partner near the grille and caught a gleaming eye peering through one of the interstices. People used to line up before the doors of the public supper-room long before they were opened. At one of the last Khedivial balls ... as many as seven hundred people were reputed to have pressed into the room at one time, forming a conglomerate mass of whom only those nearest the tables were able to obtain anything to eat. You saw elegant European ladies helping themselves from the dishes to which the more unsophisticated section of the Khedive's native guests were taking their fingers – with shocked faces averted from their shamelessly *décolletées* neighbours – and noisily ejecting from their mouths such morsels as were not to their taste.

Mabel Caillard, *A Lifetime in Egypt*, 1935.

By the end of the nineteenth century the old Cairo, the Cairo that even fifty years before had so gripped the visitor as the quintessential Eastern city of the imagination, seemed to be changing out of all recognition. Mabel Caillard observes (the Lady Butler mentioned is the painter famous for her melodramatic imperial battle scenes):

But how changed from the Egypt I remembered was the Egypt I found after five long years of absence! I had dwelt in it all the time in my thoughts, and when I saw it again I could hardly tell it for the same. Grand Cairo – 'the superb town, the holy city, the delight of the imagination, upon whose wealth and splendour the Prophet smiled' – was transformed. The process of modernization, which had been going on by slow and scarcely perceptible stages for upwards of half a century, seemed suddenly to have broken out in a riot of vulgarity and ugliness. The spaciousness, the dignity and quietude of the old residential quarters were utterly gone; the old mansions with their sombre pleasaunces and their air of secrecy and aloofness had yielded to the encroachment of rows of buildings and garish shops; the fine old avenues had been cut down and in their place were noisy streets no longer liable to be turned into lakes by a heavy shower of rain, with paved sidewalks where pedestrians no longer had to dodge the pitfalls dug around the trees for watering, of which the grilles had been removed or stolen, or perhaps had never been placed in position. Even Gezira, that green isle of recreation, had now its fringe of houses; the palace, which in the fat years of tourist visitors had been converted into the most luxurious of hotels, was closed and showing serious signs of dilapidation; and the gardens, once a scented wilderness of roses and petunias, were dried up and divided into building-plots on which some suburban villas had already made their appearance.

Elizabeth Thompson, the artist, whom we knew in Egypt as the wife of General Sir William Butler, once remarked to my father that Alexandria was too clean to be interesting. Her meaning was borne in upon me when I beheld Cairo contorted into a poor imitation of a second-rate European city. In its former picturesqueness there had been a good deal of mediæval squalor, but art had shone through like a gem lying in the dust; romance had hovered in the shadows and beauty had glowed in the high lights of the city's old magnificence. Now, its legendary grandeur was gone for ever. But its metamorphosis was, after all, no more than a veneer: for all its pretence of frankish improvement, Cairo smelt as Oriental as before.

Mabel Caillard, *A Lifetime in Egypt*, 1935.

6

Cairo: the Twentieth-century View

CAIRO'S nineteenth-century visitors – archaeologists and tutors, painters or merely curious travellers – had come in search of the exotic and unknown. A sense of magical Arabian Nights still embraced the city. Following the establishment of the British protectorate in 1882, Western administrators and merchants (largely but by no means exclusively British) settled in increasing numbers, gradually creating a colonial society that functioned almost entirely divorced from Egyptian life. Cairo remained an Eastern city, but acquired a veneer of European 'civilization'. With this there arrived a less dedicated variety of visitor. Writing in 1908, Douglas Sladen identified these as:

... swallows from London Society who see less of Egypt than they would if they remained in London and went to the Egyptian Department of the British Museum. But they enjoy themselves amazingly, having a reliable climate which never plays the deuce with engagements, and they make life in the hotels very gay. There is a dance every night of the week except Sunday at one or other of the hotels.

Life in Egypt, meaning practically life in Cairo, is very pleasant for those who do not have to think about money. In the various hotels there are enough beautiful young women in beautiful gowns, and well-bred, well-groomed, sport-loving young men to make intercourse socially interesting, and various enterprising caterers have devoted themselves with success to the task of providing all the entertainments that will be desired, except English plays and musical comedies, which are the favourite digestive to a dinner in London. There are dances, races, polo, golf, tennis, croquet, cricket, riding, motoring, shooting, excursions up the Nile, the opera, concerts, services of all kinds and creeds in churches, and club life – they can all be had for the asking – and paying.

Douglas Sladen, *Egypt and the English*, 1908.

RONALD STORRS, who joined the Egyptian Civil Service as a young man in 1904, recalls the easy informality that could characterize relations between Egyptians and British and explains how, in the first decades of the twentieth century, such 'reasonable measure of human intercourse' almost entirely vanished.

Popular reactions to casual incidents were no less un-expected. A friend was driving me down a side street in his dog-cart when we had the misfortune to knock a man over. We naturally jumped down to help him, when several passers-by collected and warned us to drive swiftly away 'lest the Police come upon you'. Sometime in 1906 I was walking in the heat of the day through the Bazaars. As I passed an Arab Café an idle wit, in no hostility to my straw hat but desiring to shine before his friends, called out in Arabic, 'God curse your father, O Englishman'. I was young then and quicker tempered, and foolishly could not refrain from answering in his own language that I would also curse his father if he were in a position to inform me which of his mother's two and ninety admirers his father had been. I heard footsteps behind me and slightly picked up the pace, angry with myself for committing the sin Lord Cromer [British consul-general] would not pardon – a row with Egyptians. In a few seconds I felt a hand on each arm. 'My brother', said the original humorist, 'return, I pray you, and drink with us coffee and smoke. (In Arabic one speaks of 'drinking' smoke.) I did not think that Your Worship knew Arabic, still less the correct Arabic abuse, and we would fain benefit further by your important thoughts.' ...

With the decline of foreign political influence and so of foreign social prestige; with the increasing numbers of minor British officials and the extension of the club and sport system; with the multiplication of the hotels, and the mass production of the peach-fed standardized tourist 'doing' the whole country in ten days and demanding indiscriminate hotel dances, there came less mixing with and understanding of Egyptians and for-eigners, and a general diminution of social caste, *cachet*, and character. Easy communications corrupt good manners, and I remember blushing to hear it said, as praise of a distinguished visitor: '*Il a même eu l'amabilité de rendre ma carte.*' ['He has even been friendly enough to return my card.'] The classic process of colonization had begun. Everybody and everything was becoming cleaner, richer, easier and more proper, but somehow (and I have seen the symptoms elsewhere) there was less fun. Once more we had multiplied the harvest but not increased the joy.

The British official in Cairo and Alexandria (upon which two cities the provincial inspectorates were now increasingly based) was a hard and honourable worker, punctual and punctilious in his Department or Ministry from early morning until well after noon. He would then drive or bicycle to the Turf Club or his flat for luncheon, play tennis or golf until dark at the Sporting Club, return to the Turf Club to discuss the affairs of the day and dine there or at his flat. All, therefore, that the Egyptian official, high or low, saw of the average British official was a daily face gazing at him across an office desk from 8 a.m. to 1 p.m., Fridays excepted. The unofficial Egyptian saw not even that. Exchanges of visits were now almost unknown and the hundred contacts and humanities that come from knowing people 'at home' – from little Ahmad's teething or Mustafa's progress in English or in football – were hopelessly excluded. Nor was there, save for one or two notable exceptions, the faintest effort on the part of the official's wife to make the acquaintance, still less cultivate the friendship, of the wives or daughters of her husband's colleagues or subordinates; and it was with an air of virtuous resignation that she steeled herself to sacrifice an afternoon for a call upon an Egyptian or Turkish lady, as likely as not better born, better bred, better read, better looking and better dressed than herself.

It would be unfair to ascribe these neglects and abstentions entirely to condescension or indifference. Between persons of different race, climate, language and religion the conversational going is not always easy, largely because of the lack of common ground; and this was especially so before the spread of European education. If in Cairo you had to exclude on the one side all knowledge of tennis golf social information and the latest English novel, and on the other of Egyptian politics (and grievances) French literature and the cotton crop, the attainment of the statutory hour on family and symptom talk was sometimes hard labour. There were of course – and even now are heard – the familiar arguments to the effect that 'Egyptians and foreigners don't appreciate visits and really prefer our keeping ourselves to ourselves' – a disingenuous depreciation of a most sociable, generous and hospitable race. I found those who saw them least most able to dogmatize about their likes and dislikes.

Ronald Storrs, *Orientations*, 1937.

IN 1925 the poet Robert Graves was appointed Professor of English Literature at the University of Cairo. Before he left England, Lawrence of Arabia wrote to him that:

Egypt, being so near Europe, is not a savage country. The Egyptians ... you need not dwell among. Indeed, it will be a miracle if an Englishman can get to know them. The bureaucrat society is exclusive, and lives smilingly unaware of the people. Partly because so many foreigners come there for pleasure, in the winter; and the other women, who live there, must be butterflies too, if they would consort with the visitors.

Quoted in Robert Graves, *Goodbye to All That*, 1957.

BRITISH officials' superciliousness towards the Egyptians, impossible teaching conditions at the University and his students' poor command of English, his children's illness – all soon combined to disillusion Graves, despite his generous salary, and he resigned after a year.

I had not realized before just how much the British controlled Egypt. Egypt ranked as an independent kingdom, but it seemed that I owed my principal allegiance not to King Fuad, who had given me my appointment and paid my salary, but to the High Commissioner, whose infantry, cavalry, and air squadrons were a constant reminder of his power. British officials could not understand the Egyptians' desire for independence, considering them most ungrateful for all the beneficent labour and skill applied to their country since the eighties – raising it from bankruptcy to riches. There was no Egyptian nation, I was assured. The Greeks,

Turks, Syrians, and Armenians who called themselves Egyptians had no more right there than the British. Before the British occupation the Pashas used to bleed the fellaheen white; and it was not the fellaheen, the only true Egyptians, who now called for freedom. National-ism, a creed derived from the new smatterings of Western education we were giving the upper classes, should be disregarded as merely a symptom of the coun-try's growing wealth. The reduction of the British official class in the last few years was viewed with disgust. 'We did all the hard work, and when we go everything will run down; it's running down already. And they'll have to call us back, or if not, the dagoes; and we don't see why *they* should benefit.' None of them realized how much the vanity of the Egyptians – probably the vainest people in world – was hurt by the constant sight of British uniform. On the other hand, I could not suppose that the morale of the Egyptian soldier would be very high in time of war; having seen one of their officers, incensed by the negligence of a sentry, pull open the man's mouth and spit into it ...

The Egyptians treated me hospitably. I attended one heavy banquet at the Semiramis Hotel, given by the Ministry of Education. Tall Sudanese waiters dressed in red robes served a succession of the most magnificent dishes I had seen anywhere, even on the films. They included a great model of the Cairo Citadel in ice, its doors and windows filled with caviare – we used a golden Moorish spoon to scoop this out. Someone told me recently that this banquet, which must have cost thou-sands, has not yet been paid for. I found little to do in Egypt (not having Lawrence's appetite for desert travel) but eat coffee-ices at Groppi's, visit the open-air cinemas, and sit at home in our flat at Heliopolis and get on with writing. Mollie, who lived near, continued sisterly. During the season of the Khamsin, a hot wind that sent the temperature up on one occasion to 113 degrees in the shade, I put the finishing touches to a small book called *Lars Porsena, or The Future of Swear-ing and Improper Language.*

The best thing I saw in Egypt was the noble face of old Pharaoh Seti the Good, unwrapped of its mummy-cloths at the Cairo Museum. The funniest thing was a French bedroom-farce at a native theatre played in Arabic by Syrian actors. The men and women of the cast had, for religious reasons, to keep on opposite sides of the stage; they sang French songs (in translation), varying the tunes with the quarter-tones and shrieks and trills of their own music. The audience talked all the time and ate peanuts, oranges, sunflower-seeds, and heads of lettuces.

Robert Graves, *Goodbye to All That*, 1957.

NOT everyone shared the disdain Graves reported. Contrast the attitudes of Alfred Butler, who spent a year in the early 1880s as tutor to the sons of the Khedive, with those of Mary Rowlatt, whose deep love for the country grew out of five generations of family involvement in Egypt. The connection began when her great-great-grandfather came to Alexandria as a merchant in the early nineteenth century and only terminated on the death of her father, who had served as Governor of the National Bank, in 1950.

There is a curious sort of democracy about an oriental court. Once I was going out driving in the train of the Khedive as was customary, when I saw a certain bey and called to know whether he would join me. After putting my question I noticed that he was with a domestic who serves the Khedive's coffee. The bey, seeing that I was in a carriage large enough to hold four persons, said, 'Have you another place to spare?' to which I promptly answered, 'No.' He got up alone, and as we drove off I said, 'Why, that man is a servant, is he not?'

'Oh, I don't know,' was the answer, 'he belongs to His Highness's service.' Another afternoon I was walking in the Great Square at Alexandria, holding the inevitable sunshade and smoking a cigar. I met the Court tailor, who, after the custom of the country, shook hands with my companion, while I stood aloof, and, armed with a cigar in one hand and sunshade in the other, declined the proffered honour. That very evening the tailor appeared in the anteroom at the palace, and, nothing daunted, proceeded to shake hands all down the line of beys and pashas who were sitting on divans round the walls. Just before he came to me I leant back on the divan, crossed my legs, and thrust both hands in my pockets. This time my meaning was clear enough: the tailor passed me with a *'Bon jour, monsieur,'* touching his forehead, and from that date he never again offered to shake hands. There were some things in which I would not play the Roman at Rome, but it is not a bad thing with orientals to stand on one's dignity.

Alfred J. Butler, *Court Life in Egypt*, 1887.

It was during these first winters [in the late 1920s] in Egypt after boarding school years, that I became aware what divergence of views and what misunderstanding could flare up between some of my English friends and the people of the land in which they found themselves. My new companions were usually the young officers and married couples of the regiments stationed in Egypt. They spoke little or no Arabic, and often misunderstood the man-in-the street. The Egyptian, on his side, would sometimes do things, which happen to madden an Englishman, things often harmless enough but occasionally harmful, such as beating his beast of burden.

When this happened, the passing young Englishman would leap out of his car and start beating the Egyptian, leaving me breathless and miserable, on the fringe of the scene. What was needed was a quiet and rational conversation, pointing out the advantages of helping your horse instead of beating it. I have seen such a conversation in which the co-operation of the driver was immediately gained; but without knowing the country or the language, it was difficult for the Englishman to get started. If an animal is found in bad condition, there are now two wonderful hospitals for animals run by joint Egyptian and English effort, the People's Dispensary for Sick Animals, and the Brooks Hospital. In many cases an introduction to either of these places is the answer to such situations.

On one occasion, several of us settled down to a picnic on an apparently vacant bit of sandy waste near the desert edge. An Egyptian peasant shortly arrived in a tearing rage. One of the men of our party stood up to him and the situation looked menacing. My requests, to let me at least find out what had upset him, were granted. It took some moments to make myself heard, during which time I waited nervously under the shower of curses and the brandishing of a mattock. When this subsided, it appeared that we had been sitting on a seed bed. Never have I seen a seed bed look more like waste ground, but none the less it made the owner's wrath understandable. It was obviously the occasion for an honest apology and a small sum to compensate. The old man slowly cooled off, and I thought we had only just made good. But we had not gone a few yards when he caught us up, this time with an apology himself and several cucumbers as a peace offering.

This ended happily; but there were other times when it did not. Incidents, often trifling in themselves, would leave hurt feelings on one side and plain rage on the other – sometimes an English fault, sometimes an Egyptian. But whichever way it was, it always left me sad and anxious, feeling equally loyal to both parties.

It is only fair to say that there was always a number of men and women from the English regiments stationed in Egypt who took a most understanding interest in the people among whom their lot had temporarily fallen.

They availed themselves of all opportunities to learn more about the country and the people. It took considerable strength of character and enterprise on their part to break away from the rut limited by bridge, cocktail parties and polo, but those who did were repaid. Any genuine friendly touch was certainly appreciated.

Mary Rowlatt, *A Family in Egypt*, 1956.

THE archaeologist Mortimer Wheeler, on wartime service in Cairo, recalls another long-standing resident of the city, who shared the characteristic English concern (quite perplexing to Egyptians) with the welfare of animals.

From Shepheard's ... I made my way for tea and talk to the rambling tenement-building on the top of which Archie Creswell lived, somewhere near the Abdin Palace. Professor K. A. C. Creswell, then Professor of Muslim Art and Architecture in the Fouad University, was and is amongst the most treasured of my friends. Not the least of his titles to fame is his monumental work on Muslim architecture, but to his familiars an abundant and tireless scholarship is merely one of his virtues. For something like thirty-five years his small, neat frame, with a collar always immaculately starched whatever the temperature, has stalked through the streets of Cairo with a benevolence that is on occasion a source of embarrassment and even peril to an innocent companion. Evangelical humanitarianism is, be it remarked, subject to misunderstanding in the East; it is a manifest shock to the Cairene carter to find that the insistent and savage belabouring of his quadruped can be regarded as other than a routine mode of progression entirely acceptable to Allah. The following is a typical convergence of events: (i) Arab carter thrashes hope-

lessly overloaded donkey; (ii) Creswell leans over the
side of his open car and thrashes Arab carter; (iii) crowd
assembles and blocks the narrow street; (iv) Creswell
spots a distant and reluctant policeman, leaps from his
car, thrashes his way through the crowd, and collars the
reluctant policeman when on the point of escaping; (v)
Creswell compels reluctant policeman to march the
offending carter in front of him to the nearest police-
station; (vi) crowd makes away with cart and donkey.
To his friends it has long been apparent that Creswell
bears a charmed life. For his prowess is not limited to
the reform of donkeymen. Whether by similar or parallel
methods, he has so impressed the Cairo municipality
that quite impossible things have been done to the civic
architecture. When I first knew the imposing medieval
walls and gates of Cairo, they were encumbered and
largely concealed by a welter of slums and shacks, at one
point by a Muslim cemetery. Today, great stretches of
these walls stand revealed in the north-eastern quarter
of the city and are one of the most dramatic sights
of Egypt. The work of clearance is a tribute to the
enlightenment of the municipality, but the prime source
of light is Creswell and none other. No greater testimony
to his powers of radiation could be found than in the
removal of that most inviolable of obstructions, a
Muslim cemetery.

Mortimer Wheeler, *Still Digging*, 1955.

WARTIME Cairo threw these contrasts into even sharper
relief. Thousands of allied servicemen and women crowded
into the city, on leave from the battlefront in the Western
Desert or filling posts in GHQ Cairo, where the strategy for
the desert war, and many other Middle Eastern campaigns,
was planned. The mixture proved heady. Regular military
personnel rubbed shoulders with writers and propagandists;
exhausted soldiers drank in the dubious pleasures of the

bazaars during all-too-brief leave from the front, while the pre-war social season of the Western establishment continued unchecked; all with the constant turmoil of the city as a backdrop. Freya Stark, traveller and writer, worked in Cairo for the first half of the War, promoting pro-Allied feeling among Egyptians.

Cairo was the centre of our world during the first three years of war, the stage on which all glances south of the Alps were focused. To see it even in 1943, when the tide of Alamein had receded, or more so today when it has returned to be one of the uneasy national provincialisms of the East, is to miss all that made it unforgettable to those who lived in it or near it during the three great years. It was the goal of the pincer movement of the Axis, the artery of our oil and our communications, the keystone of our Middle Eastern arch. It had returned to the days of the Ptolemys when Egypt was the gate to Parthia and India and all the spice trade. You would hear every European language (except German) in its streets. In the wartime epilepsy, people travelling from everywhere to anywhere would have to pass through Cairo: they would come from Scandinavia or Chungking, and salute you unexpectedly on the terrace of Shepheard's or the Continental. To describe, or even to think of it now is as difficult as to evoke the magic of dead *prima donnas*, those moments – Nijinsky poised in air or Pavlova among her white feathers subsiding – which may have been artificial but are remembered more living than anything alive, and yet they cannot be conveyed. Nor will any peace prosperity restore the incantation, for – like diamonds on velvet – it was set in danger – in the orbit of advancing armies, the drama of existence or death. Exhausted as all were at the end, the threat was an enhancement, and no one can forget the gaiety and the glitter of Cairo while the desert war went on.

Cairo: the Twentieth-century View

It changed a great deal during the time I knew it –
from September to April 1940–1 and then to and fro
at intervals during the next two years – yet it always
presented, like the two-way-facing Janus, aspects of
surprising contrast – the unobtrusive hard work and
private anxiety, and the confidence which the Army, the
Egyptians, and the outside world were made to see. It
was quiet at first – the G.H.Q. typewriters clicked from
private flats (liable to be overheard by the houses
around) and dinner parties at the Embassy were easy
among English or Egyptians who came to know each
other well. *Cawasses* in gold and scarlet bowed one into
pleasant informal evenings of talk with the Lampsons
[the Ambassador]: Miles robust and Jacqueline light as
a fairy. The Embassy gardens at that time still stretched
to the Nile, and one rested under a light rug after dinner,
on chaise-longues in the soft night, where the lisp of the
great river's journey joined the conversation.

Sometimes it would be Mena House, round a swimming-pool in the open with lights dimmed so that men
late from their offices would peer among bare jewelled
shoulders and mess uniforms that still existed to find
their party at the little tables. These dimmed blue lights
bewitched Cairo into the *Pelléas and Mélisande* remote-
ness that seemed to belong to the precarious time . . .

In and out of the official world was the Levantine
society of Cairo dripping gems and substantially
unchanged from the days when Thais wore Alexandria's
most expensive togas. It would gather in the Muhammad Ali Club where fatherly waiters and huge chandeliers preserved their Victorian solidity, into which
cheerful troops broke now and then and asked for drinks.
Having got them from the shocked fifth-columnist head
waiter, they would ask for women, and the police were
sent for; as I left once I found my fat chauffeur with his
head in his hands, rather bashed in by a South African
annoyed with him for not being a taxi.

Beyond these quarters, the whole of Cairo itself
buzzed like a hive, carrying from age to age, from foreigner to foreigner, from dynasty to dynasty, its blind

traditions and long poverties. In these crowded quarters I came to have many committees – teachers, clerks, workmen or the lesser rank of government servant, living in small alleys up narrow stairs, hard lives not untouched by dreams.

Freya Stark, *Dust in the Lion's Paw*, 1961.

NOËL COWARD, arriving in Cairo in August 1943 on an entertainment tour of the Middle East, recorded these impressions.

We had a drink before lunch sitting on the terrace at Shepheard's. The restrictions of wartime are unknown; people sat there sipping Gin-Slings and cocktails and chatting and gossiping, waiters glided about wearing Fezzes and inscrutable Egyptian expressions. There were uniforms everywhere of all ranks and services and nationalities including Constance Carpenter in a natty shark-skin two-piece with E.N.S.A. on her epaulettes. These uniforms indicated that perhaps somewhere in the vague outside world there might be a war of some sort going on. This place is the last refuge of the soi-disant 'International Set'. All the fripperies of pre-war luxury living are still in existence here; rich people, idle people, cocktail-parties, dinner parties, jewels and evening dress. Rolls-Royces come purring up to the terrace steps; the same age-old Arabs sell the same age-old carpets and junk; scruffy little boys dart in between the tables shouting 'Bourse! Bourse!' which when translated means the Egyptian 'Times'. There is a perpetual undercurrent of social and political feuds and, excepting for a brief period when the 'Flap' was on and the Germans were expected to march in at any moment, here they have all stayed, with the exception of the men on leave, floating about lazily in this humid backwater for four long years. It was odd to see all this going on again, enjoyable of course for a brief, a very brief visit but it felt rather old-fashioned and almost lacking in taste.

Noël Coward, *Middle East Diary*, 1944.

CAIRO engendered ambivalent feelings among the fighting soldiers, who had endured, and knew they might not survive, the sweltering wretchedness of the desert campaign. They resented the hollow self-indulgence of the clubs and hotels, and yet at the same time longed for the city and its entertainments as an escape from the boredom and the exhaustion of army life. Cyril Joly, who served with the Desert Rats, and G.C. Norman, who went into banking after his wartime service, reflect this ambiguity.

Cairo felt the impact of the men of the camps on her outskirts. From armoured regiments, from infantry battalions, from the artillery, the engineers and the whole array of units which backed and supported them, hundreds of men swarmed into the city each day and night, intent on enjoying themselves. They crowded the streets, the bars, the cinemas. They got drunk and fought. They broke up the dance-halls and night-clubs. They violated the virgins, appropriated the professionals and encouraged the enthusiastic amateurs. Cairo was a seething, swarming mass of soldiers, swindled, cajoled and cursed by the crowds of impoverished and grasping Egyptians. The richer Egyptians lived a life apart, ignoring the war, the soldiers and their own less fortunate countrymen. The poorer Egyptians seized the fleeting opportunity to raise themselves above their usual filthy and depressing lives; they stole, and sweated at a hundred and one menial tasks with their eyes on the main chance and with little or no concern for the wider issues of the war ...

On other occasions I joined any party who were going into Cairo for the day or the evening. I went when I could to Gezireh on Sundays for the marvellous buffet lunches, followed by a lazy afternoon watching cricket. I played tennis and had tea by the swimming-pool, bathing occasionally, and spending the rest of the afternoons 'body-watching', as the pastime came to be known.

Our experiences and the knowledge that we would soon again be in battle coloured, as they were bound to colour, our feelings for those who had not stirred from the base. In the clubs and bars, in the Staffs and depots, we met a large variety of men who not only had not seen battle, but many of whom had no intention of doing so. There were certainly a great number who were hard-working, genuine and willing to give all the help they could, and who were eagerly scheming to get themselves away from their base jobs and into the desert. But there were others who had acquired so established an air of importance that they had already convinced themselves that their presence in 'G.H.Q.' was vital to the war effort.

Cyril Joly, *Take These Men*, 1955.

It was the ideal location for a war. Hundreds of miles of empty desert, uncluttered lines of communication, a perfect climate and a civilized back-up along the Nile – it was a tactician's paradise. And there was the added bonus that it was clean. There were no muddy trenches, no atrocities that I ever heard of, and no civilians to get in the way of the professionals, apart from the totally uncommitted Senussi tribesmen wandering freely with their flocks across the lines.

At times there was even a kind of camaraderie between us and the enemy. We used their water cans, they used our lorries. We seduced Lilli Marlene, they made comic parodies of 'We'll hang out our washing on the Siegfried Line'. Breaches of the tacitly accepted rules of the game were deprecated. I recall a front-line intelligence report of a complaint by a captured German officer about the unsporting behaviour of some of our troops towards enemy wounded. We replied, probably over the field radio to which both sides were privy, that some of their supposed wounded were getting up during an advance and shooting our chaps in the back, which was certainly not British and not really Afrika Korps either.

It was all a long time ago but at this distance – and this may sound strange – my principal impression now of the desert war is of the total security. We were encapsulated in a miniature Welfare State. Naturally there were the moments of terror, the dive-bombers, the night raids, the crunch of action, but always there was full logistical support, regular rations and cigarettes, sometimes even baked bread. I never recall feeling hungry or thirsty, not seriously. And after combat came the periods of inactivity for reading, talking, brewing-up, foraging for eggs and water, mobile baths and cinemas, all inside the tight little microcosm of the unit, and bounded by the familiar and reassuring stereotypes of the ubiquitous Busty and Smudger, Lofty and Mac.

And, if you were lucky, there was leave.

Life at the base, 'the rigours of the Cairo campaign' as the English language newspaper cartoonist put it, gave us our first real taste of the totally unreal life which was being lived back there, while we were 'up the blue'. Cairo was a dream world of music, theatres and opera, cafés and cinemas, museums and mosques, where we strode the crowded, unblacked-out streets like conquerors, accepting the homage of shopkeepers, dragomen and shoe-blacks as to the manna born.

I suppose we should hardly recognise it now. Is Groppi's bar still serving Tom Collinses and real Vienna truffles? Do cool hands still take 6 a.m. temperatures in the former 62 General Hospital, and sleek modern buses glide where the crazy trams used to lurch up to Abbassia, stuck all over with people like fly-papers? What strangers now dwell in 'Music For All', that astonishing wartime outpost of the arts? Who now inhabits the Victory Club with its immense, life-giving library and a dozen other establishments created especially for us, where, as exclusive guests, we could briefly forget the war and the desert over roast chicken and miniature eggs and chips? As I turn the yellowing pages of my copy of *Oasis*, snatches of 'Saheeda Bint' and the ribald version of Farouk's anthem echo in my mind, I taste again the medicinal Stella beer which never saw the hop, the acrid flavour of Victory Vs [a cigarette produced for the Forces] and the hot, dusty, pagan smell of Cairo, unique and unforgettable.

I am not suggesting that there was not anxiety too, the pain of separation and the dark threat of the more terrible battles casting their shadow over Europe: but they were deep down, pushed out of sight and mind, except when an airgraph or air lettercard from home intruded momentarily into the fantasy. Now, in 1977, there is an air of unreality about all that past life. Did I really wander amongst the Pyramids in khaki shorts, lie fearful between bursting bombs in slit-trenches and watch, gin in hand, a stout belly dancer agitate her pelvis in some almost forgotten establishment called The Blue Melody? Was it all a dream, that bright cameo? Did it exist? . . .

G.C. Norman, 'My War', reproduced in *Return to Oasis*, 1980.

WARTIME Cairo was renowned for its vigorous literary life. Literary magazines flourished, with contributions from new and established writers – Robin Fedden, Lawrence Durrell, Bernard Spencer – appearing alongside the less polished offerings of servicemen. Many would-be writers, such as G.S. Fraser, posted as a clerk to GHQ, found that the experience of Cairo life gave them the voice they were seeking.

When I think of Cairo, now, I think of something sick and dying; an old beggar, propped up against a wall, too palsied to raise a hand or supplicate alms; but in a passive way he can still enjoy the sun ... But who can possess a city? Who can possess it, as he possesses his own body, so that a vague consciousness of its proportions is always in his mind? ...

Every street in Cairo has the character of Cairo, but hardly any street has the character of itself. Everything, every note that at first seems distinctive, is repeated again and again. The tenement which is crumbling away at one side, like a rotted tooth; the native restaurant, open to the night, from which there comes a soft clapping of palms on tables and a monotonous chanting; the maze of narrow streets that leads to a cul-de-sac, where a taxi has gone to die; the sudden green and red glitter of lights, glimpsed through a curtain, from a cabaret; the sudden patch of green wasteland, the glimpse of the river, the white glitter of buildings on the other side, the curved masts of the feluccas, pulled down at the top as if by invisible strings; these things, and not things only, but people and incidents, are repeated; the baldish purple-looking ox that has collapsed in the gutter and is having its throat cut; the street accident with twenty shouting spectators in white galabyehs; the woman in black, sitting on the pavement, nursing her baby at a dusty breast; the legless beggar propelling himself forward, on a little wooden trolley, with frightful strength, with his hands. Unknown districts of Cairo, as I used to pass them on the crowded, clattering trams, would terrify me; so much suffering, unexplored, inarticulate life. I used to go out to visit a friend in Shubra, rather far from the centre of the city. I knew where to get off the tram because beside the stop there was a great heap of pots beside a patch of wasteland; but if somebody had moved the pots, I would have been completely lost. Even as it was, when I had dismounted from the tram, I had to make my choice between three almost exactly similar sidestreets, each with a large tree beside its narrow entrance. No, I did not possess Cairo; Cairo possessed me . . .

Cairo probably seemed to me a more confusing city than it really is because I saw it through a haze of heat and odours – the smells of spice, of cooking fat, of overripe fruit, of sun-dried sweat, of hot baked earth, of urine, of garlic, and, again and again, too sweet, of jasmin; a complex that, in the beginning of the hot weather, seemed to melt down to the general consistency of smouldering rubber . . . a smell of the outskirts of hell. Ceasing, soon, consciously to notice all this, I would sometimes, in the Garden City near the Embassy, pass a lawn of thin, patchy grass that had just been watered through a sprinkler; and I would realise, for a moment, how parched and acid my nostrils were. The smell of the Nile itself, of course, was different; by its banks, at night, there was a damp, vegetative coolness, that seemed to have, in a vague, evocative way, something almost sexual about it. And it was voluptuousness, in a cool, large room, to bend over and sniff, in a glass bowl on a table, at a crisp red rose. But in such a room there would be European women; and their skins would have dried a little, in that cruel climate, and one would be aware of their powder, and their scent. Beauty, whether of body or character, lay, in that city, under a constant siege. In my memory, that hot, baked smell prevails; that, and the grittiness – the dust gathering thickly on the glossy leaves of the evergreens, and the warm winds stinging eyes and nostrils with fine sand – and the breathlessness, the inner exhaustion. Under the glaring day, one seemed to see the human image sagging and

wilting a little, and expected sallow fingers and faces to
run and stretch, as if they were made of wax.

G.S. Fraser, *A Stranger and Afraid*, 1983.

AFTER the War, Cairo's expatriate life could never be the
same again. British troops withdrew to the Suez Canal Zone,
Egyptian nationalism and demands for independence grew
ever more forceful, the last days of the cosmopolitan city
were drawing in. Doing his National Service, Philip Oakes
had a job on an army magazine produced in Cairo.

Madame Stenka, our landlady in Cairo, had a portly
brown spaniel which took its exercise on the flat roof of
the pension, ambling between avenues of flower pots
and peeing on dwarf palm trees, trays of courgettes and
tubs of morning glory with a fine impartiality.

One morning Bob Dawbarn, my colleague on the
army magazine *Parade* which employed us both as
writers, appeared at breakfast with a large gash on his
chin. 'There I was having a peaceful shave,' he said,
'when a dog flew past the window.'

The apparition was explained when the spaniel's
corpse was found four storeys below. But even before
the body was discovered the strangeness of the incident
seemed to us in no way exceptional. Cairo was an altogether strange city. That winter the first snow to fall in
Egypt for thirty years feathered down from a dark sky
and men and women ran into the streets with their
tongues out to catch the drifting flakes. At the same time
we decided that we had a spy in the pension, a mystery
woman who wore glasses so dark and opaque that her
eyes were completely hidden and who could be heard
making impassioned telephone calls in an unknown lan-

guage soon after the weekly meeting of British personnel in the sitting room.

Nothing we discussed had any military importance. The army had been withdrawn to the Canal Zone several months previously and the few soldiers who remained all had civilian jobs and dressed accordingly. There was a small contingent of military police whose main task was to keep a look out for British deserters working their way to the coast where they hoped to hitch a ride home. But there was no work for a spy. We debated whether we should lay false trails in our talks to give her something to report. But it seemed too complicated and no one wanted to get the mystery woman into trouble . . .

We ate most of our meals at the pension, but we had an office cook named George who was Sudanese and had three wives. George thought he was over sixty although he was not certain as to the date of his birth. His wives were considerably younger. 'Maybe nineteen, twenty,' he said when we asked him. 'Old wives no good.'

'How d'you manage?' asked Bob.

'Manage?'

'How do you manage to keep them happy? One man, three women.' Bob mimed fatigue by slumping forward in his chair. 'Very hard work.'

George untied a small pouch that hung from his belt and loosened the draw-string. '*Kif*,' he said. 'Makes a man strong.'

He rolled a slim cigarette between his fingers and we shared it between us, sucking in the smoke with noisy draughts of air. I felt the veins in my temples expand and I could see time flowing ahead of me like a broad, unhurried stream. All sense of urgency dissolved in the current and I wondered how George found the energy to attend to one, let alone three of his wives.

The office secretary was Edmee Cohen. She had a mane of black hair and when she combed it she threw back her head so that her throat was bared as if it was being offered to the executioner's knife. It was more than a fanciful notion. Edmee believed that the revolution was on its way. 'When it comes,' she said, 'there will be no more Jews.' For years her ambition had been to marry a British officer who would take her away from Cairo, away from Egypt. She saw herself at home in Wimbledon or Scunthorpe, places she had heard of, but could not envisage.

'Tell me what they are like,' she demanded. 'Would I be happy there?'

'They're not like Cairo,' I said. 'You'd hate the cold. It rains a lot and there's rationing.'

'Who cares about that?'

'You would,' said Bob. 'You're not used to it.'

Edmee shook back her hair and her throat shone like a column of ivory. 'I would suffer anything to leave this place.'

She believed that she was being sincere. But by temperament and upbringing she was a true Cairene and it was difficult to see her in any other setting. She belonged to a sailing club. She went to the races at Gezira. Bob and I took her to Groppi's where she ate dish after dish of ice-cream and summoned the waiters by clapping her hands, ordering them to clear the table and bring fresh glasses of iced water while she gloated over the array of cakes on the trolley at her elbow. She came with us to the cinema and we took her home by gharry, cramming ourselves into the pungent cab with portholes on either side and kissing her in turn until the driver grumbled over his shoulder and Edmee pushed us away and sat erect, her hands folded in her lap. 'He's Muslim,' she hissed. 'He doesn't approve.' The disapproval frightened her, but she despised it too. 'They're barbarians,' she said. 'They're a thousand years out of date.' . . .

We were all aware that change was on the way. There were more demonstrations. Another tram was burned outside the pension and Madame Stenka, who had fled Czechoslovakia with her husband in 1938, stood at the window and watched the coils of smoke eddy and drift towards the Blue Mosque. She was looking for someone to buy her establishment, but after a year of advertising there were still no takers. Mr Copeland, a lecturer at the university who rented a double room on the first floor,

had his classes halved and several of his private pupils –
elegant young men who joined us for coffee to practise
their English – suddenly decided that they had no
further need of tuition. 'It's very hurtful,' said Mr Copeland, 'I feel that I've failed them.'

He was an elderly bachelor who wore silk suits the
colour of lemonade and a monocle which he screwed
into his good eye while the other wept as though a
concealed pipe had sprung a leak beneath the parchment
of his cheek. He dabbed at it with a handkerchief which,
between times, he kept tucked in his jacket sleeve. He
had lived in Cairo for over forty years and had planned
to end his days there. He was not resentful about what
was happening, but puzzled. 'Where else could I go?'
he asked. He had a sister in Basingstoke, but they had
never been close. She disapproved of his attachment to
the young men he taught, and wrote to say that she
could not see him settling in Hampshire. 'She regards
me as a foreigner,' he said, toying with the notion in the
same abstracted way that he fingered a string of amber
beads looped around his watch fob ...

In one sense [Cairo] was an exciting place to be. There
was an atmosphere of intrigue and impending violence.
Revolution hung in the air like electricity before a storm.
But it offered no involvement. The cause was not ours;
we were detested by everyone concerned. The mystery
woman was right. They wanted to drive us out and I
was ready to go ...

We took Edmee for a farewell dinner at Shepheards,
but it was not a success. She flinched when the waiter
served the meal as though she already saw him in another
role, leading the mob which would drag her from her
apartment. 'You don't believe me,' she said, 'but it will
happen.'

Her arm was pebbled with cold and I stroked it in a
forlorn attempt to comfort her. 'Of course it won't.'

'You don't know. And you won't be here to find out.'

We rode home by gharry, but the only time we kissed
was when we said goodnight. 'You mean goodbye,' said
Edmee.

'We'll keep in touch.'

She shook her head. 'Oh no, you won't. No one ever writes and, anyway, what's the use?'

We watched her enter the apartment block and the door close behind her. The gharry driver clicked his tongue and the horse ambled on its way. 'She'll be all right,' said Bob.

'Of course she will.'

'Will you write to her?'

'I expect so. How about you?'

'There's not much point. She said so herself.'

Philip Oakes, *At the Jazz Band Ball*, 1983.

IN the mid-1950s two French writers, Jean and Simonne Lacouture, produced a portrait of the city in the throes of a complex and long-drawn-out political, social and religious revolution destined to produce a more homogenous, Islamic society than Cairo had ever previously known.

It is impossible to form any idea of Egypt as a whole, or of its function or its difference from the rest of the world, without some view of the great city that battens on it. Wrapped in its perennial cloud of dust and ashes, surrounded by the three Cities of the Dead, harsh, sandy, waterless as the desert, Cairo is an incongruous capital for a nation of riverside farmers, a small-holding African peasantry whose feet are never out of the waters of the Nile. Twenty million paupers, bent double over the cotton-plants and mindlessly enslaved to the seasons, have as their capital an arrogant city in which the meanest beggar can gaze out across the roof-tops, holding himself erect and bowing his head only towards the East, in homage to an abstract God.

But Cairo evokes too many such images. No one can

fail to notice the Turkish contours of the Mohamed Ali Mosque, in the Citadel. But somehow the Pyramids have lost nothing of their mystery. Loti long ago deplored the fact that they could be reached by tram or carriage, and today the city has crept up to their feet and the villas sprout like mushrooms in the shade of Cheops.

Between these two poles of ancient and modern stretches an immense city, all flat and dusty, grey and gold, rich and lice-ridden, living and dead, a town over which hundreds of kites weave an ominous net, where haughty skyscrapers are jostled by derelict hovels. It bears the name of Egypt itself, for in the vernacular there is only one word, *Misr*, for both country and capital: Cairo is Egypt yet the contrary of Egypt.

The centre of Cairo is astonishing, dazzling and disappointing. We hardly expect to find such spacious, well-kept avenues, such enormous blocks of buildings ten or fifteen stories high, these elegant shop-fronts and long American cars the colour of strawberry ices or moonlight. But turning behind some marble and concrete building you will find a sordid alley, dirty children, overturned dustbins, the old Cairo in the very heart of a business centre full of banks and cinemas. You catch a glimpse of a three-year-old child perched on a cart, on top of a heap of rubbish collected by his father. Round the corner you can again breathe the 'civilized' atmosphere of what is still known as the European quarter. The air-conditioned teashop offers some respite from the heat. July is unbearably hot – the Egyptian July, month of revolutions, strikes, sudden nationalizations. All the major events from the Hyksos invasions to Faruk's abdication have happened in July.

July is the time when fever and the Nile rise in Egypt, and especially in Cairo. In olden days at this time they used to offer the city's most beautiful virgin as a sacrifice to the river. The story goes that when General Amr, the Caliph's lieutenant, rode into Cairo, he was horrified at this barbarous custom and carried the girl off on his horse. Since then the citizens of Cairo have contented themselves with throwing a doll – the 'Nile's Bride' –

into the river. Feluccas with huge sails festooned with gaudy streamers run between the island of Gazira and the fashionable river-banks, overlooked by two palaces, the old Semiramis Palace and the modern Shepheard's.

What used to be exclusive, upper-class districts now belong, to all appearances, to the masses. This is their only clear gain from the revolution. A magnificent river-side walk has been expropriated and built up for them, though it involved a slice being cut off the British Embassy which used to jut down to the river's edge. This was achieved through one of the additional clauses to the Anglo-Egyptian treaty. This minor 'evacuation' of the Ambassador's bathing-pool has produced nothing more than a long promenade which the crowds invade at holiday-time. Their own hot and stuffy streets with hovels nestling close beside the mosques are more appreciated by tourists in search of the picturesque than by the poor who have to live in them.

The lower-class Egyptian dons his best green-and-white striped *galabiya* and strolls like a *bourgeois* along the river-bank, together with his children in flashy art-silk and his wife invisible in her black *melaya*. He walks as if he owned the street: there's no point in the motorist blowing a horn or losing his temper, for the crowd won't make room for a car. The city policeman is helpless and advises you to turn back and cross the nearest bridge. The one taken over by the gaudy crowd today, still flanked by two bronze British lions, is the one which is zealously guarded on the other side by the statue of the uniformed Zaghlul. On the left the 'people' chews sunflower-seeds and drinks its Coca-cola. It is easily pleased. In the evening the crowd crosses over the bridge and lounges all over the lawns of 'Liberation Square'. The revolution has given it all this grass, and the foun-tain – in glorious technicolour – which somehow keeps it alive. It was not far from here that the barracks used to stand, symbols of the British occupation. On the very day when the evacuation agreement was being signed – in July, of course – they were attacked with pick and shovel. Now an American cinema is rising on the same site – one occupation following another. The French-built Museum is still standing.

The holiday, like all holidays, ends tonight with a firework display. The taste for this sort of thing was begun by the Germans, when the Democratic Republic gave the city of Cairo a magnificent show. Since then festivities are never concluded without this expensive and impressive trifle which lights up the Nile, much to the joy of the mob.

Next morning it is hard at work again. The snob quarters are full of beggars, porters, car attendants and suit-pressers. Indeed, these particular jobs give a clue to the lay-out of the city. Beggars are disappearing, not because the Cairenes are getting richer but because Major Boghdadi, intent on building new boulevards and demolishing hovels, determined to thrust them out of sight. Now and then you come across a lorry packed with shameless girls, cripples and illegal barrow-boys, who have all been 'nipped'. They are merely returned to their rightful, poverty-stricken suburbs, so as not to shock the sensitive tourist. Some of them refuse to be daunted, however. One of them, particularly obstinate, has clung to his brazier for the last three years, brandishing his stump of an arm under the nose of embarrassed motorists.

Few women are to be seen in the fashionable streets. The chic upper-class women only go about in cars, taking tea at L's or G's, doing a little shopping after which their chauffeurs carry them off to the Club. The 'Gazira Sporting Club' is the heart and soul of the old and new upper-classes. It has about 250 acres of grass, always in good trim, trees, flowers, swimming-pools, a race-course, cricket-pitch, golf-course, restaurants, a 'lido' and even croquet for the more sedate ladies. There are also squash-courts to provide some violent, English exercise. Round the lido you meet diplomats wearing shorts, their methodically sunburnt wives, American babies dressed in frilly clothes that died out in Europe fifty years ago; ravishing slim girls playing the bohemian with youths in blue jeans; ex-princes, pale and disillusioned; foreign journalists on the look-out for scraps of news, and a few tennis-playing officers, friends of Nasser.

It is these officers, or those who were not admitted to the Club, who have nationalized it. The Suez affair was only a matter of international politics, but the Sporting Club did far more damage in the Cairo upper-class. Taking over the Club was proof that everything had changed and that the Bastille had fallen. Alarm and despondency were spread by this attack on privilege, merely to make sports-grounds for poor youths, when there was plenty of waste ground outside Cairo. And thereupon a wall was built across the Club's grounds, so as to remind everyone that privilege has its limits.

Jean and Simonne Lacouture, *Egypt in Transition*, 1958.

7

The Pyramids

THE inescapable first excursion out of Cairo was to the Pyramids, some six miles away on the edge of the desert at Giza. Amelia Edwards recaptures the anticipation and awe with which travellers awaited their first sight of the Egypt of the Pharaohs. It is worth noting that her chronology is uncertain at times; she adds an extra millennium and a half to the true age of the Pyramids, which date from the 26th century BC.

The first glimpse that most travellers now get of the Pyramids is from the window of the railway carriage as they come from Alexandria; and it is not impressive. It does not take one's breath away, for instance, like a first sight of the Alps from the high level of the Neufchâtel line, or the outline of the Acropolis at Athens as one first recognises it from the sea. The well-known triangular forms look small and shadowy, and are too familiar to be in any way startling. And the same, I think, is true of every distant view of them, – that is, of every view which is too distant to afford the means of scaling them against other objects. It is only in approaching them, and observing how they grow with every foot of the road, that one begins to feel they are not so familiar after all.

But when at last the edge of the desert is reached, and the long sand-slope climbed, and the rocky platform gained, and the Great Pyramid in all its unexpected bulk and majesty towers close above one's head, the effect is as sudden as it is overwhelming. It shuts out the sky and the horizon. It shuts out all the other Pyramids. It shuts out everything but the sense of awe and wonder.

Now, too, one discovers that it was with the forms of the Pyramids, and only their forms, that one had been acquainted all these years past. Of their surface, their colour, their relative position, their number (to say nothing of their size), one had hitherto entertained no kind of definite idea. The most careful study of plans and measurements, the clearest photographs, the most elaborate descriptions, had done little or nothing, after all, to make one know the place beforehand. This undulating table-land of sand and rock, pitted with open graves and cumbered with mounds of shapeless masonry, is wholly unlike the desert of our dreams. The Pyramids of Cheops and Chephren are bigger than we had expected; the Pyramid of Mycerinus is smaller. Here, too, are nine Pyramids, instead of three. They are all entered in the plans and mentioned in the guide-books; but, somehow, one is unprepared to find them there, and cannot help looking upon them as intruders. These six extra Pyramids are small and greatly dilapidated. One, indeed, is little more than a big cairn.

Even the Great Pyramid puzzles us with an unexpected sense of unlikeness. We all know, and have known from childhood, that it was stripped of its outer blocks some five hundred years ago to build Arab mosques and palaces; but the rugged, rock-like aspect of that giant staircase takes us by surprise, nevertheless. Nor does it look like a partial ruin, either. It looks as if it had been left unfinished, and as if the workmen might be coming back to-morrow morning.

The colour again is a surprise. Few persons can be aware beforehand of the rich tawny hue that Egyptian limestone assumes after ages of exposure to the blaze of an Egyptian sky. Seen in certain lights, the Pyramids look like piles of massy gold.

Amelia Edwards, *A Thousand Miles Up the Nile*, 1877.

The Pyramids

ELIZABETH CABOT KIRKLAND, wife of the former President of Harvard College, set off for the Pyramids on her second day in Cairo in 1830. Her description strikes a rare dissenting note: 'We arrived at their foot about sunset, they look much smaller than you expect, only piles resembling dirty bricks, indeed until you are so close to them as to touch them you do not realize they are stone.' A century later, the biologist Julian Huxley, travelling through the Middle East as Director-General of UNESCO, was impressed in spite of himself.

Familiarity (though at second-hand) had led me, not to despise the Pyramids, but to discount them. They had become international common-places, degraded to the level of the tourist souvenir. They had passed through so many million minds as one of the 'Wonders of the World' that their sharp edge of real wonder had been blunted. Like Niagara and Rio de Janeiro, they had been thrust down my throat so often that I was sure I was not going to be impressed by them.

But in actuality, they make an overpowering impression. It is not one of beauty, but on the other hand not one of mere bigness, though size enters into it, and there is an element of aesthetic satisfaction in the elemental simplicity of their triangular silhouette. But this combines with an element of vicarious pride in the magnitude of the human achievement involved, and with a sense of their bold novelty and their historical uniqueness, to produce an effect different from that of any other work of man.

Julian Huxley, *From an Antique Land*, 1954.

The Pyramids

THE ascent of the Great Pyramid, now forbidden to the modern tourist, was the first goal of the nineteenth-century visitor. The climb could not be accomplished unaided; several guides were necessary to help. In some cases it was more a matter of hauling each member of the party up the steep steps cut in the side. Mrs Kirkland continued unimpressed:

The fatigue was great, the charges small. We had three Bedouin Arabs, one on each side and one behind ... Many of the stones you ascend are four feet high, and it would be impossible for you to climb them without this assistance. The only objection to them, for they are very obliging and good tempered, is that they are so filthy both to the nose and the touch ... You have nothing to reward you for mounting but an idea of the vastness which you cannot otherwise acquire. We were 40 minutes in going up, and 22 in descending. Mr Coster ... cut our names in the imperishable stone, probably the most enduring memento of us (one which will survive all others) for although Mr K[irkland] was only at their foot I had his name engraved on the top. We were unfortunate in our weather, the wind from the desert excessively hot, with a scorching sun.

Elizabeth Cabot Kirkland, *Proceedings of the Massachusetts Historical Society*, 1905.

GENERALLY, at least half an hour seems to have been par for the climb. However, Mrs Dawson Damer, ten years after Mrs Kirkland, claimed that her party took only a quarter of an hour to reach the top: 'We only rested twice on our way, which was as necessary for our guides' lungs as for our own'. Carving name or initials in the top of the Pyramid was normal practice. William Holman Hunt disapproved of such frivolity, but in vain:

Before leaving the desert I engaged two Arabs to take me to the top of the Pyramids. Seddon accompanied me, declaring his determination to write his name on the top; I strove to dissuade him, but when he came down he gloried in having accomplished his object. I contented myself that mine would not be found there, but he retorted, 'Oh, isn't it, though? I took care to write yours as large as mine!'

William Holman Hunt, *Pre-Raphaelitism and the Pre-Raphaelite Brotherhood*, 1905.

In 1921, shortly before she left Egypt for boarding-school in England, the young Priscilla (Hayter) Napier, whose father was an official in the Egyptian Civil Service, tackled the climb.

I had never yet achieved our long-held ambition of going to the top of the Great Pyramid. I had once, on one of many Nanny picnics in the ruined temple below the Second Pyramid, empty of life and strewn with broken pieces of granite and alabaster brought with such expense of human effort from who knew where, climbed some way up this one. My plan had been to get anyway as far as the shiny top of this pyramid, the only part of the three which is left unstripped of its granite covering. This dream had faded. Nanny, alas, saw me in time, when I felt myself to be agonisingly nearly there. Crimson and gesticulating, she stood in the ruined temple, making imperative movements suggesting descent. There was a certain degree of redness in Nanny's face that meant business, and was discernible even from three-quarters of the way up a pyramid. Coming down a pyramid is dull, and even, when you are seven, dangerous. You have to jump off each block, and your skirt sticks on it, and you nearly fall off the edge of the next block. 'You weren't even nearly there,' Nanny said crushingly, brushing the stony dust off me, and this may have been so; it is impossible, once on a pyramid, to judge how far up there is still to go. How galling it was, this interfering conspiracy of grown-ups to prevent children breaking their necks! How they gang up, and even expect one to be interested in their stuffy hobby! I knew very well that I would never now feel the shiny top of the Pyramid of Chephren. 'There now,' Nanny said, 'run about and play. Set so much as a foot on that pyramid again and I'll spiflicate you.'

My father, surprisingly, felt rather the same. He had a thing against going up, or inside, the Great Pyramid. I never knew why; he was not superstitious, nor was he afraid of heights. Perhaps he regarded the whole thing as a tourist-fleecing racket, and a waste of time. Edward Cecil had mockingly assured him that he had carved the name of Hayter in huge letters on the summit, hoping to tease my father into going up to see whether this horrifying outrage had indeed been done; but he never went. This winter, standing at the foot of the pyramids, we had seen a bulky and portentous looking man striding up the hill from Mena, his coat-tails blowing back, his chin thrust out against the desert wind. 'Winston Churchill,' my father said. He was the first person I had ever seen wearing dark glasses, then a novelty; they made him, I thought, look like the fish footman in *Alice*. I was so preoccupied with the dark glasses that I failed to notice T. E. Lawrence, who, unromantically wearing a dark blue suit, accompanied Winston on this day. My father took me by the shoulder and whisked us firmly round the corner of the pyramid, out of range. 'I spent,' he said, 'the whole of yesterday with Churchill in the role of a local expert; and I don't want to spend the whole of this afternoon'; for Churchill, alas, was not in those years liked by his contemporaries, especially those with strong characters themselves . . .

My father was adamant about the Great Pyramid. It thus fell to the lot of Sir Frederick Rowlatt to take charge of the expedition to the top. We forgathered at the foot of the pyramid; Mary and Pamela Rowlatt neat in reefer jackets and round panama hats, Alethea and I, dressed as usual rather inconclusively. Rose Hunt was left knitting behind an immense fallen piece of alabaster, occasionally saying, 'Imshi, ya wallad,' in rather a prim voice to inquisitive intruders. Our hearts thumped wildly with anticipation, with the tremendousness of this so long awaited moment. Up above us, the angle of the pyramid stretched, an endless succession of yellow, yard-square stone blocks. I was allotted a very old Egyptian guide whom I was obliged to haul up the more difficult places, urging him on to a smarter pace in my kitchen Arabic; he imploring me to go slower and wait for him, in tones which became increasingly breathless. There are probably few things in nature more inexhaustibly energetic than a long-legged child of twelve who really wants to get somewhere. The last few steps before the top were almost unbearably exciting. Sir Frederick arrived last, slightly out of breath, but still with his habitual kindly dryness of manner. The name of Hayter was not, I was relieved to see, engraved upon the summit, but the name of Amos was; perhaps an early indiscretion of Sir Maurice's, or of his father's. A stiff wind blew, flapping the cotton skirts of our dresses and causing Sir Frederick to clutch on to his hat. 'Keep back,' he said at intervals, and in unruffled tones, 'from the edge.'

Priscilla Napier, *A Late Beginner*, 1966.

The Pyramids

PRISCILLA's friend Mary Rowlatt, who was also sent off to school at about the same time, 'piously chipped off a small corner of one of the mammoth blocks' as a reminder of home. The summit achieved, some form of refreshment was required before the splendour of the view could be properly appreciated. The American traveller David Millard and his English companion shared a simple lunch of oranges and a 'roll of good bread'. Alfred Butler, always somewhat supercilious in his attitudes, ate in rather grander style.

While we were in raptures over the sunset our five Arabs were preparing dinner, which was freshened by a huge block of ice, a thing the Arabs professed never to have seen there before. When our salt happened to be blown away by the wind, one of the Beduins offered to run down and get more. He thought less of the descent than an English servant would of running down stairs. After dinner we lay on our backs smoking, star-gazing, and talking with the Arabs. Their talk at times was rather a nuisance. As one was pondering on the awful silence of the scene, surveying the wide horizon, the skies, and the moonlit desert, thinking how grand the pyramid of Chefren looked to-night, with one side deep in shadow, the other silvered with bright light, or recalling, perhaps, quaint Herodotean gossip about the building and builders of the pyramid, it was harsh and jarring to hear an Arab voice strike up,

> Higgery diggery dugk,
> De mousenup de clugk,
> De clugk street one,
> And den come down run up!

the echo of a rhyme taught by some crazy traveller. Such chatter soon put an end to our would-be sublime imaginings. Nevertheless, when we came away, we were agreed that the pyramids are best seen under a midsummer moonlight.

Alfred Butler, *Court Life in Egypt*, 1887.

The Pyramids

THE panorama from the summit, with all its Biblical and historical associations stretching back over thousands of years, provoked the most sublime thoughts.

No man can gaze from the top of the pyramid Cheops, without emotions never to be forgotten. His thoughts roam backward through thousands of years. He gazes with astonishment on the mysterious works of art spread at his feet. He thinks of the countless thousands employed in constructing these vast monuments of human toil. He contemplates the whole as done by men who lived and moved and had a being more than four thousand years ago. Where are they now? Gone! all gone! their names lost, and even the design of their vast labor enveloped in mystery and uncertainty!

David Millard, *A Journal of Travels in Egypt, Arabia Petrae, and the Holy Land during 1841–2*, 1843.

MAKING his ascent before dawn, Gustave Flaubert was rewarded with seeing the sun rise from the summit.

We wait a good half hour for the sunrise.
The sun was rising just opposite; the whole valley of the Nile, bathed in mist, seemed to be a still white sea; and the desert behind us, with its hillocks of sand, another ocean, deep purple, its waves all petrified. But as the sun climbed behind the Arabian chain the mist was torn into great shreds of filmy gauze; the meadows, cut by canals, were like green lawns with winding borders. To sum up: three colors – immense green at my feet in the foreground; the sky pale red – worn vermilion; behind and to the right, a rolling expanse

looking scorched and iridescent, with the minarets of Cairo, *canges* [small Nile boats] passing in the distance, clusters of palms.

Finally the sky shows a streak of orange where the sun is about to rise. Everything between the horizon and us is all white and looks like an ocean; this recedes and lifts. The sun, it seems, is moving fast and climbing above oblong clouds that look like swan's down, of an inexpressible softness; the trees in the groves around the villages (Gizeh, Matariyeh, Bedrashein, etc.) seem to be in the sky itself, for the entire perspective is perpendicular, as I once saw it before, from the harbor of Picade in the Pyrenees; behind us, when we turn around, is the desert – purple waves of sand, a purple ocean.

The light increases. There are two things: the dry desert behind us, and before us an immense, delightful expanse of green, furrowed by endless canals, dotted here and there with tufts of palms; then, in the background, a little to the left, the minarets of Cairo and especially the mosque of Mohammed Ali (imitating Santa Sophia), towering above the others.

Flaubert's travel notes from *Flaubert in Egypt*, translated and edited by Francis Steegmuller, 1972.

AT ground level once again, the more adventurous visitors, not content with a day excursion from the city, pitched a desert camp around the foot of the Pyramids. Arab servants would produce an alfresco meal, and as the sun set, and the noise of the day visitors died away, this most romantic of settings could be guaranteed to produce an authentic desert experience. Mrs Haight passed a memorable if rather disturbed night, her first-ever under canvas.

Our place of rest for the night was a large tomb, excavated in the solid rock, in the side of the hill, with one end opening upon a sort of terrace. Being well swept out, and spread with carpets and mattresses around the sides, it formed a tolerably comfortable parlour, with divans, &c. In the centre a table was arranged, by placing several canteen boxes side by side, which, with a clean white tablecloth and sundry articles of dinner furniture, wore quite a promising aspect.

My impatience for dinner led me to make a domiciliary visit to the quarters of Monsieur Francois, who I found had appropriated to himself another of these chambers of the dead, which he had transformed into a pretty good *restaurant* for the living, and in which, with the aid of a little charcoal from Cairo, and sundry portions of *mummy* from a neighbouring pit, he made out to produce for us several courses of viands in his best style. This was the first time in my life that I ever *bivouacked* for a night, or made a meal seated *à la Turc* upon the ground.

A good appetite, good company, light hearts, and a consciousness of perfect security, caused our dinner and *soirée* in the tomb to pass off delightfully. The evening conversation turned unfortunately upon tombs, mummy-pits, and mummies.

My sleeping apartment, separated by a curtain from the dining-room in front, was the nook where had been the sarcophagus of some Pharaoh or other. My mattress and its occupant filled up the sacred space; nor was I at all disturbed by the wandering spirit whose three thousand years of metempsychosis can scarcely yet be over, and which might very probably have been guarding my couch in the body of the trusty dog at my feet, unconscious that my dinner had been, perhaps, cooked with its former earthly tenement.

After a day of such unusual fatigue, it is not singular that I desired to seek an early repose; and when the light of my taper disclosed to me the *locale* of my couch, its arrangements were not uncomfortable; but then, '*to sleep, perchance to dream, ay, there's the rub.*' The gentlemen spread their carpets, and, rolling themselves in their cloaks, were soon unconscious of the noisy revelry of our servants in the next-door tomb, or the unceasing jargon of the loquacious Bedouins, prowling round to catch the crumbs that fell from the tables.

As soon as the hunger of our servants was appeased and their libations had ceased, nature asserted her rights, and not a soul of them but was as silent as their companions, the mummies; none, save myself, appeared to be awake.

Whether from motives of curiosity, or from a troubled conscience like another Lady Macbeth, I seized the burning taper, drew aside my curtain, and, stepping lightly over the sleepers, reached the terrace in front of the tomb, where the night-breeze instantly extinguished my light. My first impulse was to retreat; but, aware that my husband and his friends lay within ten feet of the door, I was reassured.

The first near object that arrested my attention was our *trusty* Mustafa, sitting on a stone, with a firelock across his arm, but fast asleep. The night was one of truly *Egyptian darkness*. Such a background, together with what I then saw, formed the very *beau ideal* of a subject for the pencil of De la Notte. In the distance, a few dying embers served to throw an uncertain light on sundry forms lying about, so like the human as easily to be mistaken for man or mummy. In the foreground were several camp-fires, around which were seated the half-naked Bedouins, silently and voraciously devouring some fragments of food.

While gazing at these hideous creatures, my imagination transformed the hooded females who flitted by the blaze into Hecates and witches, the swarthy myrmidons into devils incarnate, and the half-consumed mummy-fuel into some victim they were tormenting. Now and then a shrill ejaculation from a female, or a coarse laugh from the savage-looking beings by the fire, with their lank bodies, shaved heads, sunken eyes, and endless mouths, gave the whole a more sepulchral and demoniacal appearance than anything I had ever seen before in real life, or in the mock horrors of *Der Freischutz*. To give the last finishing touch to the picture, and to exalt

my excited feelings to the highest pitch, in every direction lay fragments of mummies. Their resinous cere-
ments were scattered in all directions; each puff of wind
drove them across the embers, where instantly igniting,
they caused a transient blaze to flash a lurid glare upon
hundreds of '*death's head and cross-bones.*' At each step
of these busy demons was heard the sharp crackling of
dried human skeletons; a sound which, together with my
already surcharged vision, so overcame all my remaining
courage, that I tottered back to my sepulchral couch,
and there endeavoured to overcome my excitement, and,
if possible, partake of the repose around me. Restless and
uneasy, my thoughts wandering from one lugubrious
object to another, I endeavoured to drown them all in
ineffectual attempts to force a sleep; but all my expedi-
ents failing, I relighted my taper, and determined to
while away the remainder of the night, either in reading,
or in the most agreeable reflections I could conjure
up. To me, who had never before passed a night
out of a house, it was not a very amusing matter to
be thus lying in a *cavern of the Libyan rocks*, in the
very centre of the greatest Necropolis the world ever
knew, where were entombed countless millions of
human bodies, scarcely changed in feature, the accumulated relics of ages, and the unbroken ranks of nations
and people existent more than three thousand years
ago.

Sarah Haight, *Letters from the Old World*, 1840.

MORNING brought the expedition to the interior. If the ascent
had seemed daunting, this proved even more so. In 1900,
Murray's *Handbook* warned its readers that:

The Pyramids

A Visit to the Interior is not a very pleasant task, and, on the whole, it is perhaps more fatiguing than going to the top; the close air, the scrambling, and the dust, all contribute to make it disagreeable. Nervous people had certainly better not attempt it. Magnesium wire should be taken for the purpose of seeing the King's Chamber to advantage, and each person would do well to have a candle to himself, and matches in his pocket.

Murray's *Handbook for Travellers in Egypt*, 1900.

WRITING to his friend and fellow painter Sir John Millais in 1854 shortly after his visit, Holman Hunt provides a vivid description:

May 8, 1854.

I never had any great admiration for the Pyramids such as most people manifest, and this, and perhaps a desire to appear superior to the cockney visitors, had made me leave the duty of particular examination to the last. . . . I wish I could give you any idea of the event. It was a hot day, and when we reached the entrance I was glad to stop a few minutes in the shade before commencing my inner researches; when we started it was along an alley descending at an angle of 35°, without sufficient room to allow us to walk upright. It was a difficult matter to proceed down this slippery pavement and reach out far enough in each stride to come upon a rudely broken step which perhaps had been made at first for the use of visitors or workmen. I managed, however, here without the assistance of either the Arab before or the one behind. At the end of fifty yards we came upon a halting-place, where they stayed and lighted the candles they had each brought. Behind and upwards we looked

on the long cool passage with the hot white sky at the
end; for our further passage we had to turn on one side
and along a low tunnel requiring one to stoop double:
here my guides were divided as before, each holding
their candle towards me. I heard through their monotonous chanting shrill and sharp sounds as of creatures
frightened; but there was no opportunity for inquiry,
the men had chosen a pace and there was no interrupting
it, and when we stopped at last it was at such a strange
barrier that all my curiosity was drawn towards our own
affairs. I had not yet recovered the blindness of the sun,
and when I saw our way completely blocked up in front
and at the side, it seemed to me that there was no further
way; but I was reassured somewhat by seeing one Arab
climb the wall. I proceeded to follow his example, but as
he seemed to have restricted himself to an inconvenient
space, I turned towards the further corner; but here I
was arrested by the Arab Abdullah and the illumination
of the mouth of a dark well. 'Dat go *moush*, araf-fein;
him go down, down, no stop' – a piece of information
which induced me to place myself in his offered arm and
be quiet, while he wheeled me round as I have seen
heavy goods turned about by iron cranes in London;
and here I had the hand of Mahommed to grasp to
clamber up to a landing leading to another passage,
which, as nearly as I can guess, must run upwards at an
angle of $35°$ from the one I had just left here. I held the
hand of Abdullah in front and of the other behind, in
established order, and in spite of a liberal heat and
perspiration suffered by each, we progressed at quick
measure as again doled out by the harmonious but most
unhappy tune of the true believers. Our pace was suddenly checked by the presence of another deep well,
which here went completely across the passage; but,
fortunately, a way was left at the side on a kind of step
which runs from the bottom to the top, and this we used
to pass the terrible opening to the remainder of this and
other forgotten ascents and descents, the while I listened
to the echoes and the bat screeches, and peered forwards
as well as I could with my body bent double, to make

out the nature of our way, until at the top of a tiring ascent I was allowed to walk upright for a few paces, and then was told that the place was the central chamber of the Pyramid. My eyes were not prepared for the depth of darkness in that place, and I looked about vainly to discover the walls that I might tell its size; but I was forced to wait further initiation and employ my probation on objects within reach. There was an empty sarcophagus in the middle of the room, which had evidently been broken open for its contents, which had been taken away; nothing was left but an outer case of rude construction, perhaps designedly to deceive any who might find that hidden treasure-house. In a corner of the room was an excavation which had been commenced by some recent investigator, but which had been given up and left as fruitless. At last I could manage to estimate the size of the place, and to my disappointment, since the walls had seemed to contract in becoming visible, it was not more than 30 or 40 feet square, and it had nothing more than the two objects, except the thousands of names written upon the walls of all ages. ... The structure was still strong for ages to come to bear witness to after people. Some fruit stones have done their work when the kernel is found and their broken pieces are thrown away; while others, as cocoa-nuts and gourd rinds, are saved to commence a new office. Here I left off dreaming about the failure of the original purpose, and I chanted out: 'The dead praise not thee, O Lord: neither all they that go down into silence. But we will praise the Lord: from this time forth for evermore. Praise the Lord.' And before the sound had settled I got up to go out again, when I was startled by an echo clear as a reply: 'The dead praise not thee, O Lord: neither all they that go down into silence. But we will praise the Lord: from this time forth for evermore. Praise the Lord.'

William Holman Hunt, *Pre-Raphaelitism and the Pre-Raphaelite Brotherhood*, 1905.

HOLMAN HUNT'S expedition took place only forty years after
Belzoni (whom we shall meet later at Thebes) had excavated
the second Pyramid, the Pyramid of Chephren, which stands
a short distance south of the Great Pyramid. Belzoni always
relished an impossible challenge, particularly when, as now,
it involved doing down one of his many detractors: in this
case, the French consul Bernardino Drovetti. (Belzoni
tended to carry several chips on his broad shoulders about
his lack of formal education: 'I do not mean to say, that a
man, who has had a classical education, should think himself
under a disadvantage in regard to knowing such things,
compared with him who has not; but, that a man, who thinks
himself well informed on a subject, often does not examine
it with such precision as another, who is less confident in
himself.')

A false start led to three weeks' wasted work seeking the
entrance. Undaunted, after studying the entrance to the
Great Pyramid, Belzoni resumed work about thirty feet to
the east.

[The Arabs] were pleased at my recommencing the task,
not in hopes of finding the entrance into the pyramid,
but for the continuation of the pay they of course were
to receive. As to expectation that the entrance might be
found, they had none; and I often heard them utter, in
a low voice, the word '*magnoon*', in plain English,
madman . . .

On the 2d of March, at noon, we came at last to
the right entrance into the pyramid. The Arabs, whose
expectation had also increased at the appearance of the
three stones, were delighted at having found something
new to show to the visitors, and get bakshis from them.
Having cleared the front of the three stones, the entrance
proved to be a passage four feet high, three feet six
inches wide, formed of large blocks of granite, which
descended towards the centre for a hundred and four

feet five inches at an angle of twenty-six degrees. Nearly all this passage was filled up with large stones, which had fallen from the upper part, and as the passage is inclined downwards, they slid on till some larger than the rest stopped the way.

I had much ado to have all the stones drawn out of the passage, which was filled up to the entrance of the chamber. It took the remainder of this day and part of the next to clear it, and at last we reached a portcullis. At first sight it appeared to be a fixed block of stone, which stared me in the face, and said *ne plus ultra*, putting an end to all my projects as I thought; for it made a close joint with the groove at each side, and on the top it seemed as firm as those which formed the passage itself. On a close inspection however I perceived, that, at the bottom, it was raised about eight inches from the lower part of the groove, which is cut beneath to receive it; and I found, by this circumstance, that the large block before me was no more than a portcullis of granite, one foot three inches thick.

Having observed a small aperture at the upper part of the portcullis, I thrust a long piece of barley straw into it, and it entered upwards of three feet, which convinced me, that there was a vacuum ready to receive the portcullis. The raising of it was a work of no small consideration. The passage is only four feet high, and three feet six inches wide. When two men are in it abreast of each other they cannot move, and it required several men to raise a piece of granite not less than six feet high, five feet wide, and one foot three inches thick. The levers could not be very long, otherwise there was not space in the four feet height to work with them; and if they were short, I could not employ men enough to raise the portcullis. The only method to be taken was, to raise it a little at a time; and by putting some stones in the grooves on each side, to support the portcullis while changing the fulcrum of the levers, it was raised high enough for a man to pass. An Arab then entered with a candle, and returned saying, that the place within was very fine. I continued to raise the portcullis, and at last made the entrance large enough to squeeze myself in; and after thirty days exertion I had the pleasure of finding myself in the way to the central chamber of one of the two great pyramids of Egypt, which have long been the admiration of beholders. The Chevalier Frediani followed me, and after passing under the portcullis we entered a passage not higher or wider than the first ... Where the granite work finishes at the end of this passage, there is a perpendicular shaft of fifteen feet ... [which we descended] by means of a rope. At the bottom of it I perceived another passage running downward at the same angle of 26° as that above, and toward the north. As my first object was the centre of the pyramid, I advanced that way, and ascended an inclined passage which brought me to an horizontal one, that led toward the centre, I observed, that after we entered within the portcullis, the passages were all cut out of the solid rock. The passage leading toward the centre is five feet eleven inches high, and three feet six inches wide ...

I reached the door at the centre of a large chamber. I walked slowly two or three paces, and then stood still to contemplate the place where I was. Whatever it might be, I certainly considered myself in the centre of that pyramid, which from time immemorial had been the subject of the obscure conjectures of many hundred travellers, both ancient and modern. My torch, formed of a few wax candles, gave but a faint light; I could, however, clearly distinguish the principal objects. I naturally turned my eyes to the west end of the chamber, looking for the sarcophagus, which I strongly expected to see in the same situation as that in the first pyramid; but I was disappointed when I saw nothing there. The chamber has a pointed or sloping ceiling; and many of the stones had been removed from their places, evidently by some one in search of treasure. On my advancing toward the west end, I was agreeably surprised to find, that there was a sarcophagus buried on a level with the floor.

By this time the Chevalier Frediani had entered also; and we took a general survey of the chamber, which I found to be forty-six feet three inches long, sixteen feet three inches wide, and twenty-three feet six inches high. It is cut out of the solid rock from the floor to the roof, which is composed of large blocks of calcareous stone, meeting in the centre, and forming a roof of the same slope as the pyramid itself. The sarcophagus is eight feet long, three feet six inches wide, and two feet three inches deep in the inside. It is surrounded by large blocks of granite, apparently to prevent its removal, which could not be effected without great labour. The lid had been removed at the side, so that the sarcophagus was half open. It is of the finest granite; but, like the other in the first pyramid, there is not one hieroglyphic on it.

Looking at the inside, I perceived a great quantity of earth and stones, but did not observe the bones among the rubbish till the next day, as my attention was principally bent in search of some inscription that would throw light on the subject of this pyramid. We examined every part of the walls, and observed many scrawls executed with charcoal, but in unknown characters, and nearly imperceptible. They rubbed off into dust at the slightest touch.

Giovanni Belzoni, *Narrative of the Operations and Recent Discoveries ... in Egypt*, 1822.

A SUCCESSION of Pyramid-excavators and measurers followed Belzoni, many intent on proving the mathematical or divine significance of the dimensions of the Great Pyramid. Among them was Charles Piazzi Smyth, who devoted much energy and many volumes to his researches. Here we glimpse him (in the least technical of his works) trying to take the measurements of the Grand Gallery with a 'grand slide-rod, expressly prepared for the purpose, and capable of measuring everything up to four hundred inches in height', with his two faithful Arab assistants.

It was rather a heavy affair ... consisting mainly of square mahogany tubes firmly fastened together, standing on a strong steel spike below, and having a pointed slider above, – which slider, by means of a string worked from below, could be pulled up to touch the roof, and clamped at that precise place the instant when certain spirit-levels told that the whole rod was being held for the moment truly vertical. To hold it so was a grand struggle for us all three, for the steep incline made it difficult for any one simply to stand still, without doing anything else; but Alee Dobree straddled manfully across the floor from ramp to ramp, and Abduwahad presented his right foot, between the big and second toes of which he held the steel peg, from slipping on the floor; and thus, by dint of keeping a good look-out that the great rod did not at any time oscillate from the vertical so far as to exceed our powers of holding it up, and tip us all over with it down the north descent, – and being favoured also by no loose pieces of ceiling-stone coming tumbling down when touched by the rod (as had occurred again and again the day before with the measurement of lower side 'overlappings' of the walls), we were enabled to obtain a series of readings on the side of the great rod for the heights required. This was accomplished, too, as we hoped, with fully sufficient accuracy to clear up many uncertainties in published accounts; while, so satisfactory a result would by no means have followed, had we endeavoured to make shift with any much smaller, or less troublesome, apparatus.

Charles Piazzi Smyth, *Life and Work at the Great Pyramid, 1865,* 1867.

PIAZZI SMYTH's grandiose claims for the divine inspiration of the Pyramids – he believed that the British were the lost ten tribes of Israel – met a mixed response. They did at least fire one tyro archaeologist, William Flinders Petrie, who spent the best part of a lifetime excavating throughout Egypt and Palestine. The purpose of his first trip to Egypt, in 1880, was to determine the accuracy of Smyth's measurements, for by now Smyth's ever wilder theories had turned Petrie's initial enthusiasm to scepticism. Two seasons' measuring, during which Petrie adopted the spartan methods of working from which he never deviated, proved conclusively that Smyth's calculations were inaccurate and discredited his theories. Here is Petrie's own inimitable picture of work in the Pyramid.

Aly Gabry was a valuable helper; he had been a basket-boy in Howard Vyse's excavations of 1837, and served Piazzi Smyth and Waynman Dixon. He was very intelligent, and knew everything about the pyramid hill, and what had been done there; with much good feeling and manner, he was an excellent companion in all my work. As he was regularly in my pay, I was free of the place, and no guides or clamours for *bakhshish* ever disturbed me. Usually, measurements inside the pyramid were begun after the tourists had left at sunset, and continued till midnight so as to be undisturbed.

It was often most convenient to strip entirely for work, owing to the heat and absence of any current of air, in the interior. For outside work in the hot weather, vest and pants were suitable, and if pink they kept the tourist at bay, as the creature seemed to him too queer for inspection. After rigging up the rock-tomb with shelves, and re-making the old shutters and door, which had been left by Dixon, I found the place comfortable. The petroleum stove by the door cooked my meals, which I prepared at any time required by the irregular hours of work.

William Flinders Petrie, *Seventy Years in Archaeology*, 1931.

The Pyramids

WE conclude with an evocative description of the Sphinx from the traveller Alexander Kinglake, whose forecast, written in the 1840s, of Britain's eventual assumption of power in Egypt proved remarkably perceptive – of the 'withering away' of Islam, less so.

And near the Pyramids, more wondrous and more awful than all else in the land of Egypt, there sits the lonely Sphynx. Comely the creature is, but the comeliness is not of this world; the once worshipped beast is a deformity and a monster to this generation, and yet you can see that those lips, so thick and heavy, were fashioned according to some ancient mould of beauty – some mould of beauty now forgotten – forgotten because that Greece drew forth Cytherea from the flashing foam of the Ægean, and in her image created new forms of beauty, and made it a law among men that the short and proudly wreathed lip should stand for the sign and the main condition of loveliness through all generations to come. Yet still there lives on the race of those who were beautiful in the fashion of the elder world, and Christian girls of Coptic blood will look on you with the sad, serious gaze, and kiss you your charitable hand with the big pouting lips of the very Sphynx.

Laugh and mock if you will at the worship of stone idols, but mark ye this, ye breakers of images, that in one regard the stone idol bears awful semblance of Deity – unchangefulness in the midst of change – the same seeming will, and intent for ever and ever inexorable! Upon ancient dynasties of Ethiopian and Egyptian kings – upon Greek and Roman, upon Arab and Ottoman conquerors – upon Napoleon dreaming of an Eastern Empire – upon battle and pestilence – upon the ceaseless misery of the Egyptian race – upon keen-eyed travellers (Herodotus yesterday, and Warburton today) – upon all and more this unworldly Sphynx has watched, and watched like a Providence with the same earnest eyes, and the same sad, tranquil mien. And we, we shall die, and Islam will wither away, and the Englishman straining far over to hold his loved India will plant a firm foot on the banks of the Nile and sit in the seats of the Faithful, and still that sleepless rock will lie watching and watching the works of the new busy race, with those same sad earnest eyes, and the same tranquil mien everlasting. You dare not mock at the Sphynx.

A.W. Kinglake, *Eothen*, 1844.

8

The Nile

The River is the highway of Egypt beyond Cairo, and along this highway the traveller can proceed either in a boat of his own, or in a steamer, or by railway. The advantages of a steamer are economy of time and money; the disadvantages are the noise, the necessity of doing everything at a fixed time, sightseeing in a crowd, and that, for those interested in the archaeological remains an utterly inadequate time is allowed for their inspection. The great advantage of hiring a dahabiya is that the traveller is absolutely his own master; but as he is dependent on the wind the voyage necessarily takes longer, and is therefore more expensive. Those who are pressed for time, or who wish to save expense, can take the train the whole way from Cairo to Aswan, or can break the journey at Asyut, Nagh Hamadi or Luxor, and take the steamer thence to Aswan.

Murray's *Handbook for Travellers in Egypt*, 1900.

As Murray suggests, a *dahabiya* was undoubtedly the ideal way of making the long Nile voyage south to Aswan (590 miles south of Cairo) and back. But it was neither cheap nor simple, and definitely only for the independent-minded. The key to the entire enterprise lay in the choice of dragoman: 'the success of the trip greatly depends upon [his] character and capability'. A trustworthy dragoman could be relied on to select a suitable vessel (hire charge up to £110 a month for a well-fitted boat for six to ten people) with (just as important for the success of the voyage) an experienced captain, engage reliable servants, put the boat in order, lay in stocks of food (though not 'wines, spirits, and mineral waters', which remained the traveller's personal responsibility), organize the hire of donkeys, and do all the innumerable other tasks necessary for the comfort of his party. For all these services, the dragoman would charge a fee of about £1000 for a ninety-day trip by eight to ten people. Murray's *Handbook* cautions that 'It is of course possible to go up the Nile by lesser rates ... but in doing so the traveller would have to be content with a less efficient dragoman and run the risk of bad cooking and indifferent service.'

By the start of the twentieth century, European demands for comfort and hygiene, and for reasonably smooth service, were beginning to be understood. Even half a century earlier, travellers were liable to suffer from all manner of unpleasant irritations, as the artist W.H. Bartlett found when he hired a *cangia*, a boat smaller and less well-fitted than a *dahabiya*.

I found much difficulty in suiting myself; most were too large and too expensive for a single traveller; in fact, the price of every thing in Egypt seems to have greatly risen of late years, the wages of servants and hire of boats in particular, till it is becoming a serious drawback in the way of travellers with moderate means; – a thing much to be regretted. It is undoubtedly a compensation that more comfort is now obtainable than formerly. I found, at length, a boat of the smaller class, newly painted, and apparently quite clean, which I hired at 900 piastres (£9) per month, inclusive of the wages of the Reis and six boatmen: such provisions as were needful were then laid in, a fresh supply of eggs, bread, meat, and vegetables being generally obtainable at the villages. In order to have a regular supply of milk, which proved a great luxury, we had a goat on board, and a filtering stone for the water, besides 'goollehs,' or vases of porous clay to cool the water. I shall not give a list of the various articles we took with us; suffice it to say, that they were pretty numerous, as they must be, if a reasonable measure of comfort is to be attained. The boat, when fitted up, was quite a snug little ark, a world in itself. I went on board, proud of my floating home. I was monarch of all I surveyed, and amused myself with arranging every thing' in the nicest order; and what with books, pistols, matting carpets, and green blinds, it looked so pretty and so cheerful, and when I lay down on my bed in the cabin, the breezes were so delightful and refreshing, that I heartily rejoiced I was out of the stifling heat of Cairo and fairly embarked on my cruise.

But, alas for all human anticipations! the morning opened most inauspiciously; the boat proves to be full of bugs, and I passed a restless, a savage night; in addition, Salem has a violent attack of ophthalmia, and has been rolling about the deck in agony: fortunately, we had with us sulphate of zinc and copper, and after obtaining from the city some rosewater, I mixed them, and applied as per prescription in Sir G. Wilkinson's Hand-book, and had the satisfaction of seeing Salem rapidly improve. The extermination of the bugs was matter of more difficulty; the scoundrel of a Reis had neglected to sink the boat as he had promised, and from every chink and crevice in the old planks hundreds came forth, scenting the blood of an Englishman; books, matting, and cloth-ing were all in a swarm with the disgusting vermin, from the swollen old patriarch to the youngest of his descendant fry. We threw the mats overboard to begin with, removed all the furniture, and by dint of sundry pails of water, furious scrubbing, ferreting out the nests with an iron pike, stuffing the chinks with camphor, and then subjecting every separate article to a rigid investigation, we routed the main body the first day, and by a watchful look-out till the second evening, and cutting off stragglers, had fairly gained the victory; the rest, if there were any retreating forward to their fitting quarters near the person of the Reis and his men, and coming no more about the quarter-deck.

W.H. Bartlett, *The Nile Boat*, 1850.

BARTLETT was lucky not to have to submerge the entire boat in order to get rid of the vermin. Negotiations completed, stores loaded and the voyage at long last under way, travellers soon settled into an undemanding routine. Amelia Edwards' Nile journey in 1873–4 inspired in her a life-long enthusiasm for the antiquities of Egypt. She recounts a characteristic day with her companions on board her *dahabiya*, the *Philae*.

Thus the morning passes. We sit on deck writing letters; reading; watching the sunny river-side pictures that glide by at a foot's pace and are so long in sight. Palm-groves, sand-banks, patches of fuzzy-headed dura [a kind of sorghum] and fields of some yellow-flowering herb, succeed each other. A boy plods along the bank, leading a camel. They go slowly; but they soon leave us behind. A native boat meets us, floating down side-wise with the current. A girl comes to the water's edge with a great empty jar on her head, and waits to fill it till the trackers have gone by. The pigeon-towers of a mud-village peep above a clump of lebbek trees, a quarter of a mile inland. Here a solitary brown man, with only a felt skull-cap on his head and a slip of scanty tunic fastened about his loins, works a shâdûf [a pole with bucket and counterpoise used for raising water], stooping and rising, stooping and rising, with the regularity of a pendulum. It is the same machine which we shall see by and by depicted in the tombs at Thebes; and the man is so evidently an ancient Egyptian, that we find ourselves wondering how he escaped being mummified four or five thousand years ago.

By and by, a little breeze springs up. The men drop the rope and jump on board – the big sail is set – the breeze freshens – and away we go again, as merrily as the day we left Cairo. Towards sunset we see a strange object, like a giant obelisk broken off half-way, standing up on the western bank against an orange-gold sky. This is the Pyramid of Meydûm, commonly called the False Pyramid. It looks quite near the bank; but this is an effect of powerful light and shadow, for it lies back at least four miles from the river. That night, having sailed on till past nine o'clock, we moor about a mile from Beni Suêf, and learn with some surprise that a man must be despatched to the governor of the town for guards. Not that anything ever happened to anybody at Beni Suêf, says Talhamy; but that the place is supposed not to have a first-rate reputation. If we have guards, we at all events make the governor responsible for our safety and the safety of our possessions. So the guards are sent for; and being posted on the bank, snore loudly all night long, just outside our windows.

Amelia Edwards, *A Thousand Miles Up the Nile*, 1877.

MANY people, like Amelia Edwards, felt drawn to the time-lessness of the scenery, the *fellahin* working the land as generations had before them, the unmusical (to European ears) but haunting chants of the boatmen, the slow rhythm of day upon day. Amelia Edwards describes the glories of the Nile sunsets:

Thus the day wanes, and the level cliffs keep with us all the way – now breaking into little lateral valleys and *culs-de-sac* in which nestle clusters of tiny huts and green patches of lupin; now plunging sheer down into the river; now receding inland and leaving space for a belt of cultivated soil and a fringe of feathery palms. By and by comes the sunset, when every cast shadow in the recesses of the cliffs turns to pure violet; and the face of the rock glows with a ruddier gold; and the palms on the western bank stand up in solid bronze against a crimson horizon. Then the sun dips, and instantly the whole range of cliffs turns to a dead, greenish grey, while the sky above and behind them is as suddenly suffused with pink. When this effect has lasted for something like eight minutes, a vast arch of deep blue shade, about as large in diameter as a rainbow, creeps slowly up the eastern horizon, and remains distinctly visible as long as the pink flush against which it is defined yet lingers in the sky. Finally the flush fades out; the blue becomes uniform; the stars begin to show; and only a broad glow in the west marks which way the sun went down. About a quarter of an hour later comes the after-glow, when for a few minutes the sky is filled with a soft, magical light, and the twilight gloom lies warm upon the land-scape. When this goes, it is night; but still one long beam of light streams up in the track of the sun, and remains visible for more than two hours after the darkness has closed in.

Such is the sunset we see this evening as we approach Minieh; and such is the sunset we are destined to see with scarcely a shade of difference at the same hour and under precisely the same conditions for many a month to come. It is very beautiful, very tranquil, full of won-derful light and most subtle gradations of tone, and attended by certain phenomena of which I shall have more to say presently; but it lacks the variety and gor-geousness of our northern skies. Nor, given the dry atmosphere of Egypt, can it be otherwise. Those who go up the Nile expecting, as I did, to see magnificent Turneresque pageants of purple, and flame-colour, and gold, will be disappointed as I was. For your Tur-neresque pageant cannot be achieved without such accessories of cloud and vapour as in Nubia are wholly unknown, and in Egypt are of the rarest occurrence. Once, and only once, in the course of an unusually protracted sojourn on the river, had we the good fortune to witness a grand display of the kind; and then we had been nearly three months in the dahabeeyah.

Meanwhile, however, we never weary of these stainless skies, but find in them, evening after evening, fresh depths of beauty and repose ...

That same evening, just as the twilight came on, we saw another wonder – the new moon on the first night of her first quarter; a perfect orb, dusky, distinct, and outlined all round with a thread of light no thicker than a hair. Nothing could be more brilliant than this tiny rim of flashing silver; while every detail of the softly-glowing globe within its compass was clearly visible. Tycho with its vast crater showed like a volcano on a raised map; and near the edge of the moon's surface, where the light and shadow met, keen sparkles of mountain-summits catching the light and relieved against the dusk, were to be seen by the naked eye. Two or three evenings later, however, when the silver ring was changed to a broad crescent, the unilluminated part was as it were extinguished, and could no longer be discerned even by help of a glass.

Amelia Edwards, *A Thousand Miles Up the Nile*, 1877.

OTHERS found the journey monotonous and the scenery disappointing. A disgruntled Count Gleichen, Lieutenant in the Grenadier Guards, who accompanied the Nile Expedition to relieve Khartoum in 1884, writes:

I had been led to expect beautiful scenery on the Nile, but anything more uninteresting I never saw. The river was much broader and infinitely dirtier than I could have thought; in fact, if you let the water in your bath lie for two minutes, there was a thick deposit of mud at once.

All along the banks were unending forests of dhurra corn, beans, cotton, and all sorts of native grain; no coffee, no sugar, and no tobacco, which sadly disappointed me, as I was looking forward to unlimited supplies of these articles for daily consumption. Mud – liquid, soft, and hard – and green crops, with distant views of very hot-looking blue and pink rocks were our daily landscape for eleven days, the monotony being occasionally varied by palms and mud villages. At night we anchored off either bank, as the captain refused to go on in the dark, for fear of mud-banks.

Our chief amusement was going on shore in the evenings, and buying chickens, eggs, vegetables, and milk. The average price was – melon, one piastre ($2\frac{1}{2}$d.); eggs, ten a piastre; turkey, half-a-crown; and goose, eighteenpence.

Before long we formulated these rules, and it was only by sticking rigidly to them that we managed to get things moderately cheap:

1. Always bring a koorbash or a stick with you.
2. Bargain in the dark, so as to pass off your bad piastres.
3. Always get the article desired into your possession before you attempt to haggle.
4. Offer never more than half what they ask, and go away if you do not get it at your price; they will then follow you and conform to your wishes.

Count A.E.W. Gleichen, *With the Camel Corps Up the Nile*, 1888.

EUGÈNE FROMENTIN, the French painter and writer known for his studies of Algeria, joined the Nile cruise laid on by the Khedive for the celebrities invited to the opening of the Suez Canal in 1869. Although he found the Nile scenery magnificent, the other guests proved an irritation, and he was constantly frustrated by the rushed pace of the voyage. The 'notes' he compiled contain some marvellous descriptive pieces, as this view of Girgeh.

Morning very cool, with light, sharp wind from the north; the Nile rippled by the breeze. Girgeh occupies a turn in the river. It faces the southeast, and clings, as it were, to the Arabian chain of hills, which plunges its high stone cliffs into the Nile, which is quite narrow at this point. There is a promenade around the city, by the exterior wall, almost deserted. Dogs wandering in the great vacant spaces, birds in crowds, hawks, rooks, white herons, winging their way towards the ponds. Huge white dovecotes with their perches loaded with pigeons of slaty lilac, with throats azure green. Clouds of them leave the perches, make one or two wild flights in the blue sky, and scatter in groups around the neighboring palm-trees. They are seen from afar like a swarm of flies. The hawks circle with low cries. The roads are free from dust; the ground, still moist with the dews of night, is browner. The water-wagtails move over it with their fine silver bodices, their skipping walk, and the little cry that I have so often listened to elsewhere.

Migratory birds have this charming quality; they transport with them the living memories of many different countries. I find them here where I did not think to find them; they bring with them our West, our autumns, our ploughed fields, the meadows under the white frost, all the October mornings; while over there are Girgeh, Thebes, Assouan, the whole course of the Nile. An expatriated fellah would say to them, 'Welcome.' A thousand leagues from my country, I say to them, 'Good day, ye are welcome.'

Quoted in M.L. Gonse, *Eugène Fromentin, Painter and Writer*, 1883.

THE rich travelled in luxury, shielded from all possible inconveniences. Here are, first, W.H. Seward, US Secretary of State under Presidents Lincoln and Johnson in the 1860s, on the Egyptian stage of a world tour in 1870–1, and then Roderick Cameron, whose party hired a vessel from Messrs Thomas Cook soon after the end of the Second World War.

Each passenger has a large state-room opening into a comfortable after-cabin. The forward-cabin was arranged as a dining-room, but Mr. Seward overrules the arrangement, and causes the table to be spread always under an awning on the after-deck, and he persists also in using the same airy apartment for his own sleeping-room. It is impossible for us to be on shore in the day time, on account of the insufferable heat. We make our calculations, therefore, to move up the river in the middle of the day, resting, sleeping, trying to keep cool, and writing our notes. We go ashore at as early an hour as possible before sunrise, and at as early an hour as possible after sunset. At every landing-place the authorities, having been apprised of our coming, are found awaiting us with the chairs, horses, camels, mules, and donkeys, needed. Whether we dine on board or in a ruined temple on the shore, the servants who attend us spread the table with the same abundant and delicate supplies as at Cairo. Our captain and crew belong to the naval service, and are skilful and polite. The captain never fails personally to provide our Mocha coffee, flavored with attar of roses, as in the Turkish harem. Chibouques [tobacco pipes], exquisitely wrought and loaded with gems, are served at every meal by a personage whose sole duty in this life is to keep them safe and sweet. Instead of iced water, we have water cooled in porous earthen jars, which are hung over the stern of the boat. The wine is cooled by laying the bottles well corked in the troughs of the boat, and pouring a stream of river-water over them. A small Abyssinian monkey affords us infinite amusement by stealing these bottles, extracting the corks, pouring the wine into the gutter, and drinking it thence until he attains the height of human intoxication. We attempted to correct this habit by chastising him, but he dropped from our hands into the river, and instantly disappeared. After searching river and bank three hours for him, we gave him up for lost, when, to our surprise, he appeared squatted on the seat of the life-boat which was swinging at the stern.

W.H. Seward's Travels Around the World, edited by Olive Risley Seward, 1873.

We have chartered a private dahabieh to take us up to Assuan and back, a wonderful three weeks' trip up the Nile; the *Memnon* it was called, a fair-sized paddle steamer that could boast twelve cabins, half as many baths, a drawing-room, a sun room, a dining-room, plenty of deck space and a whole retinue of servants. A chef we had, a Greek majordomo called Starbo, three waiters, cabin boys, and a man to do the laundry. The crew were without number, little brown men with black moustaches, in white pantaloons, tightly bound turbans and dark blue woollen sweaters. Across their chests were emblazoned the words: 'Cook's Nile Service' – wonderful propaganda, for at no moment of the day could we escape this red embroidery. Go and sit down in a chair and slap, slap, slap, along comes a barefooted sailor to arrange the cushions – 'Cook's Nile Service.' When landing, a gangplank is thrown across to the bank and six smiling moustached caryatids quickly offer up two long poles by which we steady ourselves – 'Cook's Nile Service.' 'Cook's Nile Service' follows us on all our expeditions, and at night when we take a walk along the banks they accompany us with lanterns and staves. There is something rather comforting about it, but then it must be remembered it is our own dahabieh and we are the only pebbles on the beach, for it is not the season.

The star turn, however, of the whole expedition is Bakry Ahmed-Abd-El Razzah, or just Bakry as we call him, our dragoman and nurse. He is large, indeed enormous, with great big hands and a broad wise face. His hair is grey I think, but we couldn't be sure for we never saw him without his tarboosh. He is calm and dignified and never gets excited. Nothing surprises him. His attitude towards us, I feel, is that of a father. We are his children whom he is about to educate. 'But Bakry, how are we going to get there?' or 'Bakry, how much do we pay them?' A dozen of such questions we fire at him. Up will come a big brown hand which he will spread slowly before him in the air: 'Do not worry, your Ladyship,' or 'You will see, sir, everything will be all right.' The implication is; 'Now, children, run along, can't you see I'm busy,' or 'Don't you trust father?' It simplifies our lives considerably – this paternal quality of Bakry's – and he straightens out all our problems, or rather we have none for they are eliminated long before they can reach us. And with what patience Bakry explains to us all the hieroglyphics. Thank heaven, though, he does not reel off set pieces at us as do most of the guides, things they have learnt parrot-like by heart. Bakry it would seem is also a great scholar. He is also very sensitive and easily hurt, which is rather endearing: he is a servant in fact of the old school: and he is continually at our beck and call, standing away discreetly in some secluded corner of the deck, a large dignified figure in a flowing white kuftân.

The reader might gather from this that we were lapped in the greatest of luxury, and he would be right; we were. The *Memnon* was like an Edwardian country house evoked from the past, transplanted by chance to the Nile, where it churned its way slowly up through the eddying brown water. There were pens with clean nibs and engraved paper and sealing-wax on all the writing-desks. The decks were spread with carpet and set with glass-topped tables and numerous wicker chairs made comfortable with mattresses and nests of cushions. The woodwork was white and the brass shone, including the bedsteads. The dressing-tables were laid out with lace mats and the beds spread with eiderdowns (though heaven knows it was far too hot for them). Carafes of water gleamed from brackets screwed into the walls – and such meals the chef produced! Menus boasting never less than eight courses. What surprised me even more is that we were able to do them justice. One might have thought our appetites would have been impaired by all the liquids we poured down our throats. But apparently not – drinking doesn't affect you in this dry heat. Lemonades, ginger ale and ginger beer, soda water and Coca-Colas; it was not often that we were to be seen without a glass in our hands, a glass and a woven raffia fan, for the heat was terrific. Continually the ice chest on the main deck had to be replenished. I can't imagine why the ice didn't melt, I suppose the zinc lining kept the heat out.

Roderick Cameron, *My Travel's History*, 1950.

ESPECIALLY before the introduction of steam power, when an unfavourable wind could delay a boat for days at a time, the slow pace of travel brought plenty of opportunities for the inquisitive to explore the Nile countryside. Edward Lear wrote to his sister Ann from the Nile in January 1854, when he was still trying to establish his reputation as a painter:

This morning I have had a delicious walk – through never ending corn fields; at times the ground was all blue & gray with CLOUDS of pigeons; & the most beautiful little plovers & kingfishers hop just before my feet. But what pleased me very much, was to find a real vulgar old English *toad*! waddling in the field! – as for croco-diles, none have been seen yet; of course you know, that *crocodiles* are not dangerous like *alligators*; the crocodile is very timid, & is only to be seen basking on sand islands at a distance. The broad-bean fields are a great pleasure to me now; they are all in full bloom; – the Arab name for beans is Fool, – & at first the sailors used to puzzle me very much when they pointed to the fields & said – 'fool! fool!'

I am sorry I shall not be able to buy anything today for you after all – for we shall only stop at Haou, even if we do there; but I shall not forget the present whenever it turns up. You have no idea what delicious summer weather it is always! so bright, & yet with such air! – I shall now leave off, to leave room for writing more, in case we should not arrive at Kenneh so soon as we expect. – (Did you go to see the panorama of Mexico in Leicester Square? do if you didn't) – Goodbye for the present. 10.AM – 17th. Jan. 1854.

Evening of Jan. 18th., – 15 miles from Kenneh. Desnée. Here we are you see, after all not so forward as we thought to be. We have had no wind today – or only against us, so that we have been pulled by the rope all day long: – for my part, I find this very pleasant work, as I live on shore, walking slowly & sitting on the bank waiting for the boat & there is always something to look at. Last night, we arrived at one of the most beautiful places I ever saw – Casr el Saadd. I am quite bewildered when I think how little people talk of the scenery of the Nile – because they pass it while sleeping I believe. Imagine immense cliffs, quite perpendicular about as high as St. Paul's & of yellow stone – rising from the most exquisite meadows all along the river! while below them are villages almost hidden in palms. In returning, I hope to pass a day or 2 at least at Kasr el Saadd – for it is one of the most beautiful spots in the world. Tomorrow, I trust to post this at Khenneh, though if the wind is not fair, I must wait another day.

Edward Lear, *Selected Letters*, 1988.

THOMAS SEDDON paints an amusing picture of Lear on his return to Cairo. The two had intended to travel together, but Seddon remained behind to wait for Holman Hunt, and so Lear made the Nile journey on his own.

Lear returned to-day from Upper Egypt. He gave up oil painting, and has brought back an enormous number of sketches, which are exceedingly interesting. He wears a straw hat, with a brim as large as a cart-wheel, with a white calico cover. He was called up the Nile, *Abou lel enema el abiad zeidy soufra*; which being interpreted means, the father of the white turban like a table.

J. P. Seddon, *Memoir and Letters of the Late Thomas Seddon*, 1858.

CANON HARDWICKE RAWNSLEY, the energetic Lake District vicar who was one of the founders of the National Trust, took a Nile voyage in 1890 to recuperate from a heart attack. Here we join him as he hires donkeys and rides across country to visit the archaeologist Flinders Petrie, who was excavating at the Meidum Pyramid, built by King Snofru, some thirty miles south of Saqqara.

It is not so easy a matter as at first might appear, this landing from a Nile boat on a Nile bank, for the Nile mud is as slippery as grease, and what looks solid is found to be soft, and *vice versâ*. But we did not mind getting in up to the knees for the sake of good King

Seneferu; and, struggling from the slime, we got on to the hot sand, and entering the dirty little village, asked for the railway station. We did not want a train, but we wanted donkeys, and we believed that the station-master, who in these out-of-the-way villages is the centre of light and learning, would be the provider of so much ass-flesh as would bear us to the pyramid. He could talk English a little, we spoke Arabic a little, and at once he despatched a bare-legged railway porter in blue blouse and red tarboosh to harry Rekkah for donkeys. 'One donkey he knew of; Allah might give two, but of this he was not sure.' Heaven smiled upon us, for a shout was heard half a mile away, and that shout echoed another half mile; there was a running together of camels and buffaloes and sheep in a very far-off field, and a little cloud of dust upon the railway-line embankment told us that our ass had been caught and was coming down the six-foot, at its own pace, to bear the 'Khawaja' to Mêdûm.

We saddled up, and the donkey's master tapping the patient creature on the nose, for bridles are an unknown quantity in the Mêdûm donkey-world, we went back up the highway – the railway-line, for a quarter of a mile. We then turned into the pleasant green fields of beans and clover, and while the larks sang, and the paddy-birds strutted, and the kites flew high, we passed towards the sunset and the mighty memorial tomb of Seneferu.

Away to our right, as we rode over the rich plain towards the barren desert mounds, was seen the little palm-girt village of Ghurzeh; on our left, to the south, like barren islands in a sea of greenery, appeared the villages of Soft, Kafr Soft, and Haram or Haram Soft; whilst between Kafr Soft and Haram Soft was visible the tiny village that was the centre of the great religious world of the fourth dynasty in this place – the Bull Town, 'Mi Tum' – Mêdûm of to-day.

It was good to hear how the old names had clung to these villages. No one would have thought, from looking upon that little village nearest the desert, by which our path presently took us, that there had once stood close

by a pyramid; but as late as thirty years ago, the remains
of a pyramid were visible there, and the present village
is built out of the mud bricks that the old pyramid-
builders made.

We wind in and out, now west, now south, for the
lands are divided out in squares, and we go along the
edges of the allotments. Whole families are squatting by
their yellow-faced, lop-eared sheep, or their long-eared
goats or grunting buffaloes. Here a tiny tot of a child
watches a tethered camel, there a little girl carefully
collects into a palm basket the manurial products of the
day of cattle-feeding, to take home with her flock in the
evening. A slinger crouches like a black ghoul – for he
has drawn the head-shawl over his head – upon his
rough clod hillock, and in the fields men are busy with
hoe or glebe-hatchet and creaky 'shadoofs.' The land of
Seneferu has no rest, and since the King of Truth and
Goodness entered his tomb until this day, men plough
and break the glebe and lift the shadoof bucket, and
sling the stone, and take at morn the cattle to the fields,
watch them through the day with greater care than they
give to their children, and bring them back at eventide.

Now, while the hoopoe calls 'hut-hut' from the
distance, and the black and white kingfisher – 'sick-
sak' – poises over the village pond, we pass the remains
of some old offering-stool or slab used in a temple, raised
by the fourth dynasty men, but now cast out by the
wayside. Round the muddy pond we go, wherein the
ducks dabble and the brickmaker dabbles too, treading
the slime into paste, filled full with the bits of chopped
straw that have sunk down from farmyard refuse of last
year. This is the village of the pyramid we spoke of,
and brickmakers, having exhausted the fourth-dynasty
supply, must tread their own mud into brickage, and
put it in their little square wood moulds and leave it to
the sun.

We have now reached the edge of the plain, yellow
here from the flower of the 'kabbach' or ketlock, and
here is a white-domed shêkh's tomb beside a fine old
'atli,' or juniper tree: beneath it rest the bones of Shêkh

Ali Nurr – peace to his ashes. On now over the waste
we go southward towards the shining terraced pyramid.

Hardwicke Rawnsley, *Notes for the Nile*, 1892.

OCCASIONALLY more adventurous, and sympathetic, visitors
set about immersing themselves in the ordinary, day-by-day
life of the country. The Egyptologist Margaret Murray spent
part of the summer of 1920 in the little Coptic town of
Naqada, a fishing and weaving settlement on the west bank
of the Nile a short way north of Dendera. As well as Egypt's
ancient history, she was interested in contemporary customs
and ceremonies.

There was another ceremony that I saw during that
summer visit to Egypt and that was the festival of High
Nile, which has been a national festival for thousands of
years. From the earliest times of which we have any
record, the day of High Nile was accounted as the beginning of a new year, and was kept with great rejoicings
and festivity as well as religious ceremonies. In the
towns, until recent years it was a noisy affair with fire-
works, firing of guns, and other deafening sounds. The
ruler (king or *khedive*) went in procession to 'cut the
Khalig', a ceremonial cutting of an ancient canal in order
to admit the water of the Nile into irrigation canals.
There are many accounts of this ceremony in medieval
and modern times.

But there was also in ancient Egypt a belief which
preceded the Kingdom of Osiris belief of the New
Kingdom. In the Middle Kingdom (circa B.C. 2500) the
belief in the life after death seems to have been that the
dead returned to their old homes in the day-time, and
especially on the days of the two great national festivals,
when they would 'smell the sweet breezes of the North

Wind, and drink water from the swirl of the New Water'.

The festival of High Nile is now called *Nau-ruz*, two Persian words meaning New Year, and what I saw was probably the primitive method of keeping it. Though the celebration did not begin till midnight, I am sure no one slept that night. The children were all awake, and from one o'clock onwards the air was full of childish voices and laughter. The grown-up voices were subdued, and there was that curious soft sibilant sound of many feet moving in the thick dust. The people were moving in family groups, all making for the four places on the river where the animals were watered and the water for household purposes was drawn; in other words, out of the swift current of the flooded river and shallow enough to be safe for little childish feet.

It was two o'clock in the morning when I too went down to the river. It was a clear starlight night without a breath of wind. Sirius, still the Herald of the Flood, was well up above the horizon, casting a brilliant pathway of light across the river. The shallows were full of mothers and children, but the voices were subdued for this was clearly a religious ceremony. The children had water poured over their heads, some of the women apparently dipped themselves into the water. The men tried to look as if they had nothing to do with the ceremony, but I noticed that they withdrew into quiet places and washed their hands and faces, doing it in silence and their expressions often showed that they had felt that strange hush which pervaded the whole scene. It was not only the stillness of the night, but the air seemed to be full of strong emotion, for all these people were praying silently for a blessing on their loved ones. I realised then why this holy night is known as *Nau-ruz Allah*, the New Year of God.

Margaret Murray, *My First Hundred Years*, 1963.

Freya Stark also captures the unchanging spirit of another Nile township far off the beaten tourist track.

Whether it be a human being or a town, it is pleasant to meet one that has no rivalry in its heart, but lives, enjoying its own relaxations, without the gnawing feeling that some admired neighbour would probably be doing it all differently. Such a little town is Minia, a prosperous agricultural centre, with a club set in a large garden among electric lights and casual flowers, and a long, wide, well-kept promenade with green clipped hedges, where one can walk on summer evenings and watch the rising or the falling of the Nile.

For some reason which I have now forgotten, the whole town was built on one impulse in 1902. There is an older and very dilapidated Minia adjoining, but the one that matters, with straight streets planned round a centre, with markets and all the oddments of civilized life, is the Minia of 1902 built apparently by Italian architects who brought a florid stucco washed with pale pastel colours, an ornamental style of an earlier generation from Europe. The Serafim house showed this exotic influence, with white marble heads decorating grey marble stairs, and ceilings painted with lace canopies and roses, of great solidity, charming to me because they reminded me of my childhood in old-fashioned North Italian villas.

All this lived comfortably, quietly and contentedly for itself alone. Luxor, with its winter fever and summer sleep, is far up the Nile, and the nearest antiquities to Minia are neglected pyramids scarcely ever visited, that squat among cotton fields on the right as one follows a straight dusty road south from Sakkara.

The mayor of Minia was a fresh-faced, alert, twinkling Muslim in a dazzling loose snowy gown which he rightly refused to exchange for hot and ugly Western clothes. He dined with us in the garden of the hospitable Coptic house, at a long table on a strip of gravel under sweet-scented jasmine; his friend, the chief lawyer of the town, was there also, a handsome, grey-haired, cultivated man; and a number of other leading people of the town. They were evidently in the habit of seeing each other every day, and formed a friendly little oligarchy without distinction of religion, consulting in amity over the municipal affairs on which their lives revolved. There was an Englishman, they told us, then living in the town; I never heard his name, but he appeared to be one of those unhappy British whose manners are a small international catastrophe, and we avoided him; a pleasant young couple opening a British Institute promised happier relations. More influential than any of these was the Egyptian governor from Cairo, who lived in a formal modern villa with a sentry at the gate, and gave us a kindly reception.

But the real life of the town was in the group gathered at table about us. They all had houses and lands in the immediate neighbourhood, low rambling houses whose gardens melt into the fields, so that one scarce can tell where the roses end and the crops begin. To these, their country residences, a mile or two out, they go in summer, returning to Minia for the winter season.

Every extension of road, irrigation, street lighting, every municipal amenity, affects them personally. I have seen the same in Prairie towns of the West where the citizens look with feelings of achievement on improvements as they come. And this indeed is the happiness of any

'Little town by river or sea shore'

from the beginning of time. In such a way the municipal authorities of Epidaurus no doubt rejoiced in their new amphitheatre, and the elders of Mycenae congratulated Agamemnon, or whoever it was who put those ornamental lions up above the gate. There is much to be said for the little town, and all around the Mediterranean shores it came to its perfection, with life very similar, whether in the square at Tarascon, or under Tuscan plane trees, or round the café kept by some Greek in

Egypt. You can see ruins in Algiers, in Cyprus, in Syria, of the same civilized provincial life – the pavement at Tipaza with the shops below, looking out over the sea; the long fashionable street at Jerash and colonnaded piazza where young men could turn their chariots and show their skill in driving; the columned ways of Salamis which were followed by the walls of Famagusta; the mounds of Apamea deep in asphodel.

Some are in ruins now, but most little towns continue through the centuries, and their charm is that nothing of universal importance ever happens to them; the cataclysms of history sweep over and leave them, with another name perhaps, but much the same at heart; if the storm is very severe, in a few hundred years the municipal affairs will be discussed in another language; and Mr. Serafim, whose roots are with the Pharaohs, talks over the new road with the representatives of his Muhammadan conquerors in the streets whose Italian architecture of forty years ago already looks mellow, ready to melt into that long vista of small municipal events and excitements which is the history of little towns like Minia.

Freya Stark, *East Is West*, 1945.

IN the nineteenth century at any rate, most private travellers could expect some fleeting contact with Egyptians, most often local officials. In 1868 the artist Frederick Leighton journeyed up the Nile on a steamer lent him by the Khedive. He displays the elegant fastidiousness to be expected of the most patrician of Victorian Presidents of the Royal Academy and the only English artist to be made a peer.

In the evening made another sketch, and then rode to Keneh to dine with the Consul – a most interesting glimpse into a real old-fashioned Muslim interior. Si Syed Achmet (forty-five years British Agent in this town and at Khossayr) is a very wealthy old gentleman with large property in this part of the world. He is of the blood of the Prophet, a good and pious Muslim, tolerant and full of kindliness. A son, three nephews and a daughter form his immediate family circle, living with him in the house to which I was bidden – a bald, uninteresting place enough. It is entered from a narrow, irregular triangular court, ornamented on one side with some good brick and wood work, but ugly and plain on the others, and disfigured by something between a ladder and a staircase which leads to the clean but singularly naked room in which we were to spend the evening. This room was whitewashed, but so roughly bedaubed that the plain deal cupboards, the doors of which formed the only embellishment (?) of the walls, were all besmeared with ragged edges of white. Three windows, innocent of glass, and protected by a close, plain trellis-work of ordinary white wood, lighted the room, which boasted in the way of furniture the usual ugly divans, three red muslin curtains, a small deal table, two lanterns and two candles in candlesticks. Shortly after my arrival and most kindly reception by the old gentleman, who had come up from the country expressly *ad hoc*, dinner was served. The son, as the eldest, sat at table; the nephews waited on us; we squatted, I on a cushion, they on the floor, round a very low table on which was a large, round, brass tray, containing four plates, some wooden spoons, and a great many small loaves of bread arranged round it in a circle; a soup tureen, into which, after washing of hands, everybody plunged his spoon, was the central feature. After the soup, came in rapid succession several dishes containing savoury messes which were really very good, though perhaps too rich, but which I was entirely unable to enjoy in the sight of a number of hands, shining with gravy, mopping in succession at the dishes with crusts of bread, or fetching out a coveted morsel with fingers too recently licked. It is a delicate and hospitable attention to put a bit with your own hand on to your guest's plate – an attention of which I was the frequent but unworthy recipient. After the made dishes had been done justice to, half a sheep – head and all – was put on the table and *clawed* asunder by Hosseyn. The roast being disposed of, the sweets appeared, and were eaten out of the common dish with spoons, like the soup: I was not sorry when it was over, for I had gone through all the sensations of a sea voyage. I observe that Arabs make a point of eating with as much noise and smacking of lips as possible; it is as if they were endeavouring to convey a sort of oblique expression of thanks to Providence by manifesting their relish of the blessings vouchsafed. When dinner was over, and a by no means superfluous washing of hands had been gone through, we had pipes and coffee.

Diary extract quoted in Mrs Russell Barrington, *The Life,
Letters and Work of Frederick Leighton,* 1906.

By the turn of the twentieth century, the age of individual travel on the Nile was coming to an end. Its passing was mourned by the Reverend A.H. Sayce, formerly Professor of Assyriology at Oxford, who had wintered in Egypt on his private *dahabiya* for a quarter of a century.

The winter of 1907–1908 was my last winter in my floating home. Life on the Nile had ceased to be the ideal existence it once was. Modern conditions had made the sailing dahabia an impossibility. For some years I had been obliged to use a steam-launch, and therewith most of the charm of life on the Nile had disappeared. Instead of sailing beside the banks and watching the ever-changing scenes on the shore it was now necessary to remain always in the middle of the stream and to substitute the smoke of the steamer for the sights and scents of the fields. The excitement of watching the winds and the evolutions of the sailors was gone; even the great sail was folded up. The race of dahabia sailors was becoming extinct; they found it more profitable to serve on board the steamers, where wages were higher and work less. Moreover, the quietude of Upper Egypt was also gone. The population had multiplied and the waste-places of the desert were waste-places no more. The railway was now running to Assuan, the river was full of steam-craft, and it was difficult to escape from the postman or telegraph boy. Prices had risen accordingly: where I had bought twenty fresh eggs for a piastre ($2\frac{1}{2}$d.) or a turkey for fourteen piastres, I now had to give ten or fifteen piastres for the one and sixty or eighty piastres for the other. In my earlier voyages the sheep with which I presented my men at Girga cost a dollar or four shillings, in 1907 I had to pay 137 piastres for an inferior animal.

It had, too, become increasingly difficult to obtain satisfactory captains. It was the same with the crew; had it not been that some of my old men still survived it would have been difficult to work the boat.

Reverend A.H. Sayce, *Reminiscences*, 1923.

THOMAS COOK started operating Nile voyages in 1869, and the company soon achieved a virtual monopoly. Its luxury steamships catered for a very different class of traveller: those without the time or the inclination, or both, to travel independently. Douglas Sladen captures the spirit of the voyage:

I have never enjoyed anything more than my voyages up the Nile in Cook's Tourist steamers. They are luxurious without being too elaborate; their food compares with that of any hotel in Egypt; their servants are the best I have ever come across. Most of them have excellent dragomans, and their programme is skilfully adapted to satisfy both the wise and the foolish. The steamers between Cairo and Assuan accommodate about eighty people. Their cabins are large, with beds so high above the floor that an American saratoga will go underneath them; their washing arrangements and baths are particularly good, a great consideration in a hot climate like Egypt. The only fault I have to find with the cabins is that the electric light goes out at eleven, for on the Nile, more than anywhere else, you want to do a good deal of reading at night. All the best books on Egypt are in the ship library. If you read three or four hours every night you would not exhaust all that good writers have written upon the places you see on the voyage, and you can only read at night, because by day you are passing something of interest every few minutes, whether it be a city, or a Nile village, or an exquisite palm grove, or picturesque incidents of native life, or the birds which turn the large shoals into a kind of zoological gardens, and seem to know quite well that no firing is permitted from Cook's steamers.

Every steamer has a cosy little reading-room fitted with writing-tables, and supplied with the latest newspapers, as well as with a library of books on Egypt. The papers, like the letters, are brought on board every day, and there is a pillar-box on board, cleared every night, for those who wish to post letters. You simply arrange to have your letters sent to Cook's Cairo office; their post clerk knows where their steamers will be each day and forwards the letters by train. The second dragoman is postman. You find your letters beside your plate at breakfast, just as you would at home.

Breakfast is a country-house meal. It starts with porridge and its patent substitutes, and proceeds with bacon and eggs and fish and other hot dishes, and ham and tongue and chicken, and other cold fare, to jam and marmalade. And the bread and the butter are excellent. It needs to be a hearty meal, for one cannot help getting

up early when there is an Egyptian sunrise mingling
earth and heaven, and the waking life of the villages to
watch. I used to have a cup of tea brought to me at
sunrise, and then lie in my bunk, looking out of the big
window at the early morning Nile effects, until it was
time for my bath, unless we were passing through something so exciting that I felt constrained to put on a big
overcoat over my pyjamas and go and sit in the sun
gallery, glazed all round, which occupies the fore part
of the promenade deck. But this saddened the white-
robed Arab servants, who hated a passenger's seeing the
deck before they had swept off every particle of dust
with their ostrich-feather brooms, and made the brass
shine like gold. The ostrich-feather broom plays a great
part in the economy of Cook's Nile boats. The decks are
dusted with it, and your boots and legs are dusted with
it whenever you go on shore 'to shake the dust from off
your feet.'

My first bath was rather a shock to me, for the bath
and the bath-room are so very white and the Nile water
in the bath looks like a cup of chocolate. But it does not
make you muddy; it has the same cleansing properties
as other waters . . .

There is in the centre of the promenade deck of Cook's
Tourist steamers a broad lounge, which goes right across
it, awninged above from the sun by day, and awninged
all round at night till it looks like a marquee put up for
a ball. As it is full of easy chairs and tea-tables and wind-
screens, the idle and the unintelligent lounge about it all
day long when they are not making excursions (which
they like for the donkey rides), reading novels, or dozing,
or playing bridge. Their day begins with afternoon tea,
at which you have half Huntley and Palmer's pro-
ductions instead of bread and butter. Special friends
make up tea-parties, and the beautiful Arab servants,
in white robes, and bright red tarbooshes, sashes and
slippers, glide about, filling up the tea-cups as fast as
they are emptied and bringing fresh varieties of Huntley
and Palmer to compel people to over-eat themselves.
This goes playfully on till somebody discovers that

sunset is beginning. Then even the least intelligent
people on the ship hurry to the side, not for the usual
reason, and bring up ejaculations for a solid hour while
the Egyptian sky proceeds with its marvellous trans-
formation-scenes ...

In the height of the season, when the tourist steamers
are full, on the days when there are no excursions, the
particular young man sometimes breaks out into silk
suits and wonderful socks, or, at any rate, rare and
irreproachable flannels, just as the girl who has come
to conquer Cairo society rings the gamut of summer
extravagances. They have the moral courage for at least
two different costumes between breakfast and dinner;
and though a mere man is limited to his theatre jacket
for dinner, the irresponsible girl can dress as elaborately
as she pleases for the evening, and the climate tempts
her ...

By dinner-time most people are tired – tired of doing
nothing if there has been no excursion; tired of long
rides over the hot Desert, and hard sight-seeing, if there
has been an excursion. They sit down with great content
to a good dinner, and when it is over move out to the
marquee which has been improvised out of the lounge
for their coffee and cigarettes and a little light chatter;
and, if they are wise, read their guide-books. On our
steamer nobody played bridge except the two clergymen
and their wives. Most people had no time for the Devil's
picture-books; they were reading their guide-books; you
are lost in Egypt if you do not read up. I used to disappear directly after dinner and read in my bunk, where
the light was good and the quiet perfect ...

We were lucky enough, for we had chosen our ship
haphazard, to have Mohammed, the *doyen* of Cook's,
for our chief dragoman. He is a dragoman of the old
school, who knows his subject well, but is even more
endeared to the tourist by the picturesqueness of himself
and the thirty changes of raiment which he takes on
board the ship with him, and his fine manners of the
old-fashioned East. He maintains the ideals and the
atmosphere of the dragoman of the good old days when

nobody but Crœsus (for the most part a coronetted Crœsus) went to Egypt. He has a fund of good stories, which he tells with unconsciously theatrical attitudes and gestures, for the tourist; a great deal of authority for the native of the donkey-boy, guide, and curio-selling professions; wonderful tact and patience with the exacting and inquisitive or stupid people whom he has to show over ruins in which they are interested in inadequate and widely different ways; and unfailing wit and cheerfulness. Added to which, he is wholly free from the presumption which so often disfigures the attitude of dragomans to ladies.

Every night at dinner-time he used to come in and clap his hands for attention, and announce the programme for the following day, in a witty little speech, which described the nature of the monuments to be visited, and the means to be employed in getting to them – donkeys, boats, or walking – with a little useful advice as to conditions atmospheric or otherwise, and the unfailing reminder that 'monument-tickets would be very much wanted.'

Douglas Sladen, *Egypt and the English*, 1908.

MUCH the same experience, reported in a somewhat more jaundiced tone, awaited Rudyard Kipling on a Nile trip a few years later.

For three weeks we sat on copiously chaired and carpeted decks, carefully isolated from everything that had anything to do with Egypt, under chaperonage of a properly orientalised dragoman. Twice or thrice daily, our steamer drew up at a mud-bank covered with donkeys. Saddles were hauled out of a hatch in our bows; the donkeys were dressed, dealt round like cards: we rode off through crops or desert, as the case might be, were introduced in ringing tones to a temple, and were then duly returned to our bridge and our Baedekers. For sheer comfort, not to say padded sloth, the life was unequalled, and since the bulk of our passengers were citizens of the United States – Egypt in winter ought to be admitted into the Union as a temporary territory – there was no lack of interest. They were overwhelmingly women, with here and there a placid nose-led husband or father, visibly suffering from congestion of information about his native city. I had the joy of seeing two such men meet. They turned their backs resolutely on the River, bit and lit cigars, and for one hour and a quarter ceased not to emit statistics of the industries, commerce, manufacture, transport, and journalism of their towns – Los Angeles, let us say, and Rochester, N.Y. It sounded like a duel between two cash-registers.

Rudyard Kipling, 'Egypt of the Magicians', 1913.

THE age of mass tourism had truly begun.

9

At Thebes

As for Dendera and Thebes, and the remains in every
part of upper Egypt, it is useless to attempt to write
... Conceive a feverish and tumultuous dream full of
triumphal gates, processions of paintings, interminable
walls of heroic sculptures, granite colossi of Gods and
Kings, prodigious obelisks, avenues of Sphynxs and
halls of a thousand columns, thirty feet in girth and of
a proportionate height. My eyes and mind yet ache with
grandeur so little in unison with our own littleness ...

Benjamin Disraeli, *Letters*, vol. 1, 1982.

ANCIENT Thebes (the name is Greek) stretches across a large
area of each bank of the Nile. On the east bank stand the
temples of Karnak and Luxor, joined by a processional way;
on the other side, the great mortuary temples (Medinet
Habu, the Ramesseum, the Temple of Hatshepsut) and,
hidden in the hills on the western edge, the Valley of the
Kings with its tombs of the pharaohs. Like so many visitors,
Disraeli (who came to Thebes in early 1831) found himself
awed by this, the greatest concentration of ancient sites
in all Egypt. The Prussian archaeologist Richard Lepsius,
who led a three-year expedition to investigate Egypt's
ancient sites during the 1840s, describes the view from his
encampment:

At Thebes

An easy broad way leads windingly from the plain to a spacious court, the left side of which towards the mountain is formed by a long shadowy pillared row; behind this are several inhabitable rooms. At the extremity of the court there is still a single watch-tower, whence the Prussian flag is streaming, and close by it a little house of two stories, the lower of which I myself inhabit. Space, too, is there for the kitchen, the servants, and the donkeys.

Incomparably beautiful and attractive is the boundless prospect over the Thebaic plain from the wall of the court, low towards the inside and deep on the outside. Here all that remains of ancient Thebes may be seen, or still better from the battlements of the tower or from the hills immediately behind our house. Before us the magnificent ruins of the Memnonia, from the hill of Qurna on the left, to the high pylones towering over the black ruins of Medînet Habu to the right, then the green region surrounded by the broad Nile, whence on the right the lonely colossi of Amenophis rise; and on the other side of the river the temple groups of Karnak and Luqsor, behind the plain, stretches for several hours to the sharp little undulating outline of the Arabian mountains, over which we see the first rays of the sun gleaming, and pouring a wonderful flood of colours over the valley and rocky desert. I cannot compare this ever-existing prospect with any other in the world; but it reminds me forcibly of the picture, which I had for two years, from the top of the Tarpeian rock, and which comprehended the whole extent of ancient Rome, from the Aventine and the Tiber beneath it to the Quirinal, and thence over the hill to the undulating Campagna, with the beautiful profile, so strikingly like the one here, of the Alvan mount in the back ground.

K.R. Lepsius, *Letters from Egypt*, 1853.

At Thebes

SOME sixty years later, in December 1905, the American archaeologist James Henry Breasted, newly appointed to the first American Chair of Egyptology (at Chicago University), returned to Thebes after eleven years away. His son Charles, then eleven years old, recalls their arrival.

The December evening of our departure was not one of the three each week when the Luxor train carried sleeping cars, for we could not afford such luxury. In a downpour of rain – which loyal Cairo residents, like Southern Californians, always assure visitors is most unusual – we climbed sopping wet into a second-class compartment, and in company with three poker-faced Levantine gentlemen, sat up all night.

The winter rains of the Delta seldom extend far south of Cairo, and dust soon enveloped us in a choking shroud. The clatter of the train and the snoring of our companions induced a blessed semi-stupor finally broken only by the explosive opening of the door into the passage, and a guttural voice shouting, 'Dee nex' stashone LUUK-SORE!'

We pushed up slatted shutters, through darkened glass saw groves of leaning palms beyond irrigation-chequered green fields, smoke hanging low over adobe villages, flashes of the river touched here and there by a morning breeze like warm breath on gun-metal – the ruins of Karnak casting long shadows – dikes, houses – and the train drew into the station. Begrimed as so many newly exhumed, slightly animate antiques, we emerged stiff and bleary-eyed into the glorious morning brilliance of Luxor.

To my father, Thebes was one of the most inspiring sites of the ancient world. On his first visit it had surpassed his most colourful preconceptions, had remained ever since one of the favourite haunts of his daydreams. Now that he was within an hour's donkey ride of it, he could hardly wait.

He hurried us to a shabby hotel facing the Nile, then

he lure for so many travellers to the 'antique land' of Egypt – the monuments
its pharaohs and gods. Francis Frith's photograph of Abu Simbel in Nubia,
taken in 1857 (Topham Picture Source).

Paintings by artists whose writings are included in this book: *above, A Street Scene* by Frederick Goodall, see p. 19 (courtesy Mathaf Gallery, 24 Motcomb St, London SW1); *below, The Temple of Denderah* by William James Müller, see p. 48 (V & A); *right, The Mosque of Ibn Koun* by W. H. Bartlett, see p. 117 (V & A).

Opposite: Life in the Harem: one of
J. F. Lewis's Europeanized yet
seductive watercolour scenes
painted in 1858 (V & A).

The people of Egypt: *left, Cairene
Musicians* by Carl Haag, who
accompanied F. Goodall in Egypt
in 1858; *below, Fellaheen Drawing
Water, Medinet-el-Fayoum* by Jean
Leon Gerome (both courtesy
Mathaf Gallery, 24 Motcomb St,
London SW1).

Two views of the Nile: *above*, in Cairo by day by Emile Charles Wauters; *below*, a ravishing evening scene by Wilhelm Gentz (both courtesy Mathaf Gallery, 24 Motcomb St, London sw1).

Opposite: one of David Roberts' most striking lithographs, of *The Excavated Temple of Gyrshe* (courtesy Mathaf Gallery, 24 Motcomb St, London sw1).

Giovanni Belzoni (1778–1823) who penetrated the Second Pyramid, discovered several tombs in the Valley of the Kings, and uncovered the Temple of Ramasses II at Abu Simbel.

Belzoni's own drawing of the removal of the 'Young Memnon', see p. 152.

see p. 152.

Opposite: The Court of Shishak, Karnac, photographed by Francis Frith in 1857 (Topham Picture Source).

Opposite: Sir Flinders Petrie by
G. F. Watts, 1900. 'Nothing can
turn genius from his way, neither
the attractions of mammon nor the
lure of the limelight . . .' See p. 17
(National Portrait Gallery).

Left: a typical dragoman or
Egyptian guide '. . . knows his
subject well, but is even more
endeared to the tourist by the
picturesqueness of himself . . .' See
p. 143 (*Cairo*, Stanley Lane-Poole)

Below: Canon Rawnsley and party
on tour in Egypt towards the end of
the last century, see pp. 8 and 130

The statues of Memnon on the Plain of Thebes photographed by Francis Frith in 1857 (Topham Picture Source).

aboard a creaking ferry, already laden with jabbering natives, donkeys, crates of distraught chickens, some naked little girls herding four sheep and a family of geese. Sitting astern reading Baedekers as calmly as if in a peaceful French cathedral, were two green-veiled, seamy-faced English ladies convoyed by a possessive dragoman.

As our Noah's ark neared the west bank, a boarding-party of piratical donkey-boys, alternately reviling and pummelling one another, and shouting at the tops of their leather lungs the names and virtues of their respective mounts, waded out to capture our patronage by the immemorial oriental method of attrition. The moment the ferry touched the shore, their onslaught took on a lunatic fury. Even the English ladies, placing markers at 'Section B, The West Bank at Thebes,' looked up with impassive interest. Suddenly, in a cloudburst of sonorous Arabic, my father stunned the milling assemblage: 'May ten thousand wild asses,' he shouted, 'bray for ten thousand years over the graves of your ancestors.' In the silence following this dreadful curse, we chose our donkeys and trotted off across the Theban plain.

A sea of green stretched away towards a mountain of golden-brown limestone rising mesa-like above the jumble of temples and tombs at its base – the city of the dead of ancient Thebes. In his eagerness my father gradually drew far ahead, but when after some time he reached two gigantic seated figures of stone, the Colossi of Memnon now standing alone among the fields, he dismounted and waited in order to show me the one which each morning, as the first level rays of the sun touched its weather-worn, battered surface, gave out a strange melodic sound. He recalled how he and my mother had heard it on a morning eleven years before; and then with his arm resting on my shoulders, stood silent for some moments, as if hearing it again across the years of his struggle to re-achieve Egypt.

He was thinking less of the past, however, than dreaming of the future. With his first expedition hardly yet in motion, he was already planning another similar but more ambitious undertaking. As we wandered through the neighbouring ruins – the huge temple of Medinet Habu, and the Ramesseum – he was so preoccupied with making copious entries in a notebook, he quite forgot his family ...

With boyish eagerness he led us in and out of countless tombs belonging to nobles and grand-viziers, through chapels and temples on whose walls he showed me endless portraits and scenes of kings and queens with long-familiar names. He knew the exact location of every inscription, every figure, took delight in pointing out his favourites – a succession of Amenhoteps and Thutmoses; Ikhnaton – a dreamer, he said, born over a thousand years before his time, who was the first man to believe in one supreme God; a beautiful, brilliant, incredibly energetic lady named Hatshepsut, with an uncommon flare for architecture and intrigue, who confused me somewhat because apparently she should have been born a man, was for some time married to a king who was also her half-brother, and finally became a *king* in her own right! He was inclined to resent a pair of boastful kings named Ramses One and Two who seemed to be everywhere, with a penchant for vast statues of themselves. Before one of these, hewn of granite brought from Aswan, which stood in a forecourt of the Ramesseum and now lay among the ruins in enormous tumbled fragments, my father recited for me – while we ate a lunch of dried dates and native bread – Shelley's *Ode to Ozymandias.*

By the time he had led me through Queen Hatshepsut's lovely temple of Deir el-Bahri, set in a vast bay of cliffs, where he showed me the famous wall reliefs depicting treasure brought back to her by a fleet of ships she had once dispatched through the Red Sea to the Land of Punt, far south towards Ethiopia, the shadows had begun to lengthen again across this strange ruined city of the ancient dead. My mother and I both begged for mercy: our legs and eyes ached, and what with sitting up all night in an Egyptian train, we had had our fill for one day of hieroglyphs and royal profiles and the acrid stench of bat-filled tombs. With a laugh he said that our patience would now be rewarded – and asked us to follow him on foot up the steep trail leading over the mountain to the Valley of the Kings' Tombs!

Only the magic of that name could have sent me scampering after him – up and up, until the temples below grew as small as the models I had seen in museums, and the whole valley of the Nile from horizon to horizon lay spread below us. Even my mother forgot her weariness at seeing it again. He pointed out to me the ruins of Karnak far across the river, and from a still higher rock, showed me the gap in the mountains of the eastern desert through which passed the ancient caravan route between Thebes and the Red Sea. On very clear days, he said, one could sometimes see faint wisps of smoke rising from invisible ships.

We turned now and followed the crest until we looked down into a barren valley already steeped in twilight by the great cliffs which closed its western end. Jackal trails rose from it here and there, and disappeared over the high rim of the desert plateau above. Even to a small boy who had as yet witnessed death only in the shape of unwrapped, withered mummies irreverently displayed in museums, this silent, lonely place seemed a fit habitation for departed kings.

He had told me again and again of the forty and more great slanting shafts cut hundreds of feet into the solid rock at the bottom of this valley. They ended sometimes in a room, sometimes in a vertical well, in which had been placed the sarcophagus and mummy, and the richest personal belongings of a king. Each king had tried to insure his eternal rest in the hereafter by having his tomb made with the utmost secrecy and designed with false passages, impenetrable bulkheads of granite, deep, wide pits to serve as impassable moats, and other ingenious devices to thwart rapacious posterity or even contemporaries. A few tombs, including that of a young king named Tukenkhamon, had never been found by modern excavators. But the known ones had all been robbed in antiquity, he said, by the remote ancestors of

the modern natives whose little adobe villages we had
seen clinging like birds' nests among the ancient wreck-
age along the foothills of the mountain.

   Though I found all this *mechanically* fascinating, I
could never understand what he meant by 'hereafter';
nor why kings, especially, should have taken such
tremendous trouble about their tombs. But as often as
I asked him, he merely smiled and pinched my cheek,
and said that one day I would discover the answers for
myself . . .

Charles Breasted, *Pioneer to the Past*, 1943.

GIOVANNI BELZONI had come to Egypt in 1815 in order to
promote a scheme for an ox-driven water-pump which
would, he argued, revolutionize the agriculture of the Nile
valley. The Khedive, Mohammed Ali, turned down the plan,
offering Belzoni a small government allowance in compensation. At something of a loose end, Belzoni embarked
on a Nile voyage with a commission from the British consul,
Henry Salt, to remove the mammoth bust known as the
'Young Memnon' from the Ramesseum at Thebes and send
it to Cairo for shipping to England. It was a colossal task
that matched the determination even of this former music-
hall strongman. Belzoni was working in the worst of the
midsummer heat, there was considerable local resistance,
and the annual Nile flood, which would halt any attempt to
move the bust that season, was soon due. Belzoni's memoirs
take up the story when he has been requesting, in vain,
manpower to help him.

   To the Cacheff I now applied again, and at last on the
27th, he sent me a few men, but by no means sufficient
for my purpose; yet, when others saw them at work, by

permission they were easily persuaded to join the party. I arranged my men in a row, and agreed to give them thirty paras a day, which is equal to four-pence half-penny English money, with which they were much pleased, as it was more by one half than they were accustomed to receive for their daily labour in the fields. The carpenter had made the car, and the first operation was to endeavour to place the bust on it. The Fellahs of Gournou, who were familiar with Caphany, as they named the colossus, were persuaded, that it could never be moved from the spot where it lay; and when they saw it moved, they all set up a shout. Though it was the effect of their own efforts, it was the devil, they said, that did it; and as they saw me taking notes, they concluded that it was done by means of a charm. The mode I adopted to place it on the car was very simple, for work of no other description could be executed by these people, as their utmost sagacity reaches only to pulling a rope, or sitting on the extremity of a lever as a counterpoise. By means of four levers I raised the bust, so as to leave a vacancy under it, to introduce the car; and, after it was slowly lodged on this, I had the car raised in the front, with the bust on it, so as to get one of the rollers underneath. I then had the same operation performed at the back, and the colossus was ready to be pulled up. I caused it to be well secured on the car, and the ropes so placed that the power might be divided. I stationed men with levers at each side of the car, to assist occasionally, if the colossus should be inclined to turn to either side. In this manner I kept it safe from falling. Lastly, I placed men in the front, distributing them equally at the four ropes, while others were ready to change the rollers alternately. Thus I succeeded in getting it removed the distance of several yards from its original place.

According to my instructions, I sent an Arab to Cairo with the intelligence, that the bust had begun its journey towards England. From the great heat of the day I was unwell at night, having never felt the sun so powerful before in my life. Being in the hottest season, the air was inflamed; and even at night the wind itself was extremely hot. The place I had chosen in the Memnonium was worse than any, as the whole mass of stones was so heated, that the hands could not be kept on it. In the course of time these places became familiar to me, as well as the climate; for I observed, three years after, that I was often on the same spot, and at the same season, without feeling the least inconvenience, or being sensible of the intense heat I had felt on my first arrival. When the Arabs found that they received money for the removal of a stone, they entertained the opinion, that it was filled with gold in the inside, and that a thing of such value should not be permitted to be taken away.

On the 28th we recommenced the work. The Arabs came pretty early, as they preferred to work in the morning, and rest in the middle of the day from twelve to two. This day we removed the bust out of the ruins of the Memnonium. To make room for it to pass, we had to break the bases of two columns. It was advanced about fifty yards out of the temple. In the evening I was very poorly: I went to rest, but my stomach refused any aliment. I began to be persuaded, that there is a great difference between travelling in a boat, with all that is wanted in it, and at leisure, and the undertaking of an operation, which required great exertions in directing a body of men, who in point of skill are no better than beasts, and to be exposed to the burning sun of that country from morning till night.

On the next day, the 29th, I found it impossible to stand on my legs, and postponed the work to the day following. I had all our household-furniture, beds, kitchen-pottery, and provisions, put on a camel, and returned to the boat, in hopes that the air might be cool at night; but I remained very ill the whole day, my stomach refusing to take almost any thing.

On the 30th we continued the work, and the colossus advanced a hundred and fifty yards towards the Nile. I was a little better in the morning, but worse again in the evening.

On the 31st I was again a little better, but could not

proceed, as the road became so sandy that the colossus sunk into the ground. I was therefore under the necessity of taking a long turn of above three hundred yards, to a new road. In the evening of this day I was much better.

On the 1st of August we still improved in our success, as we this day proceeded above three hundred yards. I was obliged to keep several men employed in making the road before us, as we went on with the head. The Irish lad that was with me I sent to Cairo, as he could not resist the climate; but what is singular, Mrs. Belzoni enjoyed tolerable health all the time. She was constantly among the women in the tombs; for all the Fellahs of Gournou make dwelling-houses where the Egyptians had burial-places, as I shall have occasion to mention hereafter.

On the 2d the head advanced farther; and I was in great hopes of passing a part of the land, to which the inundation would extend, previous to the water reaching that spot.

On the 3d we went on extremely well, and advanced nearly four hundred yards. We had a bad road on the 4th, but still we proceeded a good way. On the 5th we entered the land I was so anxious to pass over, for fear the water should reach it and arrest our course; and I was happy to think, that the next day would bring us out of danger. Accordingly, I went to the place early in the morning, and to my great surprise found no one there except the guards and the carpenter, who informed me, that the Caimakan had given orders to the Fellahs not to work for the Christian dogs any longer.

[Prolonged negotiations with the Cacheff followed, and Belzoni carried his point only after offering him his 'pair of fine English pistols'.] Early on the morning of the 7th, I sent for the Sheik of the Fellahs, and gave him the Cacheff's order. The men were ready in an hour after, and we continued the operation. The bust advanced this day considerably more than usual, owing to the men having rested on the preceding day: and on the 8th I had the pleasure of seeing it out of danger of being overtaken by the water.

On the 9th, I was seized with such a giddiness in my head, that I could not stand. The blood ran so copiously from my nose and mouth, that I was unable to continue the operation: I therefore postponed it to the next day.

On the 10th and 11th, we approached towards the river; and on the 12th, thank God, the young Memnon arrived on the bank of the Nile. Besides their promised payment, I gave the Arabs a bakshis, or present, of one piastre each, equal to sixpence English, with which they were exceedingly pleased ...

Giovanni Belzoni, *Narrative of the Operations ... in Egypt,*
1822.

BELZONI's later excavations – if that is not too scientific a word to use to describe some of his cruder techniques – in the Valley of the Kings inaugurated a series of investigations by archaeologists that continued for well over a century. (Indeed, as these words were being written in 1990, the *Observer* newspaper carried a report of the discovery of the mummy of Queen Hatshepsut in an obscure tomb in the valley.) The most celebrated was the discovery, by Howard Carter in November 1922, of the long-sought tomb of King Tutankhamun, the smallest and by far the richest of all the royal tombs in the valley.

The history of the Valley ... has never lacked the dramatic element, and in this, the latest episode, it has held to its traditions. For consider the circumstances. This was to be our final season in the Valley. Six full seasons we had excavated there, and season after season had drawn a blank: we had worked for months at a stretch and found nothing, and only an excavator knows how desperately depressing that can be; we had almost made up our minds that we were beaten, and were preparing to leave the Valley and try our luck elsewhere; and then – hardly had we set hoe to ground in our last despairing effort than we made a discovery that far exceeded our wildest dreams. Surely, never before in the whole history of excavation has a full digging season been compressed within the space of five days.

Let me try and tell the story of it all. It will not be easy, for the dramatic suddenness of the initial discovery left me in a dazed condition, and the months that have followed have been so crowded with incident that I have hardly had time to think. Setting it down on paper will perhaps give me a chance to realize what has happened and all that it means.

I arrived in Luxor on 28 October, and by 1 November I had enrolled my workmen and was ready to begin. Our former excavations had stopped short at the north-east corner of the tomb of Rameses VI, and from this point I started trenching southwards. It will be remembered that in this area there were a number of roughly constructed workmen's huts, used probably by the labourers in the tomb of Rameses. These huts, built about three feet above bed-rock, covered the whole area in front of the Ramesside tomb, and continued in a southerly direction to join up with a similar group of huts on the opposite side of the Valley, discovered by Davis in connexion with his work on the Akhenaten cache. By the evening of 3 November we had laid bare a sufficient number of these huts for experimental purposes, so, after we had planned and noted them, they were removed, and we were ready to clear away the three feet of soil that lay beneath them.

Hardly had I arrived on the work next morning (4 November) than the unusual silence, due to the stoppage of the work, made me realize that something out of the ordinary had happened, and I was greeted by the announcement that a step cut in the rock had been discovered underneath the very first hut to be attacked. This seemed too good to be true, but a short amount of extra clearing revealed the fact that we were actually in the entrance of a steep cut in the rock, some thirteen feet below the entrance to the tomb of Rameses VI, and a similar depth from the present bed level of the Valley. The manner of cutting was that of the sunken stairway entrance so common in the Valley, and I almost dared to hope that we had found our tomb at last. Work continued feverishly throughout the whole of that day and the morning of the next, but it was not until the afternoon of 5 November that we succeeded in clearing away the masses of rubbish that overlay the cut, and were able to demarcate the upper edges of the stairway on all its four sides.

It was clear by now beyond any question that we actually had before us the entrance to a tomb, but doubts, born of previous disappointments, persisted in creeping in. There was always the horrible possibility, suggested by our experience in the Thothmes III Valley, that the tomb was an unfinished one, never completed and never used: if it had been finished there was the depressing probability that it had been completely plundered in ancient times. On the other hand, there was just the chance of an untouched or only partially plundered tomb, and it was with ill-suppressed excitement that I watched the descending steps to the staircase, as one by one they came to light. The cutting was excavated in the side of a small hillock, and as the work progressed, its western edge receded under the slope of the rock until it was, first partially, and then completely, roofed in, and became a passage, 10 feet high by 6 feet wide. Work progressed more rapidly now; step succeeded step, and at the level of the twelfth, towards sunset, there was disclosed the upper part of a doorway, blocked, plastered, and sealed.

A sealed doorway – it was actually true, then! Our years of patient labour were to be rewarded after all, and I think my first feeling was one of congratulation that my faith in the Valley had not been unjustified. With excitement growing to fever heat I searched the seal impressions on the door for evidence of the identity of the owner, but could find no name: the only decipherable ones were those of the well-known royal necropolis seal, the jackal and nine captives. Two facts, however, were clear: first, the employment of this royal seal was certain evidence that the tomb had been constructed for a person of very high standing; and second, that the sealed door was entirely screened from above by workmen's huts of the Twentieth Dynasty was sufficiently clear proof that at least from that date it had never been entered. With that for the moment I had to be content.

While examining the seals I noticed, at the top of the doorway, where some of the plaster had fallen away, a heavy wooden lintel. Under this, to assure myself of the method by which the doorway had been blocked, I made a small peephole, just large enough to insert an electric torch, and discovered that the passage beyond the door was filled completely from floor to ceiling with stones and rubble – additional proof this of the care with which the tomb had been protected.

It was a thrilling moment for an excavator. Alone, save for my native workmen, I found myself, after years of comparatively unproductive labour, on the threshold of what might prove to be a magnificent discovery. Anything, literally anything, might lie beyond that passage, and it needed all my self-control to keep from breaking down the doorway, and investigating then and there.

One thing puzzled me, and that was the smallness of the opening in comparison with the ordinary Valley tombs. The design was certainly of the Eighteenth Dynasty. Could it be the tomb of a noble buried here by royal consent? Was it a royal cache, a hiding-place to which a mummy and its equipment had been removed for safety? Or was it actually the tomb of the king for whom I had spent so many years in search?

Once more I examined the seal impressions for a clue, but on the part of the door so far laid bare only those of the royal necropolis seal already mentioned were clear enough to read. Had I but known that a few inches lower down there was a perfectly clear and distinct impression of the seal of Tutankhamen, the king I most desired to find, I would have cleared on, had a much better night's rest on consequence, and saved myself nearly three weeks of uncertainty. It was late, however, and darkness was already upon us. With some reluctance I re-closed the small hole that I had made, filled in our excavation for protection during the night, selected the most trust-worthy of my workmen – themselves almost as excited as I was – to watch all night above the tomb, and so home by moonlight, riding down the Valley.

Naturally my wish was to go straight ahead with our clearing to find out the full extent of the discovery, but Lord Carnarvon was in England, and in fairness to him I had to delay matters until he could come. Accordingly, on the morning of 6 November I sent him the following cable: 'At last have made wonderful discovery in Valley; a magnificent tomb with seals intact; re-covered same for your arrival; congratulations.'

My next task was to secure the doorway against inter-ference until such time as it could finally be reopened. This we did by filling our excavation up again to surface level, and rolling on top of it the large flint boulders of which the workmen's huts had been composed. By the evening of the same day, exactly forty-eight hours after we had discovered the first step of the staircase, this was accomplished. The tomb had vanished. So far as the appearance of the ground was concerned there never had been any tomb, and I found it hard to persuade myself at times that the whole episode had not been a dream.

I was soon to be reassured on this point. News travels fast in Egypt, and within two days of the discovery congratulations, inquiries, and offers of help descended upon me in a steady stream from all directions. It became clear, even at this early stage, that I was in for a job that could not be tackled single-handed, so I wired to Callender, who had helped me on various previous occasions, asking him if possible to join me without delay, and to my relief he arrived on the very next day. On the 8th I had received two messages from Lord Carnavon in answer to my cable, the first of which read,

'Possibly come soon,' and the second, received a little later, 'Propose arrive Alexandria 20th.'

We had thus nearly a fortnight's grace, and we devoted it to making preparations of various kinds, so that when the time of reopening came, we should be able, with the least possible delay, to handle any situation that might arise. On the night of the 18th I went to Cairo for three days, to meet Lord Carnarvon and make a number of necessary purchases, returning to Luxor on the 21st. On the 23rd Lord Carnarvon arrived in Luxor with his daughter, Lady Evelyn Herbert, his devoted companion in all his Egyptian work, and everything was in hand for the beginning of the second chapter of the discovery of the tomb. Callender had been busy all day clearing away the upper layer of rubbish, so that by morning we should be able to get into the staircase without any delay.

By the afternoon of the 24th the whole staircase was clear, sixteen steps in all, and we were able to make a proper examination of the sealed doorway. On the lower part the seal impressions were much clearer, and we were able without any difficulty to make out on several of them the name of Tutankhamen. This added enormously to the interest of the discovery. If we had found, as seemed almost certain, the tomb of that shadowy monarch, whose tenure of the throne coincided with one of the most interesting periods in the whole of Egyptian history, we should indeed have reason to congratulate ourselves.

With heightened interest, if that were possible, we renewed our investigation of the doorway. Here for the first time a disquieting element made its appearance. Now that the whole door was exposed to light it was possible to discern a fact that had hitherto escaped notice – that there had been two successive openings and re-closings of a part of its surface: furthermore, that the sealing originally discovered, the jackal and nine captives, had been applied to the re-closed portions, whereas the sealings of Tutankhamen covered the untouched part of the doorway, and were therefore those with which the tomb had been originally secured. The tomb then was not absolutely intact, as we had hoped. Plunderers had entered it, and entered it more than once – from the evidence of the huts above, plunderers of a date not later than the reign of Rameses VI – but that they had not rifled it completely was evident from the fact that it had been re-sealed.

Then came another puzzle. In the lower strata of rubbish that filled the staircase we found masses of broken potsherds and boxes, the latter bearing the names of Akhenaten, Smenkhkare and Tutankhamen, and, what was much more upsetting, a scarab of Thothmes III and a fragment with the name of Amenhetep III. Why this mixture of names? The balance of evidence so far would seem to indicate a cache rather than a tomb, and at this stage in the proceedings we inclined more and more to the opinion that we were about to find a miscellaneous collection of objects of the Eighteenth Dynasty kings, brought from Tell el Amarna by Tutan-khamen and deposited here for safety.

So matters stood on the evening of the 24th. On the following day the sealed doorway was to be removed, so Callender set carpenters to work making a heavy wooden grille to be set up in its place. Mr Engelbach, Chief Inspector of the Antiquities Department, paid us a visit during the afternoon, and witnessed part of the final clearing of rubbish from the doorway.

On the morning of the 25th the seal impressions on the doorway were carefully noted and photographed, and then we removed the actual blocking of the door, consisting of rough stones carefully built from floor to lintel, and heavily plastered on their outer faces to take the seal impressions.

This disclosed the beginning of a descending passage (not a staircase), the same width as the entrance stairway, and nearly seven feet high. As I had already discovered from my hole in the doorway, it was filled completely with stone and rubble, probably the chip from its own excavation. This filling, like the doorway, showed dis-tinct signs of more than one opening and reclosing of the tomb, the untouched part consisting of clean white chip, mingled with dust, whereas the disturbed part was composed mainly of dark flint. It was clear that an irregular tunnel had been cut through the original filling at the upper corner on the left side, a tunnel corresponding in position with that of the hole in the doorway.

As we cleared the passage we found, mixed with the rubble of the lower levels, broken potsherds, jar sealings, alabaster jars, whole and broken, vases of painted pottery, numerous fragments of small articles, and water skins, these last having obviously been used to bring up the water needed for the plastering of the doorways. These were clear evidence of plundering, and we eyed them askance. By night we had cleared a considerable distance down the passage, but as yet saw no sign of second doorway or of chamber.

The day following (26 November) was the day of days, the most wonderful that I have ever lived through, and certainly one whose like I can never hope to see again. Throughout the morning the work of clearing continued, slowly perforce, on account of the delicate objects that were mixed with the filling. Then, in the middle of the afternoon, thirty feet down from the outer door, we came upon a second sealed doorway, almost an exact replica of the first. The seal impressions in this case were less distinct, but still recognizable as those of Tutankhamen and of the royal necropolis. Here again the signs of opening and re-closing were clearly marked upon the plaster. We were firmly convinced by this time that it was a cache that we were about to open, and not a tomb. The arrangement of stairway, entrance passage and doors reminded us very forcibly of the cache of Akhenaten and Tyi material found in the very near vicinity of the present excavation by Davis, and the fact that Tutankhamen's seals occurred there likewise seemed almost certain proof that we were right in our conjecture. We were soon to know. There lay the sealed doorway, and behind it was the answer to the question.

Slowly, desperately slowly it seemed to us as we

watched, the remains of passage debris that encumbered the lower part of the doorway were removed, until at last we had the whole door clear before us. The decisive moment had arrived. With trembling hands I made a tiny breach in the upper left-hand corner. Darkness and blank space, as far as an iron testing-rod could reach, showed that whatever lay beyond was empty, and not filled like the passage we had just cleared. Candle tests were applied as a precaution against possible foul gasses, and then, widening the hole a little, I inserted the candle and peered in, Lord Carnarvon, Lady Evelyn and Callender standing anxiously beside me to hear the verdict. At first I could see nothing, the hot air escaping from the chamber causing the candle flame to flicker, but presently, as my eyes grew accustomed to the light, details of the room within emerged slowly from the mist, strange animals, statues, and gold – everywhere the glint of gold. For the moment – an eternity it must have seemed to the others standing by – I was struck dumb with amazement, and when Lord Carnarvon, unable to stand the suspense any longer, inquired anxiously, 'Can you see anything?' it was all I could do to get the words, 'Yes, wonderful things.' Then, widening the hole a little further, so that we both could see, we inserted an electric torch.

Howard Carter, *The Tomb of Tutankhamen*, 1923.

CARTER followed precise investigative methods, carefully recording each object before its removal. So it was not until over a year later, during the second excavation season, that the sarcophagus containing Tutankhamun's coffin was opened. Carter again recalls the drama of the occasion.

The tackle for raising the lid was in position. I gave the word. Amid intense silence the huge slab, broken in two, weighing over a ton and a quarter, rose from its

bed. The light shone into the sarcophagus. A sight met
our eyes that at first puzzled us. It was a little disappointing. The contents were completely covered by
fine linen shrouds. The lid being suspended in mid-air,
we rolled back those covering shrouds, one by one, and
as the last was removed a gasp of wonderment escaped
our lips, so gorgeous was the sight that met our eyes: a
golden effigy of the young boy king, of most magnificent
workmanship, filled the whole of the interior of the
sarcophagus. This was the lid of a wonderful anthropoid
coffin, some 7 feet in length, resting upon a low bier in
the form of a lion, and no doubt the outermost coffin of
a series of coffins, nested one within the other, enclosing
the mortal remains of the king. Enclasping the body of
this magnificent monument are two winged goddesses,
Isis and Neith, wrought in rich gold-work upon gesso,
as brilliant as the day the coffin was made. To it an
additional charm was added, by the fact that, while this
decoration was rendered in fine low bas-relief, the head
and hands of the king were in the round, in massive gold
of the finest sculpture, surpassing anything we could
have imagined. The hands, crossed over the breast, held
the royal emblems – the Crook and the Flail – encrusted
with deep blue faience. The face and features were wonderfully wrought in sheet gold. The eyes were of aragon-
ite and obsidian, the eyebrows and eyelids inlaid with
lapis lazuli glass. There was a touch of realism, for while
the rest of this anthropoid coffin, covered with feathered
ornament, was of brilliant gold, that of the bare face and
hands seemed different, the gold of the flesh being of
different alloy, thus conveying an impression of the
greyness of death. Upon the forehead of this recumbent
figure of the young boy king were two emblems deli-
cately worked in brilliant inlay – the Cobra and the
Vulture – symbols of Upper and Lower Egypt, but
perhaps the most touching by its human simplicity was
the tiny wreath of flowers around these symbols, as it
pleased us to think, the last farewell offering of the
widowed girl queen to her husband, the youthful representative of the 'Two Kingdoms.'

At Thebes

Among all that regal splendour, that royal magnificence – everywhere the glint of gold – there was
nothing so beautiful as those few withered flowers, still
retaining their tinge of colour. They told us what a short
period three thousand three hundred years really was –
but Yesterday and the Morrow. In fact, that touch of
nature made that ancient and our modern civilization
kin.

Howard Carter, *The Tomb of Tutankhamen*, 1923.

ONLY the most privileged visitor was able to participate in
so momentous an occasion. But even the briefest time spent
visiting the Valley of the Kings could generally be relied on
to catch the imagination and provoke solemn thoughts on
the transitory nature of human existence. Here the Reverend
Stephen Olin reflects on his visit to Thebes in 1840.

No other ancient place which I have visited makes its
instructive homily upon the madness of ambition and
the transitoriness of human grandeur, half so touching
and impressive. In Rome, and even in Athens, the
solemn lesson is perpetually interrupted by the busy
pursuits and noisy pleasures of still teeming life; and the
monuments of generations long since gone are often
blended with, and half concealed by, the habitations or
more ambitious structures of the present. At Thebes,
everything is left to the desolation to which time and
violence have consigned it. The peasants, with their
cottages and cornfields, which are seen only here and
there upon the ancient plain, are just sufficient to make
a good contrast to the fallen temples, yawning tombs,
and colossal images that look down in derision upon

their puny labours. These monuments are principal objects in the scene, and there is nothing else in the form either of improvement or wealth, or even industry, to distract the attention which they are permitted to engross, or to break in upon the converse into which they insensibly draw us with the men who, at an era beyond the age of authentic history, reared up these memorials of their achievements, literature, and arts.

I think it impossible to sojourn, even for a few days, among such venerable objects, without being inspired with the highest respect for the ancient Egyptians, though the proofs of their debasing superstitions, which so abound here, must inevitably detract a good deal from that feeling. I incline to the opinion that in point of genius they are entitled to the first place among all the ancient nations. True, these structures lack the lightness, the chaste simplicity and faultless proportions, which distinguish Grecian architecture, as exhibited in the Theseion and Parthenon at Athens. It is essential to remember, however, that the Egyptians were the inventors; the Greeks only improved upon their models – an easy task for even inferior minds. This remark is, with some modification, applicable to the statuary as well as the architecture of the two nations. In all that indicates high talent, grandeur of conception, and skill in the applications of science to mechanical operations, the Egyptians were superior, and at least equal in the lower attributes of mere handicraft skill and patient industry.

Stephen Olin, *Travels in Egypt, Arabia Petraea and the Holy Land*, 1843.

ARTHUR CONAN DOYLE, recalling a Nile cruise taken in 1896, was less responsive.

[The Egyptians'] arts seem to have been high but their reasoning power in many ways contemptible. The recent discovery of the King's tomb near Thebes – I write in 1924 – shows how wonderful were their decorations and the amenities of their lives. But consider the tomb itself. What a degraded intelligence does it not show! The idea that the body, the old outworn greatcoat which was once wrapped round the soul, should at any cost be preserved is the last word in materialism. And the hundred baskets of provisions to feed the soul upon its journey! I can never believe that a people with such ideas could be other than emasculated in their minds – the fate of every nation which comes under the rule of a priesthood.

Arthur Conan Doyle, *Memories and Adventures*, 1924.

A SUPPLY of regular meals was a major concern of the visitor. Even the indomitable Amelia Edwards, already captivated by the spirit of ancient Egypt, was not immune.

We had luncheon that morning, I remember, with the M.B.'s in the second hall of the Ramesseum. It was but one occasion among many; for the Writer was constantly at work on that side of the river, and we had luncheon in one or other of the western Temples every day. Yet that particular meeting stands out in my memory apart from the rest. I see the joyous party gathered together in the shade of the great columns – the Persian rugs spread on the uneven ground – the dragoman in his picturesque dress going to and fro – the brown and tattered Arabs, squatting a little way off, silent and hungry-eyed, each with his string of forged scarabs, his imitation gods, or his bits of mummy-case and painted cartonnage for sale – the glowing peeps of landscape framed in here and there through vistas of columns –

the emblazoned architraves laid along from capital to capital overhead, each block sculptured with enormous cartouches yet brilliant with vermilion and ultramarine – the patient donkeys munching all together at a little heap of vetches in one corner – the intense depths of cloudless blue above. Of all Theban ruins, the Ramesseum is the most cheerful. Drenched in sunshine, the warm limestone of which it is built seems to have mellowed and turned golden with time. No walls enclose it. No towering pylons overshadow it. It stands high, and the air circulates freely among those simple and beautiful columns. There are not many Egyptian ruins in which one can talk and be merry; but in the Ramesseum one may thoroughly enjoy the passing hour.

Amelia Edwards, *A Thousand Miles Up the Nile*, 1877.

VISITORS stayed in modern Luxor, on the east bank of the Nile, where they complained at being constantly pestered by guides, donkey-boys and sellers of fake *antikas*, or antiquities. Amelia Edwards had a revealing experience one day as she explored the town.

By a curious accident, L. and the Writer once actually penetrated into a forger's workshop. Not knowing that it had been abolished, we went to a certain house in which a certain Consulate had once upon a time been located, and there knocked for admission. An old deaf Fellâha opened the door, and after some hesitation showed us into a large unfurnished room with three windows. In each window there stood a workman's bench strewn with scarabs, amulets, and funerary statuettes in every stage of progress. We examined these specimens with no little curiosity. Some were of wood; some were of limestone; some were partly coloured. The colours and brushes were there; to say nothing of files, gravers, and little pointed tools like gimlets. A magnifying glass of the kind used by engravers lay in one of the window-recesses. We also observed a small grindstone screwed to one of the benches and worked by a treadle; while a massive fragment of mummy-case in a corner behind the door showed whence came the old sycamore wood for the wooden specimens. That three skilled workmen furnished with European tools had been busy in this room shortly before we were shown into it, was perfectly clear. We concluded that they had just gone away to breakfast.

Meanwhile we waited, expecting to be ushered into the presence of the Consul. In about ten minutes, however, breathless with hurrying, arrived a well-dressed Arab whom we had never seen before. Distracted between his Oriental politeness and his desire to get rid of us, he bowed us out precipitately, explaining that the house had changed owners, and that the Power in question had ceased to be represented at Luxor. We heard him rating the old woman savagely, as soon as the door had closed behind us. I met that well-dressed Arab a day or two after, near the Governor's house; and he immediately vanished round the nearest corner.

Amelia Edwards, *A Thousand Miles Up the Nile*, 1877.

As Cook's steamers, and later the railway, brought more and more visitors, Luxor began to develop rapidly during the last quarter of the nineteenth century. Hotels, promenades and a hospital were built. In winter, the town took on something of the air of a fashionable European resort, visitors studying the ruins as diligently as elsewhere they might sip the waters. It was a far cry from the town where Lucie Duff Gordon settled in 1863 for the sake of her fragile health. Scarcely another foreigner has managed to acquire so sensitive and profound an understanding of Egypt and the

Egyptian people; certainly none managed to convey that understanding as movingly as she did in her letters to her much-loved husband, Sir Alexander Duff Gordon, in London. Small wonder that she became known as *Sittee Noor-ala-Noor* (Lady Light from the Light) and *Sitt-el-Kebir* (the Great Lady) and that all Luxor mourned her death in 1869. Here is her portrait of her simple Luxor home.

The view all round my house is magnificent on every side, over the Nile in front facing north-west, and over a splendid range of green and distant orange buff hills to the south-east, where I have a spacious covered terrace. It is rough and dusty to the extreme, but will be very pleasant. Mustapha came in just now to offer me the loan of a horse, and to ask me to go to the mosque in a few nights to see the illumination in honour of a great Sheykh, a son of Sidi Hosseyn or Hassan. I asked whether my presence might not offend any Muslimeen, and he would not hear of such a thing. The sun set while he was here, and he asked if I objected to his praying in my presence, and went through his four *rekahs* very comfortably on my carpet. My next-door neighbour (across the courtyard all filled with antiquities) is a nice little Copt who looks like an antique statue himself. I shall *voisiner* with his family. He sent me coffee as soon as I arrived, and came to help. I am invited to El-Moutaneh, a few hours up the river, to visit the Mouniers, and to Keneh to visit Seyyid Achmet, and also the head of the merchants there who settled the price of a carpet for me in the bazaar, and seemed to like me. He was just one of those handsome, high-bred, elderly merchants with whom a story always begins in the Arabian Nights. When I can talk I will go and see a real Arab hareem ...

Now I am settled in my Theban palace, it seems more and more beautiful, and I am quite melancholy that you cannot be here to enjoy it. The house is very large and •

has good thick walls, the comfort of which we feel to-day for it blows a hurricane; but indoors it is not at all cold. I have glass windows and doors to some of the rooms. It is a lovely dwelling. Two funny little owls as big as my fist live in the wall under my window, and come up and peep in, walking on tip-toe, and looking inquisitive like the owls in the hieroglyphics; and a splendid horus (the sacred hawk) frequents my lofty balcony. Another of my contemplar gods I sacrilegiously killed last night, a whip snake. Omar is rather in con-sternation for fear it should be 'the snake of the house,' for Islam has not dethroned the *Dii lares et tutelares*.

Lucie Duff Gordon, *Letters from Egypt*, 1865.

SOMETHING of the same sensitivity to people and landscapes appears in Vita Sackville-West's description of Luxor.

Then there were other days at Luxor; the day when I went to the potters' village on the edge of the desert, through the fields of young corn where the white egrets stalked and the water-wheel complained, as it poured its little buckets into the irrigation trench. I liked getting away from the roads, into the region of country life, where only the peasants laboured, bending down over the dark earth. Everything there was slow, quiet, and regular; husbandry is of all ages and all countries. Nothing dates. There is a special concentration in this husbandry of the valley of the Nile; everything is drawn tightly together; there is no sprawling. The very cen-turies shrink up, and the life of man with his beasts becomes very close. They seem to have acquired the same gait and colour, through long association with each other and with the earth. In long files, flat as a fresco, they trail along the dykes, mud-coloured: the camels, the buffaloes, the little donkeys, and the man. Slouching they go, in an eternal procession; with the Egyptian genius for design, as though they were drawn with a hard, sharp pencil on the sky. First the camels' heads, swaying on their long necks; then the buffaloes, slouching as though they had just dragged themselves out of the primeval slime; then the donkeys, with a little boy sitting on the last rump, drumming his heels. Then the man, small but erect, driving the lot before him. He drives, but he is part of the procession; he brings up the rear. He completes the pattern. Yet he is not so very different from his beasts, only perpendicular whereas they are horizontal; he is the same colour, though he plies a stick. Where they are all going to Heaven knows; they all seem to be trailing on an eternal pilgrimage. It is a relief to come upon a party of peasants at work in static attitudes, bent down over the earth, not walking on towards something else; with a camel near by, safely yoked, and turning the water-wheel from morning to night in the same trodden groove; this is a kind of triumph over the camel, which (with its outstretched neck) might be an animal designed to slouch onward, always at the same gait, always over the same desert, purpose subservient to pattern. A camel yoked is nature's design defeated, for the camel looks like a natural traveller, and not like a creature intended to walk round and round in the same circle. The wooden cogs squeal as they rub against one another, in the shadow of the tamarisk, and the little pitchers come up dripping out of the deep well, spilling half their water before it gets tipped out into the trench; a wasteful process, but one upon which the centuries have not been able to improve. There is a downright, primitive simplicity about these Egyptian methods, but it appears to be effective, for enviable crops spring from the black earth. Water is the constant preoccupation, from the anxiety about the year's Nile – a good Nile, or a bad Nile – to the more controllable problem of irrigation. So the mind of the Egyptian peasant must be filled with the noise and flow of water, as the mind of every worker is shaped by the detail and exigency of his craft; he sees the pitchers dip and spill, as though they had become a part of himself, grown into his bones; he hears the shrill whining of the cogs, that sing a peculiar tune, like an incantation, all day as the feet of the camel pad round in the groove.

The peasants raised their heads at the sight of a stranger, for the tourists stick to the tombs and temples, and do not wander in the fields. The blue shirts showed above the corn as the labourers straightened their bent backs, and paused to stare. In the villages the dogs rushed out to bark, and hordes of children appeared from nowhere, with little grinning faces and out-stretched palms, and bare feet scuffling in the dust. These people live in conditions of unbelievable simplicity. Their houses are mere shelters of sun-dried mud, without any furniture of even the roughest description; there are simply four walls and a trodden floor; that is all. Sometimes a rude door keeps the entrance from the village street, but more often the entrance is just a hole in the wall, and anybody can look in. The potters' village was largely built of broken pots, embedded in mud; under a roof of plaited reeds, two potters sat at their work, the wheel spinning beneath the kick of their foot, their arms plunged up to the elbow in the dark wet clay, which in a minute was transformed from a shapeless lump into a jar of plain but faultless line – a precision of workmanship which contrasted oddly with the almost bestial condition of their dwell-ings. These are the people who can do one thing, and will continue to do it all their lives, as their ancestors did it before them, through the burning summers when no tourist dreams of going to Luxor, as through the more merciful winter when foreigners with the whole complexity of civilisation seething in their brains come to intercept for a brief moment this different current of human existence. The potters scarcely troubled to look up, they gave one dull, indifferent glance, then flung another slab of clay on the twirling wheel, and spun it out into the slender throat of the pitcher.

Vita Sackville-West, *Passenger to Teheran*, 1926.

10

Archaeologists at Work

DURING the first half of the nineteenth century many thousands of the artefacts, large and small, of ancient Egypt were shipped, often illicitly, out of Egypt to enrich public and private collections throughout Europe. Belzoni's finds, for instance, formed the basis of the British Museum's extensive Egyptian holdings, and this is only one example among many. Such plunder – the word is not too harsh – all too often involved incalculable damage to the sites concerned. Tombs would be stripped of their furnishings, mummies of their jewellery, statues and other objects would be uncovered, without any care for their surroundings; the objects, in all their richness and beauty, were valued for themselves, not for what they might reveal of the Egypt of the Pharaohs.

Gradually, some control began to be exercised. In 1858 the distinguished French Egyptologist Auguste Mariette was appointed to run the newly formed Egyptian Antiquities Service. Unrestrained excavation was controlled by the granting of specific concessions to archaeologists; ground rules for the export of antiquities were laid down; the Egyptian Museum was founded. At the same time, in place of the previous enthusiasts, a new breed of archaeologist began to arrive in Egypt, dedicated to the painstaking, precise investigation and recording of a particular site. From Britain, many of these were sent out under the aegis of the Egypt Exploration Fund, later renamed the Egypt Exploration Society. This was founded in 1882 by, to quote Professor

T. G. H. James in the volume commemorating the Society's centenary, 'a small group of far-seeing scholars and interested amateurs brought together by a concern for the ever-increasing destruction of monuments in Egypt and for the lack of properly organised excavations'. Prominent among these 'interested amateurs' was Amelia Edwards, author of *A Thousand Miles Up the Nile*, much quoted in this book, which remains a classic of travel-writing.

William Flinders Petrie (whom we have already observed at the Pyramids, see p. 113) was among the best-known Egyptologists of the late nineteenth and early twentieth century. He set new standards in meticulous site investigation and in fair dealing with his workmen, though the puritanical rigour of his working life has not been imitated by his successors.

For the 1902–3 season Margaret Murray joined Petrie's excavation at Abydos, where the royal tombs had previously been clumsily investigated by a French archaeologist named Amélineau. Here she analyses the force of Petrie's character, and goes on to explain his excellent relations with his Egyptian workmen.

Nothing can turn genius [Petrie] from his way, neither the attractions of mammon nor the lure of the limelight; he is ruthless in spending himself in his work and equally ruthless to his co-workers, so that those who do not share his enthusiasm remove themselves as soon as possible to an easier job. But to those who can stand the grade and can work for the work's sake, the flaming enthusiasm of a genius will lead them to new lines of research, new lines of knowledge and of thought, which in the end are more rewarding than a comfortable well-paid job with the work-hours of a Government office. This was the effect that Petrie had on those who came under his influence . . .

To Petrie his work was his life. When that great flood

of new knowledge [came] which, at the turn of the century, swept away all the old archaeological landmarks, Petrie alone rode the storm and reduced the chaos to order. His method of sequence-dating was a new archaeological method, and by its means he was able to divide the pre-dynastic cultures into their right chronological order. His gleanings of the bits and pieces, which were all that were left at the Royal Tombs at Abydos after Amélineau's disastrous treasure hunt, gave the chronological order of the kings of the first and second dynasties. He had thus achieved the goal which he had set himself from the beginning of his work in Egypt, which was to build up the framework of Egyptian history in its right sequence so that other workers could fit their discoveries into the correct chronological place. After the discovery of the Badarian culture (which was found under his auspices) the whole of Egyptian pre-history and history was laid bare from the earliest down to the time when that great civilisation died under the iron heel of Rome ...

Petrie was very careful of his workmen and never had a fatal or even serious accident among them. He always paid the workmen the local market price for any finds they made in the excavation, so that there was no temptation for them to secrete their finds and sell them to the local dealer. But he was adamant in dismissing on the spot any workman, even one of his best diggers, if caught out in this archaeological crime. His system of payment enraged other excavators for it increased the expenses, and I have heard some of them say, 'He has upset the labour market by paying the workmen for worthless trifles.'

As most of his early work was at a considerable distance from a bank and he could not keep a stock of money in his exiguous camp, and as there was nowhere for the workmen to spend their wages except on a little fresh food, they got into the habit of leaving their wages and baksheesh to accumulate in his hands. He kept a strict account of how much was due to each man, which he explained to the owner once a week. At the end of the season he went to a bank, brought back the cash and paid off each man. Though each man knew the exact amount he would receive, that amount in hard cash always seemed to come as a surprise in spite of having had his account drummed into him every pay day. This is the kind of thing that went on.

Petrie. 'Ahmed Ali, you had in my hands so much, *Temam* (right)?'

A.A. '*Temam.*'

F.P. 'This week your wages were so much, *Temam?*'

A.A. '*Temam.*'

F.P. 'And your baksheesh was so much, but you took out so much for your marketing, leaving so much for this week, *Temam?*'

A.A. '*Temam.*'

F.P. 'Therefore this week's earnings added to the amount I already hold comes to so much, *Temam?*'

A.A (doubtfully). '*Aywa* (yes).'

F.P. 'Listen' (and repeats the little sum).

A.A. (suddenly enlightened). '*Temam, temam,*' and he goes off quite happily.

This was a scene that took place regularly every pay day. The men did not question Petrie's figures, but liked to have their own arithmetic confirmed. This system suited both sides; the workmen had no fear of thieves, for they had no money to be stolen, and therefore could sleep soundly all night, and Petrie had no need either to keep a fairly large sum in the camp (and so attract thieves) or to make frequent journeys to the bank which was always some miles away ...

Petrie's system for paying for the finds during an excavation resulted of course in his always 'striking lucky', for then there was no incentive among the workmen to steal, and every incentive to spot even the smallest object which might bring baksheesh to the finder. If gold was found it was put into a scale-pan with gold sovereigns or half-sovereigns in the other pan in the presence of the lucky finder, who then received gold for gold in a way he understood. The process was always done in secret, otherwise the man would certainly have been robbed, possibly even murdered, on his way home if it had been known that he was carrying gold coin.

Petrie rose to fame without the training of school or university, a condition which in those days was regarded as almost without education. He knew little Latin and less Greek, yet he had a profound knowledge (obtained from good translations) of all the information about Egypt recorded in ancient authors, and thus discovered Naukratis and the Pelusian Daphnae, thereby proving the reliability of Herodotus. The accuracy of his visual memory enabled him to identify the painted pottery of the twelfth dynasty as Ægean, a statement which was laughed to scorn ('Ridiculous nonsense! Who ever heard of painted pottery in the Ægean at that date!'), until the finds in Crete silenced the scoffers.

He introduced new methods and systems into the investigation of the past, and so had converted a leisurely hobby into a subject for serious study worthy of university training. His little book, *Historical Scarabs*, must have been a shock to many an excavator as showing the vital importance of small and to them uninteresting objects, which had always been thrown away unless they were of good colour, when they could be used as a pretty little curio to set in a brooch or bracelet for a lady to wear.

Curiously enough it was his method of paying the market rate to the workmen for finds made in the dig that appears to have roused the most virulent opposition. Also his opponents never seem to realise that Petrie held strong views about subscribers' money. It was given for the dig, therefore the camp should supply the necessities of life but not the luxuries. In deference to the religious prejudices of his Moslem workers he permitted no alcohol nor 'pig-meat' in any form. As most of his helpers were young men from well-to-do comfortable Victorian homes where there were plenty of servants and breakfast was at nine o'clock, it was rather startling to breakfast before sunrise with never a sign of bacon or pork sausages, and the milk in your tea had been boiled!

Margaret Murray, *My First Hundred Years*, 1963.

PETRIE himself, looking back over a lifetime of excavating, wrote:

> I have never found it needful to chastise a workman, the eye and the power of the purse suffice; nor will I let the native use the familiar strap or lash on the children. The art of keeping the pot boiling lies in being surprisingly about. A private approach to the view of the work is so arranged that my coming up cannot be signalled along to the main body. On getting in sight of the work, it is best to stand quite still for five or ten minutes, watching everyone in turn, and looking for men or children who are not active. Then it is needful to trace out quietly what the cause may be, – usually the men waiting for the return of the basket boys. Look out the lines of discharge of the earth, and see if they can be shortened; make out the causes of delay and then rearrange matters, always pointing out the change as a favour and help to the workers, so that they feel it not as a reproach but an assistance. Usually the lines of work once started are continued blindly, running on the same course like ants, though the working face may have passed into quite a different position, and the discharge line may be shortened to half or less of the distance.
>
> Of course sheer laziness without a cause means immediate dismissal; but the break of ten minutes in the midst of the morning and afternoon seems desirable all round. If the whole work needs tuning up, then 'the devil take the hindmost,' and whoever does least is cleared out; the same may be applied to keeping up punctuality in the morning. At San, working near the village, the people used to loiter over the dinner hour, and not heed the whistle; so one day, when they were worse than usual, I went to meet them as they tardily came up, and dismissed them all for the half day. After that they all came as soon as they had their food, and sat round my huts waiting for the time.
>
> The essential spur is the quiet eye; let the workers see that you are watching and assessing them without any bluster, and never calling attention till you have exam-

ined what is going on; then every one feels the need of keeping up to the mark, as they cannot tell when a fatal dismissal may suddenly fall on them.

William Flinders Petrie, *Seventy Years in Archaeology*, 1931.

NOEL RAWNSLEY, whose father Canon Hardwicke Rawnsley had visited Petrie twelve years earlier at Meidum (see p. 130), joined the same excavation at Abydos. Here he recalls the daily routine:

At night, rolled snug in bed, one felt the pleasures of being wild. To snuff deliciously the sun-burnt blankets, to dodge the twinkling stars which peered laughingly through a gap in the plank roof, to hear a wild dog lap, lapping at the water in the canvas bath a few feet off in the dead, still night, all such experiences thrill the mind.

Soon every sense became alert. The time of night was told us by the barking of the village dogs, and every hour of the twenty-four had some distinction.

Memories of the early morning are indissolubly linked with an imperious question as to what one would like to drink with breakfast. In the first struggle of the mind to choose between the 'coffee, tea, or cocoa' there was rebellion in the heart.

'What! still another day begun? I haven't had a reasonable share of sleep. Egyptian days and nights are not proportionate.' Then came a gasp, and fists go up to eyes. Slowly one lifts the ponderous weight of sleep which sits upon the head. Death slacks her grasp, and there, before our partly opened eyes, the artist of the world is up and busy with his paint box. It is the old,

old order of the reds and orange; and while he sweeps his magic brush across the desert and splashes up the shadows of the sand hills we must begin our day.

First comes an ice-cold bath. The air is crisp and chill. How nice the prospect of a plate of porridge! What envy for the lucky ones who live on sausages and buttered eggs, and bread, and scones all piping hot! 'Futur hadr' (breakfast ready) shouts Mohammed, and off we go to breakfast.

Visions of ham and eggs are lost in the reality of other food; and though the tea is somewhat strong and scarcely nice instead of milk with porridge, and though ship's biscuits ill replace the bread, or cold tinned tongue the contents of the sizzling frying pan, we manage well enough with these. Thoughts of digestion must be set aside and, as for cold – the sun will soon be strong.

We sit on empty boxes to discuss our meals. The dining room is floored with sand. It is an oblong room and down its centre is a rough trestle table. The boards are somewhat warped and stained, and on them range the bowls of food or opened tins, covered with dishes or saucers to exclude the dust. Along each side-wall is a single plank for shelf, where lie the records of the former excavations, a few odd finds, the public ink and pens and rolls of copied hieroglyphs.

At one end near a door is an oil stove and at the other, near a second entrance are placed rough shelves for crockery and cups and plates. Through the narrow window holes which give just light enough for us to eat, we can see a few Arab boys out on the sand, beyond the well. Presently one or two of our workmen come down from their huts and stand at the compound wall asking for saws or ropes, crowbars or other special tackle. Then it is we learn one of the first rules of the camp. The compound is to be regarded as our sacred ground. No Arab is allowed to come inside the small enclosure except our servant, and all requests, complaints or salutations must be addressed from a respectful distance.

Our breakfast finished, we turn out to find the workmen tramping off in their white twisted turbans, rough brown goat hair abbas and their red boat shaped shoes, with turiahs upon their shoulders and palm leaf baskets slung behind. By twos and threes they disappear in various directions; but there remains a crowd of boys where just before we saw but one or two. These are the villagers who wish to be engaged for basket work.

The store shed must be opened, the tins of tongue and mince and salmon, pineapple and pears and plums brought out, the tough ship's biscuits and the jam. The finds of yesterday must all be marked and carefully arranged, great treasures buried in the sand, and others wrapped and packed in empty tins.

This is the work of a morning for one of the party. Others set out for their different diggings, and those who like can make their beds and hang their blankets and their towels in the sun before they go. Some forage for a lunch of the never varying biscuit, tinned necessaries and a bottle of boiled water to take along with them.

Noel Rawnsley, 'Sketches of Life and Labour in the Excavators' Camp', 1904.

ONE major, and potentially time-wasting, occupational hazard for archaeologists was visitors. Well-connected travellers came bearing a letter of introduction, perhaps even from the Viceroy, and expecting to catch some dramatic discovery. The American artist Joseph Lindon Smith, who spent many seasons painting the ancient art of Egypt, recounts one such occasion at Karnak.

One afternoon he sent for me when the head and shoulders of a large black granite statue were brought far enough out of the mud to be clearly seen. Large wooden beams were thrust beneath the statue for support. Legrain was jubilant. We spent much time down in the mud examining the fine head and face. Meanwhile a boy came with a telegram for Legrain, who read it and handed it to me. It was from Cromer saying that Lord and Lady X— would be arriving at Luxor the following day and to show them something 'particularly interesting.'

We clambered out of the hole, and Legrain screamed to his workmen, 'Pull out the beams and let the statue sink down.'

The men looked puzzled and hesitant about obeying such an unexpected order. Legrain screamed at them again louder. And down into the mud disappeared the head that had taken so much effort to raise. He said to me with a broad grin, 'I intend to "discover" a statue for Cromer's distinguished guests. You must help me in creating an atmosphere of expectancy.'

The next morning I found, commanding a view of the spot where we had seen the statue, two gilt, upholstered armchairs and over them a large sunshade. And a bit of red carpet had been spread to the chairs from the nearest point of entry. I was on hand to take part in the reception of the distinguished couple, who appeared towards the late afternoon with a dragoman, maid, and other attendants.

Legrain, looking doubtfully at her Ladyship's very high, narrow heels, asked how much walking they wished to do.

'Not much,' she said. 'Haven't you something unusual quite near at hand?'

I had my cue in Legrain's nod and asked, 'How about your new excavations, Legrain?'

She took fire at once, and we all walked together through the Hypostyle Hall, while Legrain talked briefly about Karnak. Beyond the third pylon she caught sight of the red carpet and the armchairs beyond. In obvious relief, the visitors settled themselves comfortably. And Legrain explained, again briefly, what he was doing.

'Do you mean to say in that muddy water in which

those half naked men are splashing about some object of value may be found?' she asked.

Legrain shrugged his shoulders, winked surreptitiously at me, and said, 'One never knows.'

'It's in the lap of the gods,' I added, 'and a wonderful moment when it happens.'

'It must be,' remarked his Lordship with the first spark of enthusiasm he had shown.

Legrain's timing was perfect. There was some desultory conversation before he gave a signal to his workmen submerged almost to their armpits. They at once redoubled their efforts, and louder and louder came their song, until it reached a crescendo, and their muscles strained as the head of a statue became visible. The visitors jumped from their chairs, their excited shouts mingling with the triumphant cries of the workmen as, leaning forward, they almost lost their balance and fell into the pit. Higher and higher the head was lifted until the shoulders and breast appeared out of the muddy depths.

Joseph Lindon Smith, *Tombs, Temples and Ancient Art*, 1956.

FOR every moment, real or simulated, of excitement and discovery, excavation brings countless others of monotonous labour. Here Bernard Pyne Grenfell describes the excavations he conducted for classical papyri at Bahnasa (ancient Oxyrhynchus) on behalf of the Egypt Exploration Fund in the late 1890s and 1900s.

The method of digging a mound on a large scale is extremely simple. The workmen are divided into groups of 4 or 6, half men, half boys, and in the beginning are arranged in a line along the bottom of one side of a mound, each group having a space two metres broad and about 3 metres long assigned to it. At Oxyrhynchus the level at which damp has destroyed all papyrus is in the flat ground within a few inches of the surface, and in a mound this damp level tends to rise somewhat, though of course not nearly so quickly as the mound rises itself. When one trench has been dug down to the damp level, one proceeds to excavate another immediately above it, and throw the earth into the trench which has been finished, and so on right through the mound until one reaches the crest, when one begins again from the other side. The particular mixture of earth mixed with straw and bits of wood in which papyrus is found, and which is to the papyrus digger what quartz is to the gold-seeker, sometimes runs in clearly marked strata between other layers of cinders, bricks or all kinds of debris containing no papyrus, but in many of the mounds at Oxyrhynchus papyri are found continuously down to a depth of five or even eight metres. As a rule the well preserved documents are discovered within 3 metres of the surface; in the lower strata the papyri tend to be more fragmentary, though our trenches in a few mounds have reached 9 metres at the highest parts before coming to the damp level . . .

Most of the larger pieces are found by the men working in the trench, who of course have to use their hands entirely, not the hoes, when it is a question of extricating so delicate a material; but it is inevitable that small pieces should be sometimes passed over by the man who is actually digging, and each basketful has to be examined carefully when it is emptied.

The clouds of dust and sand, which are quite inevitable when one is digging in very loose dry soil on the edge of the desert, give you an idea of the difficulties under which the excavator for papyri has to work. It is really marvellous how the men manage to keep their eyes open through it all. The brick building on the top of the mound is a much venerated shekh's tomb. The large mediaeval and modern Necropolis of Behnesa extends over part of the ancient mounds, and in this mound in particular the presence of the tombs on the summit presented considerable obstacles to our work, which however we were, fortunately for science, able to overcome. On completing our excavations in it, we restored and repainted the shekh's tomb, and this circumstance coupled with the fact that on one very windy day I was obliged owing to the dust to tie a handkerchief over one eye, has given rise to a curious legend. They will tell you if you go to Behnesa, how when we were digging that mound the spirit of the shekh appeared to me in a dream, and after vainly trying to persuade me to desist from our excavations threatened me with blindness, which duly fell upon me (there the handkerchief comes in). Afterwards however the shekh reflected that the poor people of the village had been earning very high wages by the work (one gives a bakhshish for each papyrus found in addition to the daily wage, and the luckier workmen were receiving what were for them considerable sums), and that after all we had no intention of disturbing his own tomb; so he repented and appeared again to me and consented to restore my sight on condition that I repainted his tomb and made it the finest of all the shekh's tombs in the cemetery, as indeed it now unquestionably is.

Reproduced in T.G.H. James (ed.), *Excavating in Egypt*, 1982.

FROM 1929 to 1934, many hundreds of miles further south in Lower Nubia, Professor Walter Emery led the Second Archaeological Survey, which examined all the ancient sites threatened by the enlargement of the Aswan Dam. Twenty-five years later, when the construction of the new High Dam was proposed, whose waters would occupy the entire width of the Nile valley, Emery supplied notes of his excavation procedure to assist UNESCO's rescue campaign. These notes, designed to explain 'the only practical way in which cemetery digging can be done when the expedition is constantly on the move and no time is to be lost', demonstrate the meticulous approach that, by now, was common to all archaeologists.

1. When the cemetery site is discovered the area is cleared down to the original ground-level, disclosing the grave superstructure, if any, or the top of the grave pits. During this operation, notes will be taken of stratification (a rare feature in the Nubian desert) and the position of pottery offerings outside the superstructures (a common feature in the C-group period).

2. Each grave or superstructure is numbered with the numerals painted in black on a flat stone.

3. General photographs are taken of the cemetery before any further excavation is undertaken.

4. Photographs are taken of individual superstructures with scale stick and number plainly visible.

5. The recorder then draws a plan and section on his tomb card to a scale of 1:25.

6. The recorder draws each offering pot on the tomb card to a scale of 1:5, noting the following points:

(a) Ware, slip, painted or incised decorations, etc.

(b) Position of offering in relation to the superstructure.

7. The offering pots are marked (in chinagraph) as follows:

350 (Cemetery no.); 5 (Grave no.); I Cat. no.) = 350/5–1.

8. The pottery is removed.

9. After all such surface recording is completed the workmen remove the superstructures, disclosing the mouths of the grave pits. The numbered stone marking each burial is placed at the top right-hand corner of the grave pit.

10. General photographs are taken of the cemetery when all the superstructures are removed.

11. The skilled workmen then clear the grave under the direct supervision of individual recorders, who note

on the tomb card such details as type of filling, etc.

12. When the grave is cleared and its contents disclosed it is photographed with scale stick and number plainly showing.

13. The recorder draws the plan of the grave and the contents to a scale of 1:25, inserting it in relation to the superstructure already drawn on the tomb card.

14. The recorder removes the objects, one by one, but does not disturb the skeleton. As each object is removed he numbers it (with chinagraph) and marks his tomb card drawing with the same number, showing its position in the grave.

15. As each object is removed from the grave the recorder draws it to scale on the tomb card: pottery at 1:5, beads and smaller objects at 1:2 or 1:1.

16. When all objects are removed the skeleton is examined, and general information, such as sex, age, etc., marked on the tomb card. The skull is removed for measurement, and if it or other parts of the skeleton show features of anatomical importance they are preserved. Otherwise they are left.

Note: Information of anatomical detail is not recorded on the tomb card, only sex, age and general observations.

17. After the removal of the skeleton, and any remaining objects which may be found below it, the sand deposit is sieved.

18. The orientation of the grave is taken by compass and the plan on the tomb card is marked by a large arrow drawn straight through it.

19. When all graves have been recorded the surveyor makes a map of the position of each number stone which has been placed at the top right-hand corner of each grave.

20. When this work is completed he will present a map, on tracing paper *or* linen (Scale 1:25), consisting of numbered dots. Then, placing each individual tomb card plan under its corresponding number, the card can be twisted to its correct orientation and the plan traced on to the map. Only the tomb plan and the skeleton are shown on this general map of the cemetery.

RECORDING AT THE BASE CAMP

The four essential records which must be kept on a day-to-day basis are:

1. The Diary, which must be written up at the end of each day of excavation by the Director. For this purpose each member of the expedition will give him the tomb cards and field notes that he has made during the day. From this material he will compile a short account of the progress of the work, and his observations and conclusions.

2. Pottery register (in duplicate), with each pot typed according to the Corpus. A Corpus is already in existence from the previous Archaeological Survey (1929–34) and it is the duty of the archaeologist in charge of this section to keep it up to date by adding any new type which may occur. The pottery of the Corpus is drawn to a scale of 1:5.

3. Object register (in duplicate). With this is included a bead Corpus, which again can be based on the existing Corpus of the Archaeological Survey of 1929–34.

4. Photograph register and the attachment of the relevant photographs (when printed) to the back of the tomb cards.

Walter B. Emery, *Egypt in Nubia*, 1965.

YET it would be wrong to leave Egyptian archaeology under the misapprehension that the excitement and the sense of mysterious contact with long-vanished civilizations have disappeared. In the early 1930s Mary Chubb gave up her desk job with the Egypt Exploration Society in London to work as assistant to John Pendlebury, Director of the Society's excavations at Tell el Amarna. Though her varied work included recording objects brought in to the expedition house from the dig, she sometimes assisted in the excavations themselves. Here she relates her discovery of a statue of Ankhesenpaaten, wife of Tutankhamun.

The afternoon wore on and the heap had been reduced to a foot or so above ground level, when my brush moved over something curved and hard; perhaps a big stone. I blew away the sand, and saw a grey-white ridged surface, with flecks of black paint; certainly not a stone. Hilda leaned over and looked.

'Try getting the stuff away from the front,' she said. 'We ought to get a look at it from another angle, before it's moved.' I came round and began brushing and blowing at the vertical side of the heap. Down trickled the sand between the harder bits of mud brick, like tiny yellow waterfalls, and nearer and nearer I came to the side of the buried object. A final gentle stroke with a brush tip, and the whispering sand slid away from the surface – and we could see more of the grey and white ridges, and beneath it a smooth curve of reddish-brown paint. The sand had poured away below it and left a cavity. 'Can you see inside the hollow?' Hilda asked. I lay down flat and got one eye as close as I could to the rubble.

And then I suddenly saw what the brownish paint was – part of a small face. I could just see the curved chin and the corner of a darker painted mouth. Hilda knelt up and beckoned to John, who was not far away.

'It's the head of a statue, I think,' she said quietly as he joined us. He took a long look, and then sat back on his heels. His face was very compressed and tense.

'I'll wait while you get it out,' was all he said.

Infinitely slowly we cut back the caked rubble in which it was embedded. The hardest thing on earth is to go slow when you are excited. But we had to – we could never tell how strong or how fragile a find was until it was finally detached from its hiding-place. For all we knew there might be a crack right across the unseen face, so that the whole thing might crumble into powder at a clumsy movement.

We widened the cavity just beneath it, so that John could get his fingers into it in case the head dropped suddenly. He held them here unmoving for at least five minutes, while we worked round the top. 'It's coming,' he said suddenly.

Hilda blew once more at the surface, and the head sank on to John's hand. He drew it slowly away from the debris. Then very gently he turned the head over on his palm.

Framed by a dark ceremonial wig, the face of a young girl gazed up at us with long, beautifully modelled eyes beneath winging dark eyebrows. The corners of the sweet, full mouth drooped a little. The childish fullness of the brown cheeks contrasted oddly with the tiny determined pointed chin. Somehow the sculptor had caught the pathetic dignity of youth burdened with royalty. The little head was another exquisite example of the genius of the sculptors of Akhenaten's day for perceiving more than the surface truth, and expressing to perfection what they had seen.

I looked up from the head to John's face. In those few moments it had completely lost its gaunt grey look of the past few weeks. He knelt there in the dust, brown and radiant, looking down at the beautiful thing on his hand.

'Now,' he said slowly, 'our season has been crowned.'

Mary Chubb, *Nefertiti Lived Here*, 1954.

II

Aswan and into Nubia

FROM Thebes, bolder travellers and those, in the days of sail, with ample time at their disposal, headed further upstream, first to Aswan, 140 miles to the south, and then across the border of ancient Egypt into Nubia. Aswan brought a welcome end to the long monotony of the Nile voyage and a sense, too, of unknown lands ahead. The streets and bazaars were thronged with many different races, great caravans set off across the still relatively unexplored desert. Amelia Edwards describes it.

By far the most amusing sight in Assûan was the traders' camp down near the landing-place. Here were Abyssinians like slender-legged baboons; wild-looking Bishariyah and Ababdeh Arabs with flashing eyes and flowing hair; sturdy Nubians the colour of a Barbedienne bronze; and natives of all tribes and shades, from Kordofân and Sennâr, the deserts of Bahuda and the banks of the Blue and White Niles. Some were returning from Cairo; others were on their way thither. Some, having disembarked their merchandise at Mahatta (a village on the other side of the Cataract), had come across the desert to re-embark it at Assûan. Others had just disembarked theirs at Assûan, in order to re-embark it at Mahatta. Meanwhile, they were living *sub Jove;* each entrenched in his own little redoubt of piled-up bales and packing-cases, like a spider in the centre of his web; each provided with his kettle and coffee-pot, and an old rug to sleep and pray upon. One sulky old Turk had fixed up a roof of matting, and furnished his den with a *Kafas*, or palm-wood couch; but he was a self-indulgent exception to the rule.

Some smiled, some scowled, when we passed through the camp. One offered us coffee. Another, more obliging than the rest, displayed the contents of his packages. Great bundles of lion and leopard skins, bales of cotton, sacks of henna-leaves, elephant-tusks swathed in canvas and matting, strewed the sandy bank. Of gum-arabic alone there must have been several hundred bales; each bale sewn up in a raw hide and tied with thongs of hippopotamus leather. Towards dusk, when the camp-fires were alight and the evening meal was in course of preparation, the scene became wonderfully picturesque. Lights gleamed; shadows deepened; strange figures stalked to and fro, or squatted in groups amid their merchandise. Some were baking flat cakes; others stirring soup, or roasting coffee. A hole scooped in the sand, a couple of stones to support the kettle, and a handful of dry sticks, served for kitchen-range and fuel. Meanwhile all the dogs in Assûan prowled round the camp, and a jargon of barbaric tongues came and went with the breeze that followed the sunset.

I must not forget to add that among this motley crowd we saw two brothers, natives of Khartûm. We met them first in the town, and afterwards in the camp. They wore voluminous white turbans, and flowing robes of some kind of creamy cashmere cloth. Their small proud heads and delicate aristocratic features were modelled on the purest Florentine type; their eyes were long and liquid; their complexions, free from any taint of Abyssinian blue or Nubian bronze, were intensely, lustrously, magnificently black. We agreed that we had never seen two such handsome men. They were like young and beautiful Dantes carved in ebony; Dantes unembittered by the world, unsicklied by the pale cast of thought, and glowing with the life of the warm South.

Amelia Edwards, *A Thousand Miles Up the Nile*, 1877.

MAXIME DU CAMP and Gustave Flaubert, both of whom had
a lively appreciation of the exotic and the sensual, enjoyed a
dancing display staged for them at Aswan in April 1850.

One morning in the bazaar, under a roof of mere straw
matting that filters the sun – there is many a tear made
by the heads of passing dromedaries – I was sitting
lunching on fresh fish and dates when an unveiled
woman stopped beside me. She kissed my hand respect-
fully and said:

'I am a dancer; my body is suppler than a snake's; if
you wish, I can come with my musicians and dance
barefoot on the deck of your boat.'

'The *cawadja* [master] has seen Kuchuk Hanem at
Esna,' Joseph answered her.

'Kuchuk Hanem doesn't know how to dance,' she
replied.

I told Joseph to accept; and towards evening, when
the setting sun had tempered the heat and shadows
spread over the river bank, the dancer came with her
players of the *rebec* [fiddle] and the *darabukeh* [drum].

She was a tall Nubian, born in Korosko, named
Azizeh.

She is elegant, and almost awesome, with her black
skin, like bronze in its nuances of green and copper; her
crinkly hair, full of gold piastres, is barely covered by a
yellow kerchief dotted with blue flowers; her markedly
slitted eyes seem like silver globes inset with black diamonds, and they are veiled and languid like those of an
amorous cat. Her white, even teeth glitter from behind
the thin lips of her mouth; a long necklace of sequins
hangs down to her belly, which is circled by a girdle of
glass beads that I can see through the diaphanous folds
of her clothing.

Her dance is savage, and makes one think involuntarily of the contortions of the negroes of central Africa. Sometimes she uttered a shrill cry, as though to spur the zeal of her musicians. Between her fingers her noisy castanets tinkled and rang unceasingly.

'*Cawadja*, what do you think of Kuchuk Hanem now?' she cried, as she writhed her hips.

She held out her two long arms, black and glistening, shaking them from shoulder to wrist with an imperceptible quivering, moving them apart with soft and quick motions like those of the wings of a hovering eagle. Sometimes she bent completely over backwards, supporting herself on her hands in the position of the dancing Salomé over the left portal of the Rouen cathedral.

All the sailors from the boats moored at Assuan, and the town loungers, and slaves and slave-traders, gathered opposite my *cange* and watched and applauded the strange dancer, who was proud of the admiration she aroused.

Maxime du Camp, *Le Nil, Egypte et Nubie*, from *Flaubert in Egypt*, translated and edited by Francis Steegmuller, 1972.

HAVING negotiated the First Cataract, a series of whirlpools and eddies created by rocks and rocky islands in the river, travellers now made for the sacred island of Philae, the 'jewel of Egypt', site of the lovely Temple of Isis (third century BC). Two letters written from the island, one by Edward Lear to his sister in 1854, the other ten years later by Lucie Duff Gordon to her husband, convey, in their very different reactions, something of the spirit of the place.

Temple of Isis, Philæ. 3 Feb., 7th., 1854.

My dear Ann,

Tomorrow I set out on *my return*, & I hope to post
this letter at Assouàn; I have been here 8 whole days, &
am very glad I decided on not going further south, as
this most beautiful place alone has enough to occupy an
artist for months. We did not bring our boat up here,
but, transporting a portion of luggage, beds, cookery
things etc. we came here by land, – swept out rooms in
the great temple, & have been quite comfortable in them
during our stay. 3 or 4 English boats have generally been
on the island, so we have had dinner parties, & music
every evening nearly. As for me, I have been at work
every day throughout the whole daylight hours, & so
charming is the place & the climate that I shall be very
sorry to leave it. It is impossible to describe the place to
you, any further than by saying it is more like a real
fairy island than anything else I can compare it to. It is
very small, & was formerly all covered with temples, of
which the ruins of 5 or 6 now only remain. The great
T. of Isis, on the terrace of which I am now writing, is
so extremely wonderful that no words can give the least
idea of it. The Nile is divided here into several channels,
by other rocky islands, & beyond you see the desert &
the great granite hills of Assouàn. At morning & evening
the scene is lovely beyond imagination. – I have done
very little in oils, as the colours dry fast, & the sand
injures them; water colours also are very difficult to use.
But I have made a great many outlines, & I hope my
journeys will eventually prove to have been of great
service to me; in health, it certainly has been so already, –
as I am now quite strong & well.— ...

As for Nubians, (for Philæ is in Nubia,) I cannot say
they have delighted me; – they are all so saturated with
castor oil, that I am literally sick if they come near me—;
besides they have rings in their noses. Bah! — Now I
shall leave off till I get to Assouàn, – where I will finish
& post this shabby epistle. Dinner is ready, macaroni,
turkey, rock pigeons, & pancakes.

Edward Lear, *Selected Letters*, 1988.

We spent two days and nights at Philæ and *Wallahy!* it was hot. The basalt rocks which enclose the river all round the island were burning. Sally and I slept in the Osiris chamber, on the roof of the temple, on our air-beds. Omar lay across the doorway to guard us, and Arthur and his Copt, with the well-bred sailor Ramadan, were sent to bivouac on the Pylon. Ramadan took the hareem under his special and most respectful charge, and waited on us devotedly, but never raised his eyes to our faces, or spoke till spoken to. Philæ is six or seven miles from Assouan, and we went on donkeys through the beautiful Shellaleeh (the village of the cataract), and the noble place of tombs of Assouan. Great was the amazement of everyone at seeing Europeans so out of season; we were like swallows in January to them. I could not sleep for the heat in the room, and threw on an *abbayeh* (cloak) and went and lay on the parapet of the temple. What a night! What a lovely view! The stars gave as much light as the moon in Europe, and all but the cataract was still as death and glowing hot, and the palm-trees were more graceful and dreamy than ever. Then Omar woke, and came and sat at my feet, and rubbed them, and sang a song of a Turkish slave. I said, 'Do not rub my feet, oh brother – that is not fit for thee' (because it is below the dignity of a free Muslim altogether to touch shoes or feet), but he sang in his song, 'The slave of the Turk may be set free by money, but how shall one be ransomed who has been paid for by kind actions and sweet words?' Then the day broke deep crimson, and I went down and bathed in the Nile, and saw the girls on the island opposite in their summer fashions, consisting of a leathern fringe round their slender hips – divinely graceful – bearing huge saucer-shaped baskets of corn on their stately young heads; and I went up and sat at the end of the colonnade looking up into Ethiopia, and dreamed dreams of 'Him who sleeps in Philæ,' until the great Amun Ra kissed my northern face too hotly, and drove me into the temple to breakfast, and coffee, and pipes, and *kief*. And in the evening three little naked Nubians rowed us about for

two or three hours on the glorious river in a boat made
of thousands of bits of wood, each a foot long; and
between whiles they jumped overboard and disappeared, and came up on the other side of the boat.

Lucie Duff Gordon, *Letters from Egypt*, 1865.

THE opening of the first Aswan Dam, known as the British
Dam, in 1901 all but engulfed the temple and its surrounding
buildings, as Janet Ross, Lucie Duff Gordon's daughter,
found when she paid a farewell visit to Egypt, after many
years' absence, in 1903.

The head of the works at the dam, a pleasant Scot-
chman, sent his steam-launch one morning and we went
up the river. Disembarking at the dam we walked some
way along it, and I could not help thinking how jealous
the old Pharaohs would have been of that mighty work.
The great river was bridled, stopped in its rushing,
tearing course, and instead of dangerous foaming cat-
aracts there was a large placid lake up which we rowed
to Philæ. I confess that in spite of my admiration for the
colossal barrage, and the knowledge that it had brought
food and prosperity to thousands of *fellaheen*, and would
prevent seasons of scarcity or of devastating floods such
as I had seen in bygone years, the first sight of Philæ
was really painful. The waving palm trees were all dead
and stood out yellow-brown against the blue sky; the
sunt bushes were dead, a tangle of withered branches

wrapped in withered weeds left by the receding waters
of last year; the beautiful temples no longer stood high
on a green island, the water nearly touched their steps,
and in a few weeks would rise and rise and cover them
nearly to the roofs. I sought out the Osiris chamber
where my mother slept when she went up to Philæ in
May, 1864, or rather tried to sleep, but was driven out
by the heat, and passed the night on the parapet of the
temple. The foundation of all the buildings had been
carefully strengthened with cement and all that was
possible had been done to save them from destruction –
but Philæ, beautiful, wonderful Philæ, was no more. For
a few minutes hatred of the utilitarian science which had
destroyed such loveliness possessed us.

Janet Ross, *The Fourth Generation*, 1912.

NOT until the 1970s did Philae re-emerge from the waters of
the Nile. The buildings, doomed by the construction of the
modern High Dam, were taken down stone by stone and re-
erected on the neighbouring island of Agilkia.

The great rock-cut temples of Abu Simbel, with their four
colossal statues of Ramesses II, were now the goal. In Nubia,
Amelia Edwards writes, 'the desert is ever present. We
cannot forget it, if we would. The barren mountains press
upon our path, showering down avalanches of granite on the
one side and torrents of yellow sand on the other. We know
that these stones are always falling; that those sands are
always drifting; that the river has to work hard to hold its
own; and that the desert is silently encroaching day by day.'
Amelia's enthusiasm and descriptive powers never flagged,
even after many weeks and many hundreds of miles of dedicated sight-seeing up the Nile. Here she brings us to the
Great Temple.

When we came up again, the moon had risen, but the breeze had dropped. Still we moved, impelled by a breath so faint that one could scarcely feel it. Presently even this failed. The sail collapsed; the pilot steered for the bank; the captain gave the word to go aloft – when a sudden puff from the north changed our fortunes, and sent us out again with a well-filled sail into the middle of the river.

None of us, I think, will be likely to forget the sustained excitement of the next three hours. As the moon climbed higher, a light more mysterious and unreal than the light of day filled and overflowed the wide expanse of river and desert. We could see the mountains of Abou Simbel standing as it seemed across our path, in the far distance – a lower one first; then a larger; then a series of receding heights, all close together, yet all distinctly separate.

That large one – the mountain of the Great Temple – held us like a spell. For a long time it looked a mere mountain like the rest. By and by, however, we fancied we detected a something – a shadow – such a shadow as might be cast by a gigantic buttress. Next appeared a black speck no bigger than a porthole. We knew that this black speck must be the doorway. We knew that the great statues were there, though not yet visible; and that we must soon see them.

For our sailors, meanwhile, there was the excitement of a chase. The Bagstones and three other dahabeeyahs were coming up behind us in the path of the moonlight. Their galley fires glowed like beacons on the water; the nearest about a mile away, the last a spark in the distance. We were not in the mood to care much for racing tonight; but we were anxious to keep our lead and be first at the mooring-place.

To run upon a sandbank at such a moment was like being plunged suddenly into cold water. Our sail flapped furiously. The men rushed to the punting poles. Four jumped overboard, and shoved with all the might of their shoulders. By the time we got off, however, the other boats had crept up half a mile nearer; and we had hard work to keep them from pressing closer on our heels.

At length the last corner was rounded, and the Great Temple stood straight before us. The façade, sunk in the mountain-side like a huge picture in a mighty frame, was now quite plain to see. The black speck was no longer a porthole, but a lofty doorway.

Last of all, though it was night and they were still not much less than a mile away, the four colossi came out, ghost-like, vague, and shadowy, in the enchanted moonlight. Even as we watched them, they seemed to grow – to dilate – to be moving towards us out of the silvery distance.

It was drawing on towards midnight when the Philæ at length ran in close under the Great Temple. Content with what they had seen from the river, the rest of the party then went soberly to bed; but the Painter and the Writer had no patience to wait till morning. Almost before the mooring-rope could be made fast, they had jumped ashore and begun climbing the bank.

They went and stood at the feet of the colossi, and on the threshold of that vast portal beyond which was darkness. The great statues towered above their heads. The river glittered like steel in the far distance. There was a keen silence in the air; and towards the east the Southern Cross was rising. To the strangers who stood talking there with bated breath, the time, the place, even the sound of their own voices, seemed unreal. They felt as if the whole scene must fade with the moonlight, and vanish before morning.

Amelia Edwards, *A Thousand Miles Up the Nile*, 1877.

ABU SIMBEL had only been known to European travellers since the Swiss explorer Jean-Louis Burckhardt had discovered the statues by chance, more than half buried in sand, in 1813. Burckhardt told Giovanni Belzoni about his discoveries and, attracted as always by an impossible challenge, Belzoni set out to excavate. His first attempt failed. For his second, in 1817, he was joined by two English naval captains, Charles Irby and James Mangles, who were making a lengthy journey through Europe and the Near East. Belzoni and his associates, working with little money and even less equipment in the blazing heat of midsummer, were beset with difficulties: arguments over pay and backsheesh, poor food supplies, and above all the intractable nature of the task. Let Irby and Mangles tell the story in excerpts from their journal.

July 11. – The temple is situated on the side of the Nile, between 200 and 300 yards from its western bank; it stands upon an elevation, and its base is considerably above the level of the river. It is excavated in the mountain, and its front presents a flat surface of upwards of 60 feet in height, above the summit of the sand immediately over the door, but not so much as 40 on the north side, and a little more on the south; the breadth is 117 feet. Above 30 feet of the height of the temple, from the base, is covered by the accumulated sand in the centre, and about 50 feet on either side. The surface fronting the river is hemmed in by a mountain of sand leaning against it; and the door in the centre is buried beneath this sand, which rises on each side of it, increasing the labour and difficulty of digging in a prodigious degree: for no sooner is the sand in the centre removed, than that on either side pours down, so that to gain a foot in the centre, we had to remove the whole mass of sand which leaned against the temple; this sand also was of so fine a description, that every particle of it would go through an hour-glass. In front of the temple are four sitting colossal figures cut out of the solid mountain, chairs and all: they are, however, brought out so fully, that the backs do not touch the wall, but are full eight feet from it; and were it not for a narrow ridge of the rock which joins them to the surface, from the back part of the necks downwards, they would be wholly detached ...

On the first day, the fifty men that came worked very badly, and we found that the burthen of the song which they sung, by way of stimulating each other, was, 'that it was christian money they were working for – that christian money was very good, and that they would get as much of it as they could.' This Nubian song, though cheering to them, was not much so to us. In the evening we returned to the village of Abou-Simbel; and perceiving we should never make any progress with people who, being sure of their pay whether they laboured well or ill, would only work five hours in the day, we sent to the cashiefs, and concluded a bargain with them and the natives '*to open the temple*' for 300 piastres. At this time none of us thought it would take more than four days to accomplish the undertaking; so little did we know of the real nature of our enterprise ...

Monday, July 21. – This day no men came from the opposite side of the river, but we had about forty from Abou-Simbel. They worked tolerably well, and brought to light the bend of the right arm of the statue, to the north of the door, which was much broken. The discovery was highly satisfactory to us, as it proved that the statues were seated, and, consequently, that we should not have to dig down so deep as if they had been standing figures. In the evening, the men worked pretty well; and towards the close of the day, we uncovered a projecting part of the wall roughly chiselled, uneven in its surface, and having every appearance of unfinished work. As far as we could see down, which was not more than six or eight inches, it still continued the same. The projection was about four inches from the plane surface of the front of the temple, and it appeared to fill up the whole space between the two centre statues. This being exactly the place where we expected to find the door, the sudden change from a flat finished exterior to a coarsely-chiselled uneven surface, was precisely the circumstance most calculated to give the impression that the temple was unfinished, and that there was no door. Indeed we could not in any other way account for an appearance so extraordinary and unexpected. Discouraging as this discovery was, we nevertheless resolved to proceed with our work, and to dig down till we had ascertained, beyond all possibility of doubt, whether there was an entrance or not . . .

Sunday, July 27. – At dawn of day we set to work again, and had only two assistants besides the crew, who worked remarkably well. Several volunteers came, but we rejected them on account of their laziness. One of our two assistants sang a song to cheer up the crew: this is their constant custom when working; the words were as follows: 'Oh! Nubia, my country, thou smellest like a rose; when I sleep I dream of thee, and thou appearest a garden full of flowers.' Our ideas of Nubia, where a flowering shrub is scarcely ever seen, were not in unison with this song; but it was a new proof of that happy disposition which nature implants in the breast of every man to love his native soil, be it what it may . . .

Thursday, July 31. – In the evening we resumed our labours, with the crew and two strangers; and towards sun-set we came to the corner of the door: it was rather broken. The sailors, on seeing it, expressed great signs of joy, uttering cries of 'backsheeish, backsheeish,' and immediately asked us if it was not true, that we had promised them money whenever we should find the door. We replied, that we certainly had promised them a present, and would give it when we had entered the temple. The fellows now began working hard to enlarge the entrance, appearing in high good humour, and occasionally repeating the favourite word 'backsheeish,' tyep, tyep – good good. At dusk we had made an aperture nearly large enough for a man's body; but we could not tell whether it would be necessary to draw up the sand from the entrance or not, which left us in great uncertainty as to the time when our labours would end; for, should the temple be much filled with sand, we might have a prodigious deal of work to do yet . . .

[*Friday, August 1*] As soon as we had commenced working by candlelight, one of the crew came to say that we must embark immediately and depart, or land our effects and let the boat go, as they could wait no longer. We sent word that they might go whenever they pleased; but it would be to their own loss if they did, as we would pay them nothing; and that for our part we were determined to remain till our work was completed. The crew now made their appearance in a body, dressed in their turbans and gowns, as at Elpha; this being their custom when they wish to appear of consequence. They were armed with long sticks, pikes, swords, daggers, and two old rusty pistols, which would be more likely to kill the person who fired, than him who was fired at. In reply to our inquiry of what they wanted, they made long complaints of being badly paid, and of never having received any adequate recompense for having brought us provisions from the neighbouring villages, and for all their other endeavours to please us; that they had waited here till the last moment, and must now go down the river; all at the same time joining in savage imprecations, and scraping the sand with their hatchets and swords. The reis, who was the foremost of the party, in a feigned paroxysm of anger, threw the sand up in his face, where the perspiration caused it to stick ...

As all this farce was performed to intimidate us, and to extort a sum of money as a reward for remaining till the temple was opened, we took care that they should see by our conduct that the scheme entirely failed. Avoiding, therefore, all passionate behaviour, we replied coolly and deliberately to all their lying imputations, telling them that if they studied their own interests, they would behave very differently; that this, of all others, was the most unlikely method to obtain any thing from us; and that, as they had stayed ninety-nine days, why not remain the hundredth? At length one of the crew stepped forward, and pretended to be a peace-maker. The janissary, meantime, had squeezed himself through the hole, and entered the temple during the debate, unknown to them; till one of the strangers, having stolen behind to see what work we had done, found it out, and apprised the crew ...

We were now enabled to enter the temple; and thus ended all our doubts and anxiety. We built a wall to barricade the door: it was made of stones and mud, with a foundation of date-trees driven in to prevent the sand from giving way. A toad crept out of the temple while we were thus employed, and hid himself in the rubbish at the entrance. We brought down to the boat some statues of calcareous stone, which we found in the temple. There were two sphinxes, emblematical of Osiris (lion's body and hawk's head); a monkey similar to those over the cornice, only smaller; and a kneeling female figure, with an altar, having a ram's head on it, in her lap. At three we went to work again. Two of the Abou-Simbel peasants came, and appeared astonished that we had succeeded. They said the country people had no idea we should have accomplished our undertaking. They appeared to think the temple would make a good hiding-place for their cattle, &c., whenever the Bedouins came to rob them.

Charles Irby and James Mangles, *Travels in Egypt and Nubia*,
1823.

DURING the 1960s a massive international rescue operation was mounted by UNESCO to save Abu Simbel, and many of the other temples and ancient sites of Lower Nubia, from vanishing under the waters of the new High Dam. In the quarter century to 1960, Egypt's population had doubled. The people needed food, and the original Aswan Dam and its 1930s extension could not provide sufficient water to irrigate the productive agricultural land along the Nile valley. The new dam would flood the entire width of the valley for miles behind Aswan, creating a new lake 300 miles long and 6 miles wide that would provide a constant, regular water supply for the farmers of Egypt. The temples were cut from their rock surround, lifted up 200 feet and set down again on a purpose-built mountain, carefully landscaped to replicate their original site, some 700 feet away. Meanwhile, the new dam was under construction, a mammoth, largely Russian-organized operation. In 1965, approximately halfway through the construction period, Tom Little described the project.

Each evening was like the next. The afternoon fades sharply in scarlet behind the hills of the other bank of the river, taking with it the heavy, bludgeoning heat of the day and drawing after it the first refreshing breeze to herald the evening. For a moment the desert seems cool. Then an army of men converge on the plateau by truck and spread themselves across the face of it like platoons taking position for battle, and suddenly, with the swiftness of the last fall of dark, the scene lights up with spectacular effect on man's latest and greatest endeavour on the Nile. Arc lights sharply throw a shining pool into the immensity of the night; thin strands of silvered beads trail away towards the glow of Aswan town; the headlights of cars and trucks in the distance flit like tipsy fireflies; the lights of the township prickle in the desert near by.

The work on the dam which has been numbed by the heat of the day now gets under way to the orchestrated sounds of men and machines. The main work on the rock at the diversion channel expresses itself in a ballet of grotesque shadows. The electric shovels nuzzle their long snouts into the debris and the fire of their conflict with the rock pours in blue flame from the jaws; trucks groan with granite loads up improvised escarpments and men looking no bigger than insects crawl about everywhere ...

The plateau was broken by a series of monstrous cavities which, one could see, were blending together

as the work proceeded. At the downstream side the
diversion had already the shape of a deep valley but it
was still being excavated at different levels and a natural
block of rock stood across the mouth to keep the river
from the workings. Roads improvized on temporary
escarpments at the levels of work led only to the excavators, which chewed and groaned and sometimes
screamed as they bit into the granite left loose by the
day's dynamiting. The excavators filled a 25-ton truck in
anything from a minute and a half to two minutes and a
half and moved 130 cubic yards of rock an hour. The art
of the excavating was to ensure that a truck was always
waiting while another was filling so that the flow of rock
from the site never paused. Each digger had its line of
trucks, the empty ones rattling and bumping up the
escarpment and the loaded ones screaming in low gear as
they crawled down past them, often edging hazardously
close to the rough-cut edge of the road and the 'drop'
into the valley below.

On the upstream side of the channel, where they
had started from the natural depression in the plateau
running from Khor Kundi, the digging levels were lower
than downstream and shelved steeply from the entrance
to the 200-feet rock face of the central section, where
bays cut into the face already marked the proposed inlets
of the tunnels. This work was protected by a sand coffer
dam 65 feet high and 270 yards long, which had been
constructed in a month by sluicing over 300,000 cubic
yards of sand through pipes on the west bank, the
method that the Russian engineers intended to use for
the upstream coffer of the main dam. It was the first
time this method had been used on the Nile and was on
a small scale but it demonstrated the solidity that could
be achieved. It was firm enough to serve as a road even
for heavily laden trucks going round the excavations and
for as long as it was left in position it served as one of
the main highways at the site.

Meanwhile, men were hard at work in the belly of
the plateau cutting the tunnels. A tubular subterranean
'highway', 650 yards long and 25 yards wide had been

bored from its starting-point near the river-side on a gentle gradient until it bisected the line of the tunnels and as each in turn was reached excavation of that tunnel started immediately in both the upstream and the down-stream directions. About half the tunnel excavation had been done. Work was proceeding on four tunnels by digging out the top half of the tunnel-cylinder, leaving the bottom half of the cylinder as a temporary road for the trucks and a rock floor for the mobile drilling and concreting platforms. The difficult part of this operation was breaking into the virgin granite; the removal of the lower half of the tunnels was a normal and relatively simple job which, when the time came, proceeded at great speed. The dump trucks moved freely in both directions in and out of the workings.

Not a moment was now being wasted. As each section was excavated the teams moved in to reinforce the rock; first, the Soviet drilling teams to bore and fit the steel rods; then the placing of the seven-ton steel frames which had been erected sectionally above ground and were welded together below ground to fit the semi-cylindrical roof; and, finally, the concrete was moulded on these frames to a thickness of one yard.

As this work spread underground, the heart of the plateau acquired a nightmarish quality of light, shade and noise: the harsh glare of the floodlights and the dark brown caverns of shade, the intermittent, blinding blue light of the welding and drilling plants, dripping water and the myriad reflections on murky pools, grotesque shadows of men and machines, mud; the screech of the drills, and the throb and clank of trucks in the enclosed passages. Below ground just as much as in the channel outside the race with time was at last engaged in most spectacular fashion.

Tom Little, *High Dam at Aswan*, 1965.

12
The Suez Canal

THE Pharaohs constructed a canal from the Nile to the Red Sea at Suez. The idea of creating a physical link between the Mediterranean and the Red Sea – the seas of Europe and Asia – was much discussed in the seventeenth and eighteenth centuries. Among the party of *savants* accompanying Napoleon's invasion force in 1798 was an engineer, Charles le Père, who investigated the possibility of building a canal across the low-lying Isthmus of Suez. Although he rejected the idea – largely because of the commonly held but entirely erroneous belief that the level of the Red Sea was some thirty feet higher than that of the Mediterranean – the seeds were sown.

By the mid-nineteenth century the economic potential of the Canal was becoming increasingly obvious. European trade was expanding, the European empires were developing. That the Canal was finally built, however, was almost entirely the result of the unceasing efforts of one man, Ferdinand de Lesseps. He won the assent of the Khedive, Mohammed Said, secured finance for his Suez Canal Company against the considerable (and remarkably ill-informed) opposition of the British government, and supervised the entire construction works. Here de Lesseps recalls the November day in 1854 when his proposals were accepted.

The Viceroy's presence served to draw me out of my reverie, as he came to wish me the 'top of the morning,'

and to ask me to take him round the country which I
had ridden over the day before. Preceded by two lancers,
and followed by the staff, we reached an eminence where
the ground was strewn with stones which had formed
part of some ancient building. The Viceroy deemed this
a very suitable place to prepare for the morrow's start,
so he sent an aide-de-camp to have his tent and carriage
brought up, the latter being a sort of omnibus drawn by
six mules and fitted up as a bedroom. We rest under the
shade of the carriage, while the chasseurs build up a
circular parapet formed of stones which they had picked
up, and in this parapet they make an embrasure into
which a gun is placed to salute the troops from Alexandria which are just coming in sight. When I leave the
Viceroy to go and get my breakfast, in order to show
him how well my horse can jump, I put him over the
parapet and gallop off to my tent. You will see that this
foohardy act was one of the reasons which induced the
Viceroy's *entourage* to support my scheme, the generals
who came to breakfast with me, and who had seen the
feat, telling me as much ...

At five o'clock I again mounted my horse and came
up to the Viceroy's tent by way of the parapet. He was
very bright and good tempered, and taking me by the
hand, he led me to a divan and made me sit by his side.
We were alone, and through the opening of the tent I
could see the setting of the sun which, at its rising that
morning, had so stirred my imagination. I felt inwardly
calm and assured at the moment of entering upon a
question which was to be decisive of my future. I had
clearly before me my studies and conclusions with
regard to the canal, and the execution of the work seemed
so easy of realisation that I felt little doubt as to being
able to convince the Prince of this. I set out my project,
without entering into details, dwelling upon the principal facts and arguments set out in my memorandum,
which I had by heart. Mohammed Said listened with
evident interest to what I had to say, and I begged him
if there were any points which did not seem clear to
him to mention them to me. He, with considerable

intelligence, raised a few objections, with respect to which I was able to satisfy him, as he at last said to me: 'I am convinced; I accept your plan; we will concern ourselves during the rest of our expedition as to the means of carrying it out. You may regard the matter as settled, and trust to me.' Thereupon he summoned his generals, bade them seat themselves upon some folding chairs which were just in front of the divan, and repeated the conversation we had had together, asking them to give their opinions as to the proposals of his 'friend,' as he was pleased to call me to these improvised advisers, better suited to give an opinion as to a cavalry manoeuvre than a gigantic enterprise, the significance of which they were incapable of understanding. They stared at me and looked as if they thought that their master's friend, whom they had just seen put his horse over a wall, could not be otherwise than right, they raised their hands to their heads as their master spoke in sign of assent.

The dinner was brought in upon a salver, and just as we had all been of one assent, so we all dipped our spoons into one and the same tureen, which contained some excellent soup. Such is the faithful and true narrative of the most important negotiation I ever undertook, or am likely to undertake.

Ferdinand de Lesseps, *Recollections of Forty Years*, 1887.

THE canal promised to bring economic fortune to Suez, described by de Lesseps a few weeks later as 'an isolated point ... its population a very miserable one, having only brackish water to drink. Our canal will bring it water and activity, which it lacks.' The town was already a busy crossroads. Travellers from Palestine to Cairo passed though, it was a meeting-point for the annual pilgrimage to Mecca, and, from the 1840s onwards, the embarkation-point for travellers on the Overland Route, via Alexandria and Cairo, to India. Mrs Dawson Damer arrived on 26 December 1839, *en route* for Cairo.

The place did not possess any sort of beauty; but it borrowed a temporary interest from the circumstance of its being the season at which Hadjis of every country had assembled to embark for their pilgrimage to Mecca, and the varied form and colour of their encampments (chiefly made on the sea-shore) produced the most picturesque effect it was possible to imagine. This pilgrimage included specimens of every variety of national and oriental costume. To these Hadjis we (perhaps uncharitably) attributed the *extraneous* population of every *un*-nameable insect; for Greece, Turkey, and Syria, were clean and sweet, in comparison with this our first introduction to Egyptian plagues and customs.

During our walk homewards, we were accosted by two good-humoured-looking men, who had picked up half a dozen words of Italian, and, inquiring if we were English, added, '*Buona perchè Inglesi sempre sempre bravi.*' This acknowledgment proved quite an agreeable little incident, as the people of these countries are in general little *prévenant* or communicative, and we felt quite proud of this courteous appreciation of the English character.

In passing through the very dirty street which led to our inn, we heard a very pretty Tyrolese air, sung by some hidden performer, which national music had the effect of quite affecting the doctor, and after the dreadful discord of Arab music, even our *un*-German ears were very agreeably refreshed.

Our dinner was exactly what we might meet with at Canterbury, rather better than it would have been at Dover, and on a most liberal scale; but mulligatawny soup, round of beef, and heavy plum-pudding, were too substantial substitutes for our good and wholesome Desert fare. Before it was quite ended, the sound of drum and tabret attracted us to the door of the hotel, and we found that an Arab marriage was taking place, by the light of coloured lamps and torches, the former hung on poles, and the cry of – 'the bridegroom is coming,' was another instance of the constant recurrence of familiar images used in Scripture; and he was thus announced, as going forward to meet the bride at the mosque, where both processions were to join. The bridegroom was conducted between the other Arabs, dressed like himself, in scarlet *caftans* and white turbans, but he looked the very image of grief, and appeared more like a criminal pinioned for execution, than a *nouveau marié*.

Fancy had full scope to imagine blighted hopes and forced marriage, but the excessive din of drumming and singing made one very unpoetical.

Hon. Mary Dawson Damer, *Diary of a Tour in Greece, Turkey, Egypt and the Holy Land*, 1841.

CONSTRUCTION of the canal lasted ten years and cost about £20 million (well above the original estimate); additional money had to be raised on several occasions to enable the work to continue.

To begin with, as the *Fortnightly Review* reported, the canal was largely dug by hand. In 1864, however, the Egyptian government withdrew the compulsory labour force of 20,000 men it provided each month. The Company turned this potential setback to its advantage by using the compensation it received to mechanize. According to some commentators, without the new machinery it developed the Canal would never have been completed. The *Fortnightly Review* reports:

The principal machinery in use consists of large dredgers, with iron buckets fastened to an endless chain,

revolving over two drums – one at the end of a long
movable arm, to regulate the depth at which the scoops
are to dredge, the other at the top of a strong iron
framework which rests on the hull of the machine. These
dredgers vary in size, according to the work for which
they are required, and the ulterior disposal of the dredgings. Those more recently constructed are much larger
and more powerful than those at first employed. The
lesser ones are 15-horse power; there is also an inter-
mediate size; and then follow the largest machines of
75-horse power, 110 feet in length, with 27 feet beam,
and having their drums 48 feet above the water-line.
The cost of these is £20,000 each ... A large proportion
of the dredgings is discharged from the machines into
either an apparatus which has been named the *long
couloir* (long duct), or into the *élévateur* (elevating duct).

These two machines have been successively introduced for facilitating the disposal of the excavated soil.
As soon as the present contractors undertook the work
in 1865, up to which date comparatively little had been
accomplished, the magnitude of the enterprise would
seem at once to have determined them to avail themselves of the only mode by which it could have been
successfully accomplished within the stated time,
namely, by the application of mechanical power on a
scale hitherto unknown in any single undertaking, but
in this case, only proportionate to the results necessary
to be obtained. One of the most important machines is
the *long couloir* ... With the aid of a *long couloir*, a
dredger can work in the centre of the canal; and by one
movement the dredgings are deposited at a considerable
distance beyond the water-line, on either side, as may
be required.

The shorter *couloirs* are placed on the dredging
machine itself, and are balanced by a counterpoise on
the opposite sides. In situations where the advanced
stage of the works brings the dredgers too far below the
summit level of the embankments to render the *couloir*
any longer available, the *élévateur* is introduced. This
machine somewhat resembles in principle the one just

described, but the inclination of the plane is in the opposite direction – that is to say, upwards, instead of downwards. This duct consists of an inclined plane, about 52 yards long, and carrying two lines of tram rail. The inclination is 1 in 4, and it is supported in the middle by an iron frame, which rests on a carriage, running on rails laid for the purpose, along the bank of the canal, at an elevation of 6 feet above the water-line. The lower end of the *élévateur* reaches over the water, where it is again supported on a steam float. When this machine is at work, the lower extremity of the duct is 3 yards above the water; whereas the upper end is about 52 yards distant, with an elevation of 12 yards, thus reaching over the embankments. A lighter, containing seven boxes of dredgings, is floated under the lower extremity of the *élévateur*. Each box is raised in succession on to a truck by an endless steel-wire rope, which is adjusted in a few seconds, and it then travels to the upper end of the incline. On reaching this point the box swings vertically, when, by a self-acting contrivance, the door opens, and the contents are thus completely emptied. The empty box then runs down, suspended by its hook and chain, on the under side of the line of tram rails, which it previously traversed on its upward course.

Captain J. Clerk, *Fortnightly Review*, January 1869.

In the spring of 1869 the Prince and Princess of Wales visited the Canal after a Nile voyage. The journalist William Howard Russell, who accompanied the royal tour, reported from Ismailia, on the shore of Lake Timsah, midway along the Canal.

On the borders of the newly-created Lake, there lie stretched out magazines, storehouses, cafés, restaurants, boulevards, church, cemetery, set in a border of bright verdure fresh and blooming. The limits are sand and rock, the veritable Desert itself. Wood can be worked by Egyptian carpenters and French designers into pretty and fanciful outsides, and the necessity of procuring as much air as possible, and of keeping out sunshine and dust, conspire to the production of such fantastic contrivances in architecture, that, on the whole, the châlets are like nothing that I have ever seen. And then the gardens, where there are growing in their newly-found homes the banana, the orange, the cactus, and tropical plants in great abundance, form a charming ornament, and contribute to the light and graceful aspect of the town ...

One of the greatest charms, however, of the life of the colony is to be found in the Desert itself. The stables of the Company furnish excellent horses for the use of visitors; the chief employés have their private studs of fiery Arabs, and the young ladies have become bold and hardy horsewomen, whose greatest pleasure is to go on what is called a fantasia into the Desert, galloping over stone and sand to some spot selected for a pic-nic, and returning, after a long day, or perhaps two, to their homes. M. de Lesseps is a true hippodamos, and pushes his equestrian powers to the limits of human and equine endurance, and the gentlemen who assist him emulate his capacity. Life is 'fast' at Ismailia – at least that portion of it which the stranger sees – for the men are nearly always galloping, ventre à terre, with groups of ladies, flying like the wind; and speed – constant speed – by land and water is a necessity of existence. Early hours and constant exercise have enabled the inhabitants to resist the effects of climate and the high temperature to which they are subjected part of the year; and, to judge from their looks, they are in robust health.

The Frenchman must have his café and his billiards wherever he goes, when he has settled down to take a lease of the soil. There are several in Ismailia, as well as hotels and estaminets; and in an evening you would be tempted, as you hear the click of the billiard-balls and the rattle of the dominos, and look in through the gauze blinds and see the smoking crowds, to imagine that you were in some country quarters of La belle France, but for the deep sand, which, rising ankle deep, tells you that the city is built in the heart of the Egyptian Desert.

William Howard Russell, *A Diary in the East*, 1869.

THE opening festivities, presided over by the Empress Eugénie of France, were attended by a large party of celebrities invited by the Khedive. Every European nation and every profession was represented, though the French, as might be expected, predominated. Before the Canal celebrations began, the guests were received by the Khedive in Cairo, fêted at a grand reception and then treated to a three-week trip up the Nile to Aswan, all at the Khedive's expense (baksheesh included). That must have been a curious voyage. The Norwegian dramatist Henrik Ibsen, who shared a cabin with a Swiss army captain and composer named Knorring, recalled the journey in an unfinished prose piece written on his return to Europe.

It was a motley picture that now unfolded before us; Europe and the East in a picturesque composition. Directly in front of us stood a minaret, erect and sparkling in the sunlight. Beside it lay the ruin of a Coptic monastery, the whole front of which had collapsed into the river. For the rest, Arab huts, mounds of gravel, palms and sycamores. Inside the ruins of the monastery an Egyptian coffee-house proprietor had established himself; the coffee-room itself lay outside beneath a roof of withered palm-branches. Here we see a great concourse; long beards and long pipes are dominant; long Eastern silence and, too, long European chatter.

And familiar faces. That handsome, brown-eyed man, who at a distance so strikingly resembles Abdul Kader, and who cannot be acquitted of playing the coquette a little in his elegant silk *koffie* and white-striped Beduin *burnous*, is the archaeologist Lenormant. Beside him, alert and friendly, with red fez and sky-blue flannel shirt, sits Dr Lambert, the Murray and Baedeker of Egypt in one person. That distinguished little white-haired man, with no parasol and his felt hat pulled down like Kilian in *Ulysses von Ithaca*, is the chemist Ballard. Out on the farthest slope of the shore stands Dr Bertholet, short, robust and jovial, with a thousand items of news to shout to us. A lady glitters, the sole representative of her sex in the party; her dress is European, her proportions oriental. She is of course Madame Collet, the Parisian *littératrice*. For the moment her attention is taken up with her diary, in which our arrival is noted, that the information may be transmitted to an important French magazine. A score of baying dogs send us the usual greeting from the housetops. In doors and corners stand Arab women, staring motionlessly from behind their long black veils, and up the high gravel mounds hasten the humbler members of the populace, the *fellahs*, amid laughter and cries, pursued by policemen who, with the aid of long palm staves, seek to persuade them to lend us a hand with the mooring of the ship.

On the voyage up the Nile I felt for the first time that to belong to a small nation can have its advantages. Europeans bring bickering with them wherever they go, and so it is here. The Germans and French were, however, kind enough to take care of that, so that the rest of us had our time, and peace of mind, undisturbed. As things turned out, a few hours of intrigue and counter-intrigue ensured that our departure to Abydos should be postponed until the following morning. Only a rebellious minority of seven or eight broke away during the evening to spend the night among the ruins.

Quoted in Michael Meyer, *Henrik Ibsen*, vol. 2, 1971.

ANOTHER guest was the poet Théophile Gautier, who despite his vivid writings on the East was making his first visit to Egypt. On board ship a few hours out of Marseilles, he fell down a coal hole and broke his arm. Instead of joining the Nile voyagers, he remained despondently in Cairo, exploring the city and watching the world go by from the balcony of Shepheard's Hotel. He did manage to attend the Canal celebrations, however, and set down his impressions in a letter to his friend Carlotta Grisi.

Our expedition to the Isthmus of Suez was very picturesque and very entertaining. To avoid the long way round by Alexandria and Port Said, I went from Cairo to Ismailia, and there we camped under canvas like Arabs, as the town wasn't big enough to lodge all the guests. I was lodged, with my friends, in tent 3, facing M. de Lesseps' chalet, on the bank of the sweetwater canal encumbered with *cangs* and *dahabiehs*, local vessels very like the boats on Lake Geneva with their great scissor-sails. We had a square ante-room and an octagonal *salon*, all in canvas stretched out on stakes and held up by an ingenious system of rigging. There were five of us in it, and we got on as well as could be. We had our meals in huge tents at the expense of the Khedive or the Suez Canal Company. The assault on the table was comic and human voracity appeared in a quite bestial light. There were three services of dinner and at the last there was hardly anything but radishes, ham bones and Chester cheese. We went to meet the Empress on Lake Timsah, at the place where the maritime canal coming from Port Said, that's to say from the Mediterranean, flows into it. We went with a few Frenchmen on one of the company's steamers. When we arrived at the mouth of the canal, below the Viceroy's chalet, the cannon thundered and the imperial yacht, *l'Aigle*, made her majestic entrance into the lake. The Empress, in white with a blue veil, was standing on deck with De Lesseps at her side. At the same moment, at the other end of the lake, two big packet-boats of the Messageries, coming from Indo-China, and a Dutch vessel coming from the Red Sea through the Suez Canal, made their appearance. The effect was magic, irresistible, and so fine that there were tears in everybody's eyes; the Empress, extremely moved, had an attack of nerves and withdrew into her cabin where she relieved her emotions in abundant tears. She soon re-appeared wiping her eyes amid the acclamations of all the boats which (in spite of protocol) had closed about her. The Emperor of Austria followed on his ship, then the Crown Prince of Prussia. It was magnificent. In the evening there were illuminations, an Arab fantasia, performances by howling, groaning and spinning dervishes, pantomimes, a reception of the sheiks of the desert installed in picturesque striped and lit-up tents. The celebrations, entirely European in Cairo, were entirely Egyptian in Ismailia. It was the Viceroy's idea and did credit to his good taste. The Empress disembarked from her yacht and rode on a dromedary, which she did with consummate grace; it isn't easy, considering the animal's extremely brusque reactions. Next day we embarked on *la Péluse*, the biggest boat of the Messageries impériales, which is 105 yards long, 24 wide, weighs 2,500 tons and draws $19\frac{1}{2}$ feet. In spite of a few mishaps, next morning found us in the roads of Suez, when the sun rose on some fifty vessels, fifteen or twenty of which had been in the Mediterranean the night before. And so this ancient barrier is overcome, and when they have cut through the Isthmus of Panama, we shall sail in a matter of weeks around the world.

Quoted in Joanna Richardson, *Théophile Gautier, His Life and Times*, 1958.

SOME eighty years later the Suez Canal provided the setting for the last act of the British Empire in Egypt. In 1946 British forces were withdrawn from throughout Egypt to the Canal Zone. The presence there was substantial (some 88,000 troops during the 1950s), designed to protect the vital sea route through the Canal to British bases and colonies in Asia and the Far East. A posting to the Canal Zone was not a welcome prospect. Living conditions were primitive, there was the nagging threat of sporadic attacks by Egyptians, and the rest of Egypt was generally off-limits. Edmund Ions, who served briefly in the Canal Zone towards the end of a five-year commission, recaptures the atmosphere.

The normal consolations of a foreign posting were absent. There were no women in Falaise Camp and, according to a subaltern's reconnaisance party, none in TEKBLOC [the ordnance and supply depot] either, except for one or two nurses and WRACs whose favours were already pre-empted. We were beleaguered in an arid stretch of desert guarding a gigantic supply and arms dump half way between Ismailia and the Nile Delta. The local villages were out of bounds because of the worsening political situation, and in any case the abject poverty in the mud hovels would have made female company there an immediate health hazard, even if the Arab menfolk had not closely guarded their thin, under-nourished daughters.

After a couple of months, one came to accept Tel el Kebir for what it was: one of the worst foreign postings in the world. It was intriguing, partly saddening, to see the effects on newly arrived officers as this truth began to tell. Among our newly arrived officers was a rotund, amiable, idle captain, of independent means, who had finally been edged out of some sedentary posting in Britain to rejoin the regiment at Tel el Kebir. He liked good food, good wine, and enjoyed the temptations of the flesh when these were available. He stood with a whisky in his hand after his first dinner in the mess at Tel el Kebir, somewhat crestfallen, the food having plunged him into despondency. He asked whether the locality did not at least offer other forms of satisfaction and addressed the subalterns sitting stirring their coffee. He had a nice turn of phrase.

'Anyone know a place round here where one can put the meat, then?' The answer was no, unless he wanted to risk a pox in Ismailia, thirty miles away.

He looked glum, and called for another whisky. There was something of the philosopher and the good-natured fatalist in him, however, and he accepted the common lot. Most regiments have, or had, one of him in their midst. Indolent, slightly eccentric, a private income relieving him of ambition, he was liked by his fellow-officers, by the NCOs, and also by the men, who regarded him as a sort of mascot. His military deficiencies had to be concealed for the good of the company and sometimes for the honour of the regiment. But the incipient philosopher in him could fetch up a pithy, telling commentary on military life or on our present predicament. One evening he returned to the mess after completing his rounds as orderly officer of the day. His whisky safely lodged in his hand, he pronounced a neat summary of life for the ordinary soldiers at Falaise Camp.

'Poor buggers,' he observed. 'They come off twelve hours' guard duties; they get their sausage and mash in the cook-house; they stagger over to the NAAFI canteen to fill up with bangers and beans; they down five bottles of warm beer; they stagger across to their tents, climb under their mosquito nets, have a bloody good wank, and drop off to sleep. End of a perfect bloody day.'

To relieve the tedium a generous use of army transport was allowed to ferry the men into Ismailia when they were not on guard duties. The officers also went into Ismailia, sometimes with the troops, more often in a landrover. There was a reasonably good NAAFI club for the men, a YMCA club, and some bars still in bounds, as well as cinemas.

The officers used the three or four sailing and beach clubs sprinkled around the shores of Lake Timsah. The French Club was favourite. It was built for the French colony of technicians, engineers, and canal pilots who serviced the canal and its complex installations. British officers were allowed to join though the language barrier kept national groups apart. The French had no intention of making the further concession of speaking English. Very few British officers could manage French, so there was little rapport.

There was also a Greek Club, where the food was worse, but the music and cabaret more interesting and exotic. Nearby there were beaches where one could lie under the sun between swimming in the slightly brackish water of Lake Timsah. On most days, ships would be moving slowly across the lake as they passed between the various reaches of the canal, and small sailing boats from the clubs would be dotted about the lake. There was a timelessness about life here.

Edmund Ions, *A Call to Arms*, 1972.

FOLLOWING negotiations with the Egyptian government, the last British troops left the Canal Zone on 31 March 1956. Seven months later, in the ill-fated Suez campaign, they invaded the Canal Zone, following President Nasser's nationalization of the Canal. Having failed to win American support, Britain was plunged into immediate financial and political crisis, and was forced to withdraw after six weeks. Edward Farson served with the forces that occupied Port Said.

In a remarkably short space of time our soldiers adjusted themselves to a life of constant patrols and guards. They learnt to be suspicious, cautious and extremely observant. I shall never forget watching one Royal Scot patrol working its way slowly along the wide street that separates Arab Town from Shanty Town. It was a patrol of seven, operating in the rough shape of a diamond. The rear Jock walked slowly backwards, his loaded Bren gun, slung from the shoulder, was held at the hip. Slowly and continuously the barrel traversed the street, but I am sure it was his expression that made for the perfect behaviour of the crowd. His bonnet was back a little on his head; his young sunburnt face was set; it was quite clear to everyone – 'There will be no nonsense here.' There wasn't . . .

The success of the occupation was largely due to the high standard of junior leadership. It was the young corporal, sometimes just a private soldier, who led the patrol and got to know his area as well as the village policeman does at home. A grenade on a café table in Arab Town was seen by a passing Royal Scot. The printing press that produced most of the anti-British leaflets was discovered down a side street by Lance-Corporal Furniss of the West Yorkshires, all because he spotted that only two out of four shop shutters were padlocked. Corporal Armour of the Argylls became suspicious of two Arabs carrying baskets from a rowing boat. He gave chase and, as a result, unearthed a large dump of ammunition and explosives smuggled from the Nile Delta into the fishing village of El Qabuti. Sometimes it was the junior officer, like Tony Moorhouse, who, by patience and observance, captured seven Egyptian fedayeen in a house on the day before his abduction . . .

It was interesting to watch the reactions of the Egyptians as the time of our occupation lengthened. For the first few days, the streets were practically deserted, and the majority of shutters were closed. Gradually young men appeared, mostly, we suspected, Egyptian Army soldiers in civilian clothes and Intelligence agents sent out to pick up every available scrap of information about us. They would hang about outside unit billets, with the persistence of flies. If you drove them away, within two minutes they, or others, would be back. One map we subsequently captured showed most of our Brigade positions, so they did their work well! Many of them posed as traders, and carried a stock of wallets and necklaces. The more traditional ones had the famous postcards. As all the shops were closed, through fear of intimidation and reprisals, their trade was quite brisk. A little later, in an effort to get the shops to open, it was arranged that the soldiers could draw some of their pay in Egyptian currency. For a brief few days the real traders came out in force, and a roaring trade was established in the Rue El Gamhouriah. French parachutists, British sailors, Jocks in kilts were soon buying up every souvenir there was. Camels, pouffes, wallets, watches, Spanish fly – the whole repertoire of Port Said was displayed. One Lance-Corporal even fell for the old trick of buying a sealed bottle of gin for £2, finding to his dismay, on opening it, that it was just water!

Edward Farson, 'Musketeer', in *The Unquiet Peace*, 1957.

IN the late 1970s the writer Gavin Young set out to travel by boat from Piraeus to Canton, recording his adventures in his memorable book *Slow Boats to China*. Here he arrives in Port Said to search for a ship willing to carry him through the Canal to Suez.

I had reached Port Said from Alexandria about an hour before, after 7.00 p.m. It is a long drive, but a rewarding one and, when I told the driver not to hurry, it was not because of the wrecked cars at the side of the road. The delta of the Nile is a wide expanse of glimmering greenness, water, villages and animals.

Everywhere men and women walk behind ploughs, or sit in groups under eucalyptus trees or the weeping willows that bow over scores of canals and rivulets – all the myriad waterways that make up the miracle that has nourished old Egypt since before the building of the pyramids. You drive through white-pink fields of cotton dotted with the larger blobs of pink, white, red and blue that are the robes, turbans and dresses of villagers working in the sun. Behind mud-coloured village walls, pencil outlines of minarets rise from screens of palm trees. Men and boys wash naked in streams by the roadsides, the silt-thickened water modestly encircling them as if they stood waist-high in a mudpack. One sees railway lines, factory chimneys and pylons carrying high-tension wires that connect the industrial towns of the delta with Alexandria or Cairo, but the great rich greenness flows away to the skyline, never interrupted for long. It is a landscape with moving figures of count-less men and animals and a restless profusion of egrets, kites and waders.

As evening fell, on the straight coast road between Damietta and Port Said, the taxi ran full tilt into a rock no smaller than the foundation stone of an average-sized bank, shattering the front axle. The stone was difficult to see at dusk against the asphalt road. My driver waved down a private car, and its owner drove us, crying, 'No problem, no problem. You do same for me,' to the Holiday Hotel, the hotel recommended to me by Captain Roncallo. The taxi driver, who had friends who owned a garage in Port Said, didn't seem worried about his front axle, and said goodbye in good spirits.

The hotel was quite modern. On a card in my room I read that television involved an additional charge but, when I turned it on, it showed nothing on seven of its eight channels and, on the eighth, a snowstorm from which came garbled American voices. After a shower I asked the receptionist if he would either remove the television charge from my bill or the set from my room.

He seemed astonished. 'But TV is compulsory,' he said.

'But there is no TV reception in Port Said.'

'You see here, sir, our card, it says – room service so-much, with breakfast compulsory so-much more. And then TV compulsory so-much more. And a fridge and radio and air-con, all so-much more. Tax extra, ten per cent.'

'Have you a room without TV, please?'

'Sir, all rooms have TV, fridge, and radio. No one ever said before what you say about not wanting.'

Another receptionist joined in. 'TV is like breakfast. Breakfast is compulsory. So is TV.'

'Yes, but breakfast is food – to eat, to live. TV actually doesn't exist here. Breakfast exists; you eat it!'

But there was no comprehension. It was written on the card ('What is written is written,' Muslims say), so I paid for the nonexistent television. I didn't begrudge it much. Egypt is a very poor country of great charm and spiritual resource, and it deserves better times and at least minimal riches. The receptionists had charm too – like most Egyptians – and deserved a richer country. In any case, I hoped I wouldn't have to wait too long at the hotel. The following morning I would go to see Mr Karawia at the Aswan Shipping Company with my letter from Captain Rashad.

Like the other canal towns, Port Said is still con-valescent. The Six-Day War of 1967 closed the canal, and until 1975 the port was paralysed, like a busy man felled by a stroke. It still had an empty look, despite the groups of tourists from the cruise ships that lay alongside the quay. These days the city is a free-trade zone, and you can buy luxury goods cheaper than at most other ports. This is why the tourists come ashore. Their ships – handsome white ships belonging to Cunard or Greek lines mostly – couldn't help me. They were either going north to Naples or to Casablanca or across the Atlantic, or going south in long smooth strides to Mombasa or Cape Town. In any case, their captains seldom, if ever, pick up stray travellers like me. They like groups. All the world, those Patmos landladies had reminded me, loves a group.

The tourists wandered the streets, occasionally bending to peer at a window full of tape recorders or calculators. The women wore straw hats with small, coloured pompoms hanging from the wide brims. I could catch snatches of their chatter as they struggled after their guides in the north Mediterranean streets: 'We did the Valley of the Kings last year. Wasn't it adorable, Wilma?'

Port Said was also, I found, a surprisingly courteous city which had not been my recollection of it twenty years earlier. The Egyptian who had cycled up to me outside the Ritz Bar to offer joy had shown no irritation when I'd turned him down; I'd expected a stream of abuse. I was considering this phenomenon when a small boy put his head out of the door of the bar, hissed at me, grinned and stabbed his finger in the direction of a fat girl in a green shift and headscarf nearby who must have weighed about thirteen stone. When I shook my head politely, the girl smiled and said, 'Never mind,' with no hint of rancour for business lost, and waddled away.

Gavin Young, *Slow Boats to China*, 1981.

13

Desert Excursions

NOBODY in Egypt can escape the presence of the deserts. They constantly overshadow and confine all life: the cosmopolitan sophistication of Alexandria, Cairo's teeming streets, the dusty provincial towns and villages strung along the fertile lands of the Nile valley. To travellers they have always seemed exotic and alluring yet threatening, a world apart to be broached only in the company of Arab guides familiar with the traditional caravan routes.

The characters of the two deserts are very different. The narrow Eastern Desert, squeezed between the Nile and the Red Sea, consists largely of a sandy plateau cut through, towards the Red Sea, by a range of rocky, unwelcoming peaks. The Western Desert, which at times extends to the very banks of the Nile, forms the fringe of the Libyan Desert, which itself joins the Sahara to run across the whole of North Africa. Occasional oases punctuate monotonous stretches of drift sand and identical undulating ridges; in the north lies the great Qattara Depression, 120 metres below sea level.

Of the two, the Eastern Desert was the more frequently explored, not least because of its ancient gold and breccia (granite) mines. Cosseir, on the Red Sea coast, was a traditional port for Arabia and India, and the hardier travellers on the Overland Route from Europe would journey up the Nile as far as Qena or Qift, below Luxor, and then hire camels and guides for the three- or four-day trip. Mrs Elwood recorded her trip in 1825 in a tone of somewhat astonished rapture. Some twenty-five years earlier, Vivant

Denon had also crossed to Cosseir with a troop of French soldiers.

It is not easy to conceive the sterile grandeur of the scene, and the singularity of our position, encamped in the heart of the Desert, surrounded by wild Arabs, every moment liable to an attack from some wandering tribe, and totally dependent upon the good faith of our Ababdè guide for safety, and yet, from the novelty of all around, and the excitement incident to travelling in such uncommon regions, I may truly say, I never enjoyed myself more, despite the thermometer at 105°, and the numerous petty inconveniencies I was necessarily obliged to submit to. Certainly, no fine lady, who could not do without her everyday luxuries and comforts, should attempt the Desert of the Thebaid [around Thebes]; but I believe I was born under a roaming star, and I must say, I infinitely preferred this patriarchal style of life, free and unshackled as it was, to the artificial stupidity of civilization. I no longer was surprised at the ardent love of the Bedouin for his wandering life; the marvel is, how those Arabs who were ever free to roam the pathless desert in liberty, could submit to the trammels of society, to the forms of a city, and to the mandates of an arbitrary tyrant ...

The Arabs were so alert in their movements, that this afternoon we fairly started by four P.M. There was no water in the neighbourhood, which probably expedited our departure; and this was the last night's journey to Cosseir. Dr. Johnson observes, we seldom do any thing for the last time without regret; and, as we wound along the noble and majestic mountains, I really felt quite sorry this was to be our last night in the Desert. Since I had become inured to the rough motion of the Takhtrouan, I had been quite delighted with our nocturnal marches. The serenity of the scene, the purity of the air, the exquisite beauty of the stars, all contributed their *agréments*, and the novelty and excitement of spending the day in the patriarchal fashion under tents in the Desert, amply compensated for the heat and inconveniencies we encountered.

The intensity of the heat was such, that, without exaggeration, water spilt upon the ground or upon a table evaporated *instantaneously*; and tea, some of which we generally preserved from our evening's repast to assuage our thirst before breakfast was prepared on the following day, literally remained quite warm during the whole night.

At midnight the defile began to widen; the mountains, gradually diminishing in height, lost their sublime and picturesque appearance, and by degrees sank into hills; we perceived ourselves rapidly descending – the air lost its purity and elasticity, and became moist and clammy. About three A.M. we passed the Well of Ambaseer, which is strongly impregnated with salt and sulphur, to which however the camels, much to the annoyance of their riders, who were not prepared for the movement, rushed with the utmost eagerness. Soon as 'the morn began to tremble o'er the sky,' our caravan came to a sudden halt, and looking out, my eyes first fell upon the blue waters of the Red Sea!

Mrs Colonel [Anne Katharine] Elwood, *Narrative of a Journey Overland ... to India*, 1830.

Two days after our arrival, not to famish the garrison which we were to leave, we commenced our return: we were always preceded by our Arabs, to whom the desert seemed to belong: on their march, they did not neglect a single product of their empire: we saw two ghazals, running along the desert; four of their party were detached, with bad match-locks; some minutes after, we heard two single reports, and presently saw them returning with the two ghazals, fat as if they had inhabited the most abundant pasture: the Arabs invited me to eat of the product of the chase; and, curious to see their mode of dressing it, I went to their camp: the chief, haughty as a sovereign, found a palace wherever he spread his carpet; his kitchen-furniture consisted in two plates of copper, and a pot of the same material; butter, flour, and a few sticks of wood furnished all the provisions of his household; a little stale camel-dung collected, a kiln erected, and the flour moistened, some baked cakes, which, while they were hot, I thought very good, were prepared in a few minutes; soup, boiled-meat, and roast-meat, composed a repast, very tolerable for an hungry man; but this, in the desert, I was wholly without: I lived on lemonade, which I generally made on my camel, putting slices of lemon, with sugar, into my mouth, and drinking water upon it. Our Arabs knew, to the obscurest nook, what each pasture produced; they were aware to what degree of growth such and such plants must have arrived in a spot at a league from where we were, and they sent their camels to feed: this regale excepted, these poor animals ate only a small ration of beans once in the day, on which they ruminated for the rest of the twenty-four hours, either as they marched, or as they lay on the burning sand; and they never testified the least impatience.

Vivant Denon, *Travels in Upper and Lower Egypt*, 1803.

On the same route the extreme conditions led to violent disagreement between Maxime du Camp and Gustave Flaubert, normally boon travelling companions, so that they did not speak for forty-eight hours. Comic as it seems, the incident reflects the genuine hazards of desert travel.

My mouth and lips were dry, and the vermin which infested my dromedary had attacked me. No one spoke as our little caravan moved forward, neither Flaubert nor myself, nor the dragoman nor our camel-drivers, who swayed from side to side as they rode upon their camels. Suddenly, it was about eight o'clock in the morning, as we were passing through a defile formed by pink granite rocks covered with inscriptions – a place like a furnace – Flaubert said to me—

'Do you recollect the lemon ices we used to eat at Tortoni's?'

I nodded my head affirmatively. He continued—

'Lemon ice is first-rate. Confess, now, that you would not object to a lemon ice at this moment?'

'Yes!' I replied, in rather a rough tone.

Five minutes later he resumed—

'Ah! those lemon ices; all over the glass there is a kind of mist, which looks like a white jelly.'

I interrupted—

'Supposing we were to change the subject?'

'It might be as well, but really lemon ice should have its praises sung. You fill the spoon so that there is a little dome of ice which goes into your mouth, and is gently crushed between the tongue and the palate. It melts slowly, coolly, and deliciously caresses the uvula and the gullet, then slips down into the diaphragm, which is not displeased, and is greeted finally by the stomach with joyful laughter. Between you and me, there is a decided lack of lemon-ices in the desert of Qôseir.'

I knew Flaubert well, and that nothing could stop him when he was possessed by one of these moods. I tried not speaking in the hope that my silence would check him. But he began again when he saw that I would not answer, louder than ever—

'Citron ices! Citron ices!'

I felt I could not endure it. Terrible thoughts passed through my brain. I said to myself, 'I shall kill him.' I pressed against him with my dromedary, and took hold of his arm.

'Where do you mean to ride? In front or behind?'

He replied—

'I will go forward.'

I stopped my dromedary, and when our little company had advanced some two hundred yards in front of me I resumed my march. At nightfall I left Flaubert among our men, and made my bed in the sand at a distance of more than two hundred metres from our encampment.

At three o'clock on Sunday morning we started again, still as far apart as on the previous day, and without exchanging a word. About three in the afternoon the dromedaries began to stretch out their necks and to show signs of emotion. We knew that water was not far off. At half-past three we made Bir-Amber, and we drank. Flaubert threw his arms round me and exclaimed—

'Thank you for not having blown out my brains. In your place I should have done it.'

The next day we were enjoying something better than Tortoni's lemon ices, for we were drinking the water of the Nile, better than the costliest wines, especially after you have broken your water-skins.

Maxime du Camp, *Recollections of a Literary Life*, 1893.

THE desert exerted a strong attraction on many of Egypt's long-standing European residents as a place of true escape. Here Sir Thomas Russell, who devoted all his working life to the Egyptian Police (he retired as Chief of the Cairo Police in 1946), describes hunting for ibex.

Of all the strenuous and uncertain forms of hunting, I doubt if there is anything to beat ibex-hunting in this Nubian Desert. Motor-cars, I am glad to say, are of no use, and the whole trip must be done by camel and on your feet. Water, guides and trackers are the three prime necessities. Before doing a trip the wise man sends an

Arab scout round the country a month beforehand and
bases his water and hunting plans on his report. If your
projected trip is in a green year, you can base yourselves
on one of the temporary water-holes which still hold the
spate water from which the camels can be watered with
ease: if the year is a dry one you must carry your own
drinking-water for the whole trip and limit your range
of hunting so as to send your camels after ten days or so
to one of the few permanent holes like the famous Bir
Shetun. Next in importance are the guides: they must
be local Arabs who know not only the main wadis but
who can also take you by day or night over the tops from
wadi to wadi: it is no joke to be left out on a freezing
night in a shirt wet with sweat after a ten-hour day in
the hot sun. Such guides are rare, and in all my years I
only knew three men on whom I could rely completely.
It is foolish to treat the desert lightly, a slip might break
a leg or worse and entail a week's delay till a doctor
could be brought up, so reserves of food, water and
medicines must be taken.

Having made certain of your water supplies and your
guides, you have done all you can for your personal
safety, but you still have your hunting to ensure, and
this will depend on your trackers. Any desert Arab can
track more or less, but they cannot compare with the
Bisharin trackers of the Camel Corps Police who are
recruited as experts from the Hamedorab and other
subsections of the Sudan Bisharin who are all indi-
vidually first class at the job.

Once on a track, speed is essential, if you are to catch
up during daylight. Having fitted his stride to that of
the ibex, the tracker puzzles it out step by step at a jog-
trot on easy ground, and slowly where the tops are a
pavement of flat flints sunk into a clay surface: here,
often for hundreds of yards at a time, the only suggestion
of a footmark is where the ibex has trodden on the edge
of a flint and loosened it in its setting. All you can do to
help is to cast well ahead when you can see some soft
ground where even you can spot the track, then with a
wave of the hand you lift the trackers on and gain valu-

able time. Where again your expert tracker is essential is in dating the tracks found at dawn in the wadi bottom: he will say whether the track is under the dew or over the dew and decide accordingly as to how far ahead of you your game may be, and thus gauge your chance of catching up in daylight. The tracker, too, is the most interesting member of your party if you can get him to open out: many trackers cannot explain what they are doing, but Hamed, my chief tracker, who was with me on every trip I did, could make the tracks talk and almost show you what the animal was thinking about ...

The hunting is of a nature peculiar to itself. The country is vast, the head of game small, the wadis twist and turn every few hundred yards and to spy every fresh length of wadi with the field-glass is simply a waste of time as, in the first place, the game is not there during the day, or if it is, is lying up in the rocks five hundred feet above you where not even an Arab's eye can see it, unless it moves. In the second place, you cannot use a field-glass from a camel's back; when you halt him he won't stand still like a horse but swings and squirms his neck, making spying from the saddle impossible, and to get off your camel on every turn in a wadi entails a lengthy and noisy proceeding on the part of the camel which may scare game over a mile away. Spying is equally useless if you are travelling the tops that lie between the big wadis where you might search for a month of Sundays and never see a living thing. The one and only method is tracking. The game feeds in the wadis at night and leaves for the tops in the morning: the hunter's business is to be on the move at daylight, each man leading his camel to work off their frozen stiffness of the night and, with the trackers lined across the wadi, carefully examining the ground for traces of the previous night. If game exists at all in the neighbourhood, it will be in the wadis that you will find the tracks and, when found, you must decide whether these are fresh enough and of a size to make them worth following.

An hour or more may be spent following the footmarks from bush to bush where a few hours ago they had been grazing, until the spot is reached where with the dawn the ibex or sheep had decided to leave the wadi and seek the safer shelter of the top desert. At this point you say good-bye to your riding-camels, load up with rifle, camera, food and water for the day, give orders to a guide as to where, with luck, he is eventually to meet you with the riding-camels and up the face you go in your rope-soled shoes and settle down to following the track. On the rare occasions when your luck is in, after several hours' hurrying at the fastest pace you can manage, you will be closing in on the track with your nose in the wind: twigs nibbled and dropped are wet at the broken stalk, droppings are moist and warm; excitement is tense: be wise now and leave the tracking to your men and walk on the toes of your rope-soled shoes, casting your eyes well ahead, with your rifle ready; remember the dead silence of the desert and that a rattling stone can be heard a mile away. Then, if the fates are kind, you may, if you are very lucky, catch a glimpse of your ibex as he wakes from his noon siesta and dashes off at your sound, giving you a galloping chance at three hundred yards, immediately to outsight himself in the most amazing manner. It is all a question of luck. Walk and work as you will, you can make sure of nothing. In any other form of hunting your first consideration is the wind, but in this desert hunting, once you are on tracks, you are at the mercy of chance, for the tracks wander along, turning now this way and that, according to the grazing, sometimes up wind, sometimes down, but stick to them you must and trust to luck that when you do get within distance of your game you will be approaching it with the wind in your face. Nor must you be unduly disgusted with fate if, after hours of hard work, you find that your ibex had got your wind long before and gone off at the gallop ...

Bir Shetun, with its never-failing supply of sweet water, was the pivot of many of my trips and is one of the most romantic features of this desert. It is the only permanent hole in this waterless area in a radius of a

hundred miles to the north, east or south. Geologically
it is a fault in the floor of the Wadi Shetun. If you are
following this shallow rocky wadi down from where it
starts to the north, you suddenly come to a narrow crack
in the rock floor and down below you at seventy feet you
can see the water. This cleft widens out to some ten
yards in width and continues south for forty-five yards
with an average depth of water of twenty feet. The deep
reservoir thus formed has no doubt been hollowed out
from prehistoric times by millenniums of occasional
rainstorms pouring down from the desert above and
cutting their way through some softer rock. From the
top the only approach to the water is by a rock staircase
of about ninety steps, cut at some time by man and
leading to the southern end of the waterhole, after which
the wadi gradually widens out between two-hundred-
foot cliffs until two hours later it joins the main Wadi
Qasab, some five hours' ride from the Nile Valley.
Camels can be watered at Shetun by bringing them up
the lower wadi from Wadi Qasab but they must then
return the same way they came as there is no way out.
If the waterhole is approached from the high-level desert
from the north, water can only be brought to the camels
by the men climbing down the stair and bringing the
filled water-skins up to the camels on their backs, or by
a bucket and forty feet of rope, which no Arab ever
possesses. The amount of water in Shetun varies slightly
according to the rains, but has no relation to the rise and
fall of the Nile. On one of my visits there had been no
spate down the wadi for seven years, and after measuring
the depth with a hundred-foot length of rope and a
bucket, we calculated that there were forty-six thousand
gallons of clean, sweet rain-water stored in this interesting chasm. It has never been known to dry up and,
even after a seven-year-old drought, was little lower
than when we last saw it, the reason being, no doubt,
that the water is in almost perpetual shade and is thus
not exposed to evaporation.

As can be imagined from this description, such a
permanent water is of vital importance to man and beast

in this desert: there are other holes of varying capacity and endurance, all depending on how far the water is hidden from the summer sun, but none of them are permanent and none of them have the clean, sweet, sand-filtered water of Shetun.

Sir Thomas Russell Pasha, *Egyptian Service, 1902–46*, 1949.

WILFRID SCAWEN BLUNT, poet, traveller and fervent supporter of Egyptian nationalism, wintered in Egypt each year at his country home, Sheykh Obeyd, outside Cairo. He often undertook lengthy desert explorations, far from the regular camel routes. This extract from his diary recounts one difficult journey in the Western Desert in 1897.

23rd Feb. – After a delightful night I walked at sunrise to the top of the highest *nefud* [sandhill] from which the whole lake can be seen. It is very interesting. Clearly the Oasis has been inhabited, but has been overwhelmed by the *nefuds* advancing on it from the south and west. The lake may be seven miles long, and is very beautiful. The northern shore is bounded by low cliffs, the ancient limit doubtless of the lake, which is shrinking, and will some day be a mere chaos of *nefud*, as so many others are. It was somewhere in this desert, they say, that Cambyses disappeared with his army. I can well believe it, for we were within a little of such a misfortune two days ago. If the weather had been less clear and cool I could not have seen the valley, and with a sand wind we might easily have perished. Now all seems easy and delightful. In the afternoon I went out for a ride, intending to visit the pyramidal hill, but got into a quicksand, crossing over a half dry arm of the lake, out of which I had some difficulty in dragging my mare. The blackbird I saw again at the same place, and a kestrel.

It is so hot to-day that I had the tent pitched for a shade – the first time we have used it, as I sleep under my carpet shelter. The barometer shows the lake to be 120 feet below sea level.

24th Feb. – Started at sunrise, believing our difficulties to be now over, but we took a wrong track, which led us south-west instead of farther north, towards some distant palms we had sighted an hour after leaving. This took us to what I believe to be the oasis of Bahreyn – at least such an Oasis is marked on my map. (N.B. A very excellent German map.) This Oasis is very like Síttarah, though with two lakes instead of one – whence its name. Osman pronounced this to be Araj, and said we were now close to Zeytoun and Siwah, which I knew could not be the case, and was sure when we came to the second lake it could only be Bahreyn. The road, too, westwards, we found blocked by a great *sebkha* (a dry salt marsh), and we were obliged to turn north and travel several hours to recover the right road. Fortunately we fell in soon with the track of a donkey, and two men who had been to the oasis, we think, to gather dates, a track of about ten days old, which we followed. The barometer at Bahreyn showed exactly o° above the sea. The donkey track led us to a *nukbeh*, where we fell in with a well-marked road bearing north-west by north over a plateau of limestone hillocks, each about ten feet high, like the crested waves of the British Channel in rough weather, with the space between them sand. The road was carefully marked with *rijms* (cairns), and easy to follow, and I cantered gaily on to find a camping place, where we now snugly are, screened from the north-east wind. It is fortunate we found the donkey track, or we might not have hit off the road. Yemama is now in excellent condition, and ate up her two *melwas* of corn during the night. The camels were all watered before starting. At Bahreyn to-day I saw a kite and a raven ...

25th Feb. – To-day we are in a worse plight than ever. We started very early, taking up our path of yesterday, which brought us in a couple of hours to the end of the limestone plain, and to my great delight to the edge of a new and very deep oasis which I knew must be the Araj we were looking for. Araj has no lake, only a little standing water and a tamarisk marsh. But a vast number of palms are scattered over a wide basin with many isolated clumps, very beautiful, in the sand. It was no case here of the *nefud* having destroyed the villages, as in the other oases, but of abandonment, one cannot say why. There are palms enough left to support many villages. The cliffs here are on the south and west sides, the sand slopes on the north and east. Still on the track of the donkey and the two men we chevied along the edge of the jungle north westwards, the ground covered with the tracks of gazelles, hares, and jackals. Of birds I saw only three, mourning chats, black with white beaks and rumps – nothing else alive. The depth of the oasis puzzled my barometer. It must be about 150 feet below the sea. From the bottom the track led up by some clumps of palms, where I am sure there must be water underground, across deep *nefuds* to the opposite *nukbe* marked by some wonderful rocks – one quite square, white as marble, and with curious architectural markings, another like a tall chessman, both 100 feet high at least, their tops level with the plain above, a splendid hermitage where one might find shade and shelter at all hours and in every weather. They are geologically of limestone, with layers of shells, their tops black, like lava. One layer of the chessman, one of those round white flakes, Suliman calls *dirahem* (money). This place was the wildest, the most romantic, the most supernatural in its natural structure I have ever seen, an abode of all the *jan* [spirits].

I cantered up the sand slope to the top of the pass, elated at having found Araj corresponding so well with my map, and being in front forgot to give orders for water to be looked for, and the girbehs filled. Hence our present trouble. For on gaining the upper plain, instead of the well-marked track we had expected, we found nothing but a windswept plateau of *nefud* interspersed with mounds of stone, where the donkey track speedily disappeared or was lost, nor could we ever again find it.

We were left now to our sole wits and the mercy of God, for the wind was blowing hard from the north-east and was drifting the sand hopelessly. Suliman, now in command, recommended descending towards some hills to the north-west, and this brought us to a new formation of limestone ground, arranged in flat masses with sharp edges, the most abominable imaginable interspersed with sand. Across this we floundered with our camels for several hours, when Suliman, having climbed to the top of a low tell, announced that he had seen a valley with palms, and it was resolved, much against old Osman's wish, that we should cross the whole valley on the chance of striking a track near the hills. The trend of the valley was westwards, and if it was the beginning of the Siwah valley, Suliman argued, it must have a road passing up it. So Suliman and I went scouting with the tall buttresses of a crag to west-north-west for our object. Now we have almost reached these, but have found no sign of road or life – only a poor wagtail lost in the strong wind. We have camped for the night, feeling ourselves to be out of all reckoning (for this according to the map should have been the Siwah valley, yet it is absolutely without trace of human passage, old or new). We are camped in a hollow near two *seyyal* trees, ill screened from the wind, and in very miserable plight.

26th Feb. – I spent a restless, uncomfortable night, disturbed at finding that of our five water skins three were already empty, and reproaching myself with having let the men pass Araj without replenishing. I felt myself responsible, too, from having taken the direction of our route out of Osman's hands. Old Beseys and the rest, except my own Bedouins, were clearly of opinion that I was wrong. The wind, too, raged furiously, and kept me waking, and in the darkness I imagined all kinds of disaster, more especially when I found the stars over-head obscured with drifting sand. I said prayers to all my saints and repented of my sins, and so I think did all the party. Once in the night the sky cleared and I got a sight of the Pole Star and made a line on the ground

with my camel stick as a guide in the morning, for my
pocket compass is out of order and cannot be relied on.
There were even moments when I thought gloomily of
ordering a retreat to Araj.

In the morning, however, more courageous counsels
prevailed, and we took our due course west towards the
khusm (the headland) determined to go straight forward
and solve the question of this being the Siwah valley or
no. Nor were we long in suspense. We had hardly gone
a mile when, riding in front, I came upon a little single
path leading to some *seyyal* trees which had been pol-
larded by Bedouins, a sign of human neighbourhood,
and presently, to my delight, to the old caravan road,
reappearing plain and unmistakable. It relieved us from
all anxiety, and following it we found ourselves by mid-
day at the first bushes of the Siwah oasis ...

Soon afterwards we came to *sebkhas*, where there were
tracks of many pasturing camels, and then within sight
of the oasis of Zeytoun and the Senussi Zaghwiyeh
standing on high ground a mile or more from its palm
trees. As it was near sunset we resolved to rest here
and have made a pleasant camp under some *ghurkhud*
bushes. *El hamdul Illah.*

Wilfrid Scawen Blunt, *My Diaries*, 1919.

FOR three years of the Second World War the Allied and
Axis armies pursued each other across the 600 miles of the
Western Desert between Alexandria and Benghazi in Libya.
The culmination of many bloody encounters was the battle
of El Alamein, in October 1942, when Montgomery's Eighth
Army inflicted a decisive defeat on Rommel's Afrika Korps.
Within little more than half a year the Axis forces, caught
between the British advancing from the east and the Ameri-
cans, newly landed in Algeria, from the west, had been swept
from North Africa.

Cecil Beaton spent three months in the Near East in the spring of 1942 on a photographic mission. His diary records the peculiar atmosphere of the desert battleground, barren territory repeatedly fought over by the opposing armies.

The road was clear for a bit, the sun hidden by sand; but putting your hands outside the car windows you felt the heat of the wind coming laden from the south. This wind could drive one to desperation, especially when the hot sand pricks into the pores of one's skin. The nerves are upset.

The sand storm had abated when we got to Sollum, a badly bashed fishing village. The waves were washing through the skeleton of a wrecked ship by the shore. The houses were pock-marked with shell wounds, and not a roof remained. We drove by hairpin turns up Sollum Pass, past long-haired, immaculate turbanned Indians, running glibly over Halfaya Pass in pistachio-green tanks. The relics of the battle of Halfaya are now half buried in sand. The salvage people have cleared much from these forlorn remains, but a phenomenon still exists that is far stranger than anything to be found in Surrealist books. A clothing stores must have been blown up; hundreds of shirts, neatly folded, are strewn on the sand; some tanks are blown up, so that a rhythm of circular disks stand in diminishing recession. The ground is littered with ammunition, gasmasks, water bottles, old boots and letters. The Surrealists have anticipated this battle ground. In all their paintings, now proved to be prophetic, we have seen the eternal incongruities. The carcases of burnt-out aeroplanes lying in the middle of a vast panorama: overturned trucks: deserted lorries: cars that have been buckled by machine-gun fire, with their under parts pouring out in grotesque, tortured shapes: some unaccountable clothing blown into the telephone wires, or drapery in a tree: the shattered walls: the sunsets of bright, unforgettable

colours. All these have been faithfully reproduced by
Dali, Max Ernst, Joan Miro, long before the war. At an
abandoned Italian aerodrome, where dozens of aircraft
had been destroyed on the ground, their skeletons looked
like prehistoric animals – and one, in particular, was like
a sphinx painted by Picasso.

Often one sees aircraft wearing floating draperies, or
veiled in fluttering nets; but this is for camouflage.

A north country soldier was wandering casually
among the graves of the German soldiers, their topees,
rotting in the sun, thrown over the crosses that bear the
beastly swastika. A beer bottle, with a piece of paper
inside, up-turned with its neck dug into the sand was all
there was to identify the young man who had died in
obedience to the abortive inspiration of the paper-
hanger-house-painter – 'Adolf Gross, born 14.11.19,
died June 1941'. The north country soldier put back the
bottle. 'It makes you think', was all he said.

Cecil Beaton, *Near East*, 1943.

To end with, two recollections of desert service: Cyril Joly
describes a tank advance across the Egyptian desert into
Libya in the early months of the desert campaign, while Erik
de Mauny, who served with the New Zealand Expeditionary
Force, recalls the battle of El Alamein.

At this stage – after our long period of relative inactivity and the softness and delights of leave – those of
us in the tank crews found hardest to bear the continual
lack of sleep and the physical effort required to meet the
perpetual rolling and pitching of the tanks across the
uneven desert. Our days started with the first flush of
morning, and not until the sun was well below the
western horizon did we normally withdraw to leaguer.

Even then the work did not finish. Breakdowns to the tanks and casualties among the crews entailed hard work and reorganisation within the squadrons. The tanks had to be filled with ammunition and fuel. The engines and tracks, suspensions and transmissions had to be inspected and repaired or adjusted as necessary. Orders, codes and wireless call-signs for the morrow were issued and memorised or filed away. Clean clothes were available sometimes from the squadron quartermasters; the doctor was at hand for minor wounds and ailments. In addition to these numerous duties and tasks, this, too, was normally the only time when we could get a hot meal and drink. During the day we existed on biscuits, margarine and cheese, occasionally varied by jam and tins of cold bully-beef. There was usually no time nor chance for even a quick brew of tea, so that the evening stew of tinned meat and vegetables and the brew of tea, sometimes with a tot of rum added if the Divisional Commander authorised it, assumed considerable importance in the minds and lives of each of the tank-crew members. It was seldom that the leaguer was quiet and asleep much before midnight, so that, with a turn of guard duty to perform and reveille a quarter of an hour before first light, each man got between four and five hours sleep each night at the most. If there were repairs to be done to the tank, then that crew, as well as the fitters who normally helped, got little or no sleep at all. And if the repair was of a major part of the tank, the crews of the tanks nearest on each side of the damaged one had their sleep disturbed by the inevitable noise and movement.

During the days of the battle and the subsequent chase, when the tanks were on the move for most of the hours of daylight, it was a test of endurance to exert the continual physical effort required to prevent actual injury caused by the rolling and pitching. The dust and heat of the engine, the fumes from the empty cases of the main armament and the more trying acrid smell of the Beza machine-gun cartridges were the least of the worries. Even so, looking ahead, I dreaded to think what hell of discomfort these would cause in any prolonged battles fought in the heat of full summer. These trials, in a very mobile campaign, were less exacting than those imposed by the movements of the tank. The rolling of the tank was the easiest of the unexpected movements to counter; a side slope of a hill or the more violent slopes of the small depressions in the ground were usually visible some way off, if one happened to be looking in the right direction at the right time. Forewarned, each member of the crew who could see could brace himself for the essentially limited sideways movement of the tank. The operator, working his set or loading the guns in any battle movement, and even at other times provided with very little vision, suffered most through being unprepared. It was the pitching and tossing movements which were the most violent, most unexpected and least possible to guard against. We usually moved fast, sometimes at a speed of between fifteen and twenty miles an hour, across all types and surfaces of desert, through the solid tufts of the sand-choked roots of scrub, over boulders often a foot in diameter and across ground of which every crevice and dip, undulation and hole was flattened to the eye by the almost perpendicular rays of the sun, which, except at the extreme ends of the day, cast no shadows at all. In these circumstances it was impossible for the driver to avoid most of the crashing bumps which we suffered and equally difficult for the crew members to brace ourselves in time. It was tremendously exhausting never being able to relax completely without being bruised or hurt. Even with the tank at rest, while we sat in watch on the enemy, the crampedness of our several positions gave us no chance to relax, so that, though only the commander needed to be always on the alert, the other members could doze only fitfully.

Another factor which contributed in no small measure to the exhaustion of tank commanders and operators was the wireless. From the moment we stood to at first light until we were finally settled into our positions in leaguer an hour or so after last light, the commanders and operators had to be fully on the alert. We only courted the vilest and most vehement abuse if, after failing to catch fully any message when it was first transmitted, we had to answer 'Say again'. The realisation of the need for this instant and continual alertness and the degree to which it was achieved were the measures of efficiency and effectiveness of any armoured regiment. Laxness in this respect or undue volubility on the wireless detracted from the speed of manoeuvre of a regiment and could, and often did, make it a prey to any unforeseen quick move by the enemy. The alertness was not the only cause of exhaustion. When no messages were being transmitted and, in the early evening and first half of the night as a background to the messages that were being passed, there was a continual crackling, wheezing, whining, whistling noise in the head-phones, which had to be kept close to the head in case a distant faint transmission was missed. The concentration needed at all times and the persistent noise often gave to each commander and operator a violent headache which the glare of the sun on the sand did nothing to relieve.

Cyril Joly, *Take These Men*, 1955.

My El Alamein? A blurred jumble of noise, dust, confusion, and a desperate lack of sleep!

Having done my basic training earlier on with the New Zealand Medical Corps, I was by then with No. 1 NZ Casualty Clearing Station. This was, in effect, a small but well equipped mobile hospital, operating as near as possible to the front line, and moving forward every few days to deal with the latest intake of casualties.

Everything had been pared to the bone for the sake of speed and mobility. Our transport consisted of three-tonners, from the back of which canvas awnings could be slung to form tented wards. There was a special blood bank truck, a well-stocked dispensary, and a large generator to provide power for the operating theatre. It was an extremely efficient outfit, staffed by a small team of surgeons who operated round the clock, and a great many badly wounded men undoubtedly owed their lives to their skill and devotion.

Once the battle had begun, with its mind-numbing barrage, ambulances started arriving in a steady stream from the forward RAPs [regimental aid posts], jolting over the rough desert tracks to the additional agony of their suffering occupants. No distinction was made between friend or foe, but only in the varying degrees of injury inflicted. This was indicated by discs of various colours hung round the necks of the wounded. Those not in urgent need of treatment would be given a hot drink, food, a cigarette, and despatched by ambulance convoy back to a base hospital. But those with stomach wounds or grave damage to other vital parts would be rushed as quickly as possible onto the operating table.

I had several spells as a theatre orderly, and among the mingled odours of blood, diesel fumes and anaesthetic, I saw some prodigies of battle surgery. It was always an eerie experience, especially at night, when the ground shook with the impact of high explosives, the sky behind the tent flaps an arterial crimson with gun flashes, and our overhead light blinking and flickering as the generator groaned in the background. Only the surgeons, their eyes dark with fatigue, seemed unperturbed, cutting away sections of blood-soaked uniform, trimming, probing and sewing up the gaping flesh with calm and studious concentration.

But in that first phase of the battle, the entire unit had to make do with a minimum of rest. My main job was to look after one of the tented wards. While the wounded snored and groaned in the darkness, I sat at a small table on the back of the truck, surrounded by medical paraphernalia, and devised desperate stratagems to fight off the encroaching waves of sleep. The only one that seemed to work was to light a cigarette, then catnap with my head on the table until the smouldering butt burned my fingers; whereupon I would light another one and repeat the process. At four o'clock one morning, the RC padre, making one of his rounds, found me asleep on a pile of sandbags beside the truck. I had no recollection of lying down there. The padre pumped up the primus, and restored me with a scalding mug of black coffee.

What struck me most was the dramatic contrast in the way the wounded reacted to their predicament. I saw a lengthy operation on a young German soldier with multiple stomach wounds, in which yards of intestine were hauled out onto a metal side tray, each perforation neatly sutured, then the whole lot unceremoniously shovelled back into the open cavern of the abdomen. It was like watching a seemingly impossible repair of a badly punctured bicycle tyre: but the seemingly imposs- ible worked. A day or so later, in the intensive care ward, I saw the young German, full of drainage tubes, but sitting up in bed and smiling cheerfully. He would survive.

Others wouldn't. A man might have only a minor injury. But bad news from home – the desertion of a wife or girl friend – could be as lethal as a bullet. One says that the spirit is willing but the flesh is weak. At Alamein, and in its aftermath, I learned that the reverse is also sometimes true. The flesh was willing to heal itself; it was the spirit that weakened and withdrew. One knew it from a peculiar expression on a man's face – and that he was about to turn his face to the wall.

Erik de Mauny, 'Picking up the Pieces at El Alamein', in *From Oasis into Italy*, 1983.

14

Farewells

It was only a few days since I had quitted Thebes, and
I seemed already within sight of Paris: my departure,
which I looked for only in the future, was appointed for
the morrow; I was favoured with the realization of a
dream; suffered to move in the direction of my desires,
I felt as if in their vortex: I know not whether I was not
alarmed: but a sentiment for which I could not account
made me regret Caira; I had scarcely ever lived there,
and nevertheless I had always quitted it with sorrow. I
felt at length to what a degree, naturally and without
perceiving it, we are sensible of the mild and equal
enjoyment which a delicious temperature imparts, and
which, in the absence of other pleasures, causes us to
feel, instant by instant, the happiness of existence; a
quotidian sensation, to which must be attributed what
has often happened in this country, and this is that
Europeans, arrived for a few months at Caira, have
grown old in that city, without ever persuading themselves to leave it.

Vivant Denon, *Travels in Upper and Lower Egypt*, 1803.

We have not been able to get access to any of the harems,
only seen the ladies muffled up on donkeys, sitting
astride as the men, taking an airing. They seem huge
clumsy bodies. Egypt is undoubtedly a curious country,
differing from Europe in everything, but it has no attrac-

tions for me. I shall leave it without regret, though
with grateful recollections of the great kindness we have
received from many individuals. The famed magician
that we had hoped to have had an opportunity of seeing
in Cairo was in prison, so that I could not ascertain how
susceptible a subject I might have proved for being
wrought upon. Though I believe it all humbug, yet I
was sorry not to have seen the farce. Some Europeans,
after living a good while in this country, seem to believe
in magic.

Elizabeth Cabot Kirkland, *Proceedings of the Massachusetts
Historical Society*, 1905.

BOULAK
June 15, 1869.

DEAREST ALICK,

Do not think of coming here. Indeed it would be
almost too painful to me to part from you again; and as
it is, I can patiently wait for the end among people who
are kind and loving enough to be comfortable, without
too much feeling of the pain of parting. The leaving
Luxor was rather a distressing scene, as they did not
think to see me again.

The kindness of all the people was really touching,
from the Kadee who made ready my tomb among his
own family, to the poorest fellaheen. Omar sends you
his most heart-felt thanks, and begs that the boat may
remain registered at the Consulate in your name for his
use and benefit. The Prince has appointed him his own
dragoman. But he is sad enough, poor fellow, all his
prosperity does not console him for the loss of 'the
mother he found in the world.' Mohammed at Luxor
wept bitterly and said, 'poor I, my poor children, poor
all the people,' and kissed my hand passionately, and
the people at Esneh, asked leave to touch me 'for a
blessing,' and everyone sent delicate bread, and their
best butter, and vegetables and lambs. They are kinder

than ever now that I can no longer be of any use to them.

If I live till September I will go up to Esneh, where the air is softest and I cough less. I would rather die among my own people in the Saeed than here.

You must forgive this scrawl, dearest. Don't think please of sending Maurice out again, he must begin to work now or he will never be good for anything.

Can you thank the Prince of Wales for Omar, or shall I write? He was most pleasant and kind, and the Princess too. She is the most perfectly simple-mannered girl I ever saw. She does not even try to be civil like other great people, but asks blunt questions, and looks at one so heartily with her clear, honest eyes, that she must win all hearts. They were more considerate than any people I have seen, and the Prince, instead of being gracious, was, if I may say so, quite respectful in his manner: he is very well bred and pleasant, and has the honest eyes that makes one sure he has a kind heart.

My sailors were so proud at having the honour of rowing him *in our own boat*, and of singing to him. I had a very good singer in the boat. Please send some little present for my Reis: he is such a good man; he will be pleased at some little thing from you. He is half Turk, and seems like whole one. Maurice will have told you all about us. Good-bye for the present, dearest Alick.

Lucie Duff Gordon, *Letters from Egypt*, 1865.

It has been a hot day, and there is dead calm on the river. My last sketch finished, I wander slowly round from spot to spot, saying farewell to Pharaoh's Bed – to the Painted Columns – to every terrace, and palm, and shrine, and familiar point of view. I peep once again into the mystic chamber of Osiris. I see the sun set for the last time from the roof of the Temple of Isis. Then, when all that wondrous flush of rose and gold has died away, comes the warm afterglow. No words can paint the melancholy beauty of Philæ at this hour. The surrounding mountains stand out jagged and purple against a pale amber sky. The Nile is glassy. Not a breath, not a bubble, troubles the inverted landscape. Every palm is twofold; every stone is doubled. The big boulders in mid-stream are reflected so perfectly that it is impossible to tell where the rock ends and the water begins. The Temples, meanwhile, have turned to a subdued golden bronze; and the pylons are peopled with shapes that glow with fantastic life, and look ready to step down from their places.

The solitude is perfect, and there is a magical stillness in the air. I hear a mother crooning to her baby on the neighbouring island – a sparrow twittering in its little nest in the capital of a column below my feet – a vulture screaming plaintively among the rocks in the far distance.

I look; I listen; I promise myself that I will remember it all in years to come – all the solemn hills, these silent colonnades, these deep, quiet spaces of shadow, these sleeping palms. Lingering till it is all but dark, I at last bid them farewell, fearing lest I may behold them no more.

Amelia Edwards, *A Thousand Miles Up the Nile*, 1877.

The last morning arrived, and was as heartlessly beautiful as ever. I dressed with an unforgetting, photographing eye fixed upon the pyramid of Cheops. My footfalls sounded sadly round the garden, even the squeak of the last swing had a melancholy fall. The leaves of the apricot grove glittered in the brilliance of the morning, datura flowers hung richly in their green gloom. Mohammed smiled as ever, the kindness of his pock-marked face was an ache against the heart.

The birds still sang as my new luggage was loaded at the gate. 'If you can manage not to cry,' my mother had said, 'it will make things easier for your father.' But would it be possible? In theory I was coming back, perhaps for some distant Christmas holidays, in spite of the ten days' journey from England. In theory I was coming back, grown-up, to enjoy the sweets and splendours of adult Cairo life. In theory this was no good-bye. But children, like dogs, sometimes know things in their bones, and what my bones were saying this bright morning was good-bye for ever.

It was impossible to look back at the green-shuttered house, at the stone steps leading up to the front door with their pots of freezias and cinerarias and pelargoniums, at the stone gate posts on whose broad tops Alethea and I had so often sat, two non-matching heraldic beasts. The road was spattered with bright sunlight and deep shadow, with the lozenge shaped leaves of the leboc trees spreading out into the sun. The timeless Nile rolled under, the horses' hooves rang out again across the iron of the Boulac Bridge. As the train drew out of Cairo station, leaving my father's grey-flannelled figure on the platform, leaving the comprehending faces of Mohammed and Suliman, I reached the end of this particular tether, and the fields of the Delta dissolved before my eyes. 'Well done,' my mother said, 'you lasted out.' I was pleased that she was pleased, but otherwise this victory seemed of little worth. From her corner Rose Hunt sniffed sympathetically; Alethea, glancing up from *Little Folks*, seemed to look faintly diverted. By Tanta I was deep in *The Viper of Milan*, and half-way through a box of Turkish Delight, and for once no one seemed concerned about my spoiling my lunch.

Priscilla Napier, A Late Beginner, 1966.

We finally sailed from Port Said in mid-June 1945 after several tiresome weeks of waiting for the embarkation order to come through. There had therefore been plenty of time to detach myself from the life I had created in Cairo, which in any case had become increasingly tedious ever since it had become certain that demobilization could not be more than six months ahead. Strangely I could hardly bother to wave a farewell as Alexandria and the north coast of Africa as far as Mersa Matrup melted away. What had passed was in the past, and in another place. Now suspended, as it were, between sea and sky, in time and space, it was better to become merely a parcel – one of several hundreds similarly posted home. To hide from myself the difficulty of thinking in any concrete terms about the future I read James Joyce's *Ulysses* (for the first time) and did not put it down until after Gibraltar and the Pillars of Hercules had closed the Mediterranean and we were in the grey Atlantic.

Robert Medley, *Drawn from the Life*, 1983.

Sources and Acknowledgements

All places of publication are London unless otherwise stated.

Mrs Russell Barrington, *The Life, Letters and Work of Frederick Leighton*, 2 vols., 1906.

Cecil Beaton, *Near East*, 1943. Reproduced by permission of the Literary Executors of the Estate of the late Sir Cecil Beaton.

Giovanni Belzoni, *Narrative of the Operations and Recent Discoveries Within the Pyramids, Temples, Tombs, and Excavations in Egypt in Nubia*, 3rd ed., 1822.

Wilfrid Scawen Blunt, *My Diaries*, 1919.

Charles Breasted, *Pioneer to the Past: the Story of James Henry Breasted, Archaeologist*, New York, 1943. Reproduced with permission of Charles Scribner's Sons, an imprint of Macmillan Publishing Company. Copyright 1943 Charles Breasted; copyright renewed © 1971 Charles Breasted.

Alfred J. Butler, *Court Life in Egypt*, Oxford, 1887.

Mabel Caillard, *A Lifetime in Egypt 1876–1935*, 1935.

Roderick Cameron, *My Travel's History*, Hamish Hamilton, 1950. Reproduced by permission of the author and publishers.

Maxime du Camp, *Le Nil, Flaubert in Egypt*, translated and edited by Francis Steegmuller, Bodley Head, 1972. Reproduced by permission of McIntosh and Otis, Inc.; *Recollections of a Literary Life*, 1893.

John Carne, *Letters from the East*, 1830.

Howard Carter, *The Tomb of Tutankhamen*, 3 vols., 1923–33, reprinted Century, 1983.

François René Chateaubriand, *Travels in Greece, Palestine, Egypt and Barbary during the Years 1806 and 1807*, 2 vols., 1811.

Ellen Chennells, *Recollections of an Egyptian Princess by her English Governess*, 2 vols., Edinburgh and London, 1893.

Mary Chubb, *Nefertiti Lived Here*, Geoffrey Blès, 1954. Reproduced by permission of the author.

Captain J. Clerk, 'Suez Canal', *Fortnightly Review*, January 1869.

Noël Coward, *Middle East Diary*, 1944. Copyright Estate of Noël Coward, 1944. By permission of Michael Imison Playwrights Ltd.

Hon. Mary G. E. Dawson Damer, *Diary of a Tour in Greece, Turkey, Egypt and the Holy Land*, 2 vols., 1841.

D. Vivant Denon, *Travels in Upper and Lower Egypt during the Campaigns of General Bonaparte*, 2 vols., 2nd ed., 1803.

Benjamin Disraeli, 'The Court of Egypt', *New Monthly Magazine*, June 1832, reprinted in *Tales and Sketches* edited by J. Logie Robertson, 1891; *Letters*, Vol. 1, 1815–34, edited by J. A. W. Gunn, John Matthews, Donald M. Schurman, M. G. Wiele, University of Toronto Press, Toronto, 1982. Reproduced by permission of the publishers. Copyright University of Toronto Press, 1982.

Arthur Conan Doyle, *Memories and Adventures*, 1924.

Lawrence Durrell, *The Durrell–Miller Letters, 1935–80*, edited by Ian S. MacNiven, Faber and Faber, 1988. Reproduced by permission of the author and publishers.

Amelia Edwards, *A Thousand Miles Up the Nile*, 1877, reprinted Century, 1982.

Mrs Colonel [Anne Katharine] Elwood,

Narrative of a Journey Overland from England by the Continent of Europe, Egypt, and the Red Sea to India; including a Residence There, and Voyage Home, in the Years 1825, 26, 27, and 28, 1830.

Walter B. Emery, *Egypt in Nubia,* Hutchinson, 1965. Reproduced by permission of the Random Century Group.

Edward Farson, 'Musketeer', in Maurice Tugwell (ed.), *The Unquiet Peace,* Allan Wingate, 1957. Reproduced by permission of W. H. Allen & Co. plc.

Gustave Flaubert's travel notes quoted in *Flaubert in Egypt,* translated and edited by Francis Steegmuller, Bodley Head, 1972. Reproduced by permission of McIntosh and Otis, Inc.

E. M. Forster, 'Between the Sun and the Moon', in *Pharos and Pharillon,* 1923. Reproduced by permission of King's College, Cambridge, and the Society of Authors as the literary representative of the E. M. Forster Estate.

G. S. Fraser, *A Stranger and Afraid,* Carcanet Press, Manchester, 1983. Reproduced by permission of the publishers.

Théophile Gautier, *L'Orient,* Paris, 1877. Excerpt translated by Suzanne Bosman.

Count A. E. W. Gleichen, *With the Camel Corps up the Nile,* 1888.

M. Louis Gonse, *Eugène Fromentin, Painter and Writer,* Boston, 1883.

Frederick Goodall, *The Reminiscences of Frederick Goodall, R.A.,* 1902.

Lucie Duff Gordon, *Letters from Egypt,* 1865, reprinted Virago, 1986.

Robert Graves, *Goodbye to All That,* revised edition Cassell, 1957. Reproduced by permission of A. P. Watt Limited on behalf of the Trustees of the Robert Graves Copyright Trust.

Sarah Haight, *Letters from the Old World by a Lady of New York,* New York, 1840.

David Holden, 'Letter from
Alexandria', *Encounter,*
August 1963. Reproduced
by permission of *Encounter*

William Holman Hunt, *Pre-
Raphaelitism and the Pre-
Raphaelite Brotherhood,*
1905.

Julian Huxley, *From an
Antique Land,* Max
Parrish, 1954.
Reproduced by
permission of the author's
estate.

Edmund Ions, *A Call to
Arms,* Newton Abbot,
David & Charles, 1972.
Reproduced by
permission of the author.

Captains Charles Irby and
James Mangles, *Travels in
Egypt and Nubia,* 1823.

T. G. H. James (ed.),
*Excavating in Egypt: the
Egypt Exploration Society
1882–1982,* British
Museum Publications,
1982. Reproduced by
permission of the
Committee of the Egypt
Exploration Society.

Cyril Joly, *Take These Men,*
Constable, 1955.
Reproduced by
permission of the author.

A. W. Kinglake, *Eothen,*
1844.

Rudyard Kipling, 'Egypt of
the Magicians', 1913, in
*Letters of Travel (1892–
1913)*, 1920.

Elizabeth Cabot Kirkland,
from *Proceedings of the
Massachusetts Historical
Society,* second series, Vol.
XIX, 1905, Boston, 1906.

Jean and Simonne
Lacouture, *Egypt in
Translation,* Methuen,
1958. Reproduced by
permission of the
publishers.

Stanley Lane-Poole, *Cairo,*
1892.

Edward Lear, *Selected
Letters,* edited by Vivien
Noakes, Oxford,
Clarendon Press, 1988.
Reproduced by
permission of Vivien
Noakes.

K. R. Lepsius, *Letters from
Egypt, Ethiopia & the
Peninsula of Sinai,* 1853.

Ferdinand de Lesseps,
*Recollections of Forty
Years,* 1887.

Tom Little, *High Dam at
Aswan,* Methuen, 1965.
Reproduced by
permission of the
publishers.

Erik de Mauny, 'Picking up
the Pieces at El Alamein',

in Victor Selwyn (ed.),
From Oasis into Italy,
Shepheard Walwyn for
Salamander Oasis Trust,
1983. Reproduced by
permission of The
Salamander Oasis Trust.

Robert Medley, *Drawn from
the Life,* Faber and Faber,
1983. Reproduced by
permission of the author.

Michael Meyer, *Henrik
Ibsen,* Hart-Davis/
Granada, 2 vols., 1969,
1971. Reproduced by
permission of the
translator and the
publisher.

David Millard, *A Journal of
Travels in Egypt, Arabia
Petraea, and the Holy
Land during 1841–2,*
Rochester, NY, 1842.

William Müller, 'An Artist's
Tour in Egypt', *Art
Union,* September 1839,
quoted in H. Neal Solly,
*Memoir of the Life of
William James Müller,*
1875.

Margaret Murray, *My First
Hundred Years,* William
Kimber, 1963.
Reproduced by
permission of Thorsons, a
division of the Collins
Publishing Group.

Murray's *Handbook for
Travellers in Egypt,* 7th
ed., 1900.

Priscilla Napier, *A Late
Beginner,* Michael Joseph,
1966. Reproduced by
permission of the author.

Florence Nightingale,
Letters from Egypt, edited
by Anthony Sattin, 1987.
Reproduced by
permission of Sir Ralph
Verney and the Claydon
Papers Trust.

G. C. Norman, 'My War', in
Victor Selwyn (ed.),
Return to Oasis, Poetry
London for Salamander
Oasis Trust, 1980.
Reproduced by
permission of The
Salamander Oasis
Trust.

Philip Oakes, *At the Jazz
Band Ball,* André
Deutsch, 1983.
Reproduced by
permission, copyright ©
1983 by Philip Oakes.

Stephen Olin, *Travels in
Egypt, Arabia Petraea and
the Holy Land,* New York,
1843.

William Flinders Petrie,
*Seventy Years in
Archaeology,* 1931.
Reproduced by

permission of Miss Lisette Petrie.

Sophia Poole, *The Englishwoman in Egypt*, 1844–6.

John Pudney, *Who Only England Know*, 1943. Reproduced by permission of the author's estate and The Bodley Head.

Hardwicke D. Rawnsley, *Notes for the Nile*, 1892.

Noel Rawnsley, 'Sketches of Life and Labour in the Excavators' Camp', in Hardwicke D. Rawnsley, *The Resurrection of Oldest Egypt*, Laleham, 1904. Reproduced by permission of Conrad Rawnsley.

Joanna Richardson, *Théophile Gautier, His Life and Times*, 1958. Translation copyright © Joanna Richardson 1958. Reproduced by permission of the Curtis Brown Group Ltd., London.

Janet Ross, *The Fourth Generation*, 1912.

Mary Rowlatt, *A Family in Egypt*, 1956. Reproduced by permission of Mrs Pamela Pelham Burn.

Sir Thomas Russell Pasha, *Egyptian Service 1902–46*, John Murray, 1949.

William Howard Russell, *A Diary in the East*, 1869.

Vita Sackville-West, *Passenger to Teheran*, 1926. Copyright 1926 Vita Sackville-West. Reproduced by permission of Curtis Brown Ltd., London.

Reverend A. H. Sayce, *Reminiscences*, 1923.

Olive Risley Seward (ed.), *W. H. Seward's Travels Around the World*, New York, 1873.

P. Seddon, *Memoir and Letters of the Late Thomas Seddon*, 1858.

Douglas Sladen, *Egypt and the English*, 1908.

Joseph Lindon Smith, *Tombs, Temples and Ancient Art*, University of Oklahoma Press, Norman, Oklahoma, 1956. Reproduced by permission. Copyright © 1956, 1984 by the University of Oklahoma Press.

Charles Piazzi Smyth, *Life and Work at the Great Pyramid, 1865*, 3 vols., 1867.

Sources and Acknowledgements

Freya Stark, *Dust in the Lion's Paw,* John Murray, 1961; *East is West,* John Murray, 1945. Reproduced by permission of the author and publishers.

Ronald Storrs, *Orientations,* 1937.

Mortimer Wheeler, *Still Digging,* Michael Joseph, 1955. Reproduced by permission of the author's estate.

Gavin Young, *Slow Boats to China,* Hutchinson, 1981. Reproduced by permission of the author and publishers.

While every effort has been made to secure permission, we may have failed in a few cases to trace the copyright holder. We apologize for any apparent negligence.

Index

Index